The New Fiction Technologies

T0197968

The New Fiction Technologies

Interactivity, Agency and Digital Narratology

SHAWN EDREI

McFarland & Company, Inc., Publishers

Jefferson, North Carolina

This book has undergone peer review.

ISBN (print) 978-1-4766-7914-3
ISBN (ebook) 978-1-4766-4564-3

LIBRARY OF CONGRESS AND BRITISH LIBRARY
CATALOGUING DATA ARE AVAILABLE

Library of Congress Control Number 2021046205

Front cover image © 2021 Tithi Luadthong/Shutterstock

Printed in the United States of America

*McFarland & Company, Inc., Publishers
Box 611, Jefferson, North Carolina 28640
www.mcfarlandpub.com*

Acknowledgments

This book is dedicated to my mentor, Prof. Elana Gomel, for her years of insight, advice and education that I will carry with me always, and to Shira Kaplan, who kept me going all this time through equal parts love and terror.

The research project this book is based on originated in the School of Cultural Studies at Tel-Aviv University, an institution to which I owe a great debt: special thanks go out to Revital Zippori and Dr. Hedda Ben-Bassat for their patience, understanding and support.

Table of Contents

Preface

Narrative rules the world.

As an undergraduate, studying narratology was the kind of eye-opener any burgeoning scholar hopes for: here was a key to taking apart, piece by piece, the stories I'd loved all my life, and understanding them on a level far deeper than simple reading could achieve. Structuralism—often referred to as "classical" narrative theory—seemed perfect to my mind, a way of clearly charting the myriad components of both fiction and the stories we tell ourselves, the most fundamental aspects of our identities and everyday lives. Best of all, these methods could be applied to any medium … or so I thought.

During my graduate studies, I couldn't help noticing blind spots in the existing critical corpus. Key texts had, of course, been published which touched on the Internet's function as a storytelling platform, and how online writing might differ from anything previously recognized in narrative; game studies, academically discussed only in whispers at the time, were just beginning to shed their long-standing stigma and warrant closer scrutiny. But information moves quickly online, and new literary trends and phenomena were forming even as the ink was drying on those important theoretical works. More significantly, scholarly attempts to bridge the gap between disparate products of "the digital age" were and remain few and far between; as an observer of online fandoms at the turn of the millennium, and with some modicum of direct experience with gaming, I believed I was in the perfect position to contribute to the ongoing discussion.

This book, based on research conducted for my doctoral dissertation, attempts to establish essential common ground between three forms of digital fiction thought to be unique and self-contained: fan fiction, video games, and webcomics. As a narratological study, there are of course major components of these media that must be left by the wayside—ludology, for example, is crucial for a complete understanding of game studies but less relevant to understanding how games contend with narrative paradigms;

film theory could no doubt provide great insight into the production of fan films but would practically require another volume to fully incorporate theories of the camera, the use of sound effects and CGI, and so on.

I also found myself facing an obstacle familiar to many scholars of digital fiction: the sheer size of the corpus makes any kind of comprehensive, all-inclusive study all but impossible. How does one choose fan fiction texts for analysis when a single online archive contains more than six million works? How does one discuss games as narratives when the hardware and software used today bear almost no resemblance to games ten years ago, let alone to the material available at the time of the medium's inception?

It is my hope that this text serves as a useful primer for narratology researchers seeking to explore digital fiction, by breaking down these three platforms to their basic narrative components and drawing attention to the points where they intersect. Even those foundational aspects have evolved in new and fascinating ways thanks to extant digital technologies, but if you can track the common ground and impetus these modes of fiction share, you'll be that much closer to understanding how stories are being told in the 21st century, and what the future of narratology may hold in store for us.

Introduction

A New Narratology for the Digital Age

In his introduction to *Narratologies*, David Herman notes that the evolution of narrative theory from its classical/structuralist roots was not a teleological process, with each new development representing a net improvement over the last. Rather, sub-disciplines such as cognitivist, rhetorical and feminist narratologies evolved as attempts to address perceived flaws, blind spots and gaps in existing theory:

> Feminist narratology, for example, has suggested that the older narratological categories do not necessarily capture how issues of gender inflect the production and processing of stories. Other researchers have refined our understanding of narratives as complex rhetorical transactions between authors, narrators, and various kinds of audiences. Still other narrative theorists have drawn on fields such as Artificial Intelligence, hypertext, psychoanalysis, film studies, and linguistics (including possible-world semantics and discourse analysis) to broaden and diversify our conception of stories and to provide new ways of analyzing their structures and effects [Herman, 2].

As such, it must be acknowledged that these innovations in the field were conceived, at least in part, as responses to an established template. We cannot overlook the fact that the scope of narratology has expanded exponentially since the forays of critics such as Roland Barthes and Gerard Genette: "Narrative theory, over the years, has become increasingly concerned with historical, political, and ethical questions. At the same time, it has moved from its initial home in literary studies to take in examination of other media (including film, music, and painting) and other nonliterary fields (for instance, law and medicine)" (Phelan/Rabinowitz, 2).

How best, then, to conduct a narratological analysis of contemporary digital fiction, the many variants of which seem to defy existing critical theories? Certainly it cannot be denied that the "Digital Age" and the technologies it has produced thus far have had a significant impact on the construction, reception and interpretation of narrative, particularly with regards to the spectrum of interactivity as defined by H. Porter Abbott:

> Interactivity is a matter of degree, ranging from comparatively passive to comparatively active forms of reader engagement.... At one end is the minimal freedom enjoyed by readers of hypertext fiction to create the order of the narrative discourse by selecting from a palette of hypertext lexias fabricated in advance by an author. At the other end is a reliance on readers or gamers actually to produce segments of the narrative discourse in an individual or collaborative enterprise, the outcome of which is not known in advance [Abbott, 530].

The interactivity to which Abbott refers presents itself differently, and to different extents, depending on the medium in question; but Marie-Laure Ryan has explicitly linked these manifestations to specific technological developments:

> It is evident that developments on the level of hardware had a crucial impact on the features of digital texts: for instance, faster processors and expanded storage capabilities allowed the integration of text, image, and sound, while the creation of large computer networks allowed communications between multiple users and the collaborative construction of the text. But the form and content of digital texts, as well as the reader's experience, are also affected by the underlying code [Ryan, 515].

Here, then, is a point of contention, and a possible lacuna in the theoretical corpus: discussions of digital fiction, interactivity, and the narratological principles which inform them tend to view disparate types of digital media in isolation; for example, computer-based fiction (e.g., video games) is rarely, if ever, discussed as part of a broader phenomenon which encompasses other manifestations of interactivity and the reader's desire for diegetic agency. The varied fields of digital creation (and appropriations of new and extant technologies for that purpose) have each generated their own body of critical thought, but relatively little attention has been paid to the points where these new narrative platforms intersect, and where experimentation with new literary forms and techniques in one digital medium has drawn on the tools of another to further its own progress. This book will delineate the essential narrative features, modes of production and methods of distribution for three forms of digital media; in doing so, foundational assumptions pertaining to what James Phelan and Peter Rabinowitz call the "theoretical bedrock of the fundamental and unchanging principles on which narratives are built" (Phelan/Rabinowitz, 1) will be re-examined, such as the value of the Author (constructed or real) in relation to the text; the creation, projection and reception of fictional worlds; the arrangement of the narrative plot; the configuration of time and space as setting; and the presence and deployment of textual actants. This breakdown and analysis will ultimately draw out and highlight the common ground these supposedly singular digital platforms share and make a case for a more holistic and inclusive approach to the narrative works of the "Digital Age."

Communication and the Implied Author

Roman Jakobson's "Closing Statement: Linguistics and Poetics" breaks down the basic act of communication thus:

> The *addresser* sends a message to the *addressee*. To be operative the message requires a *context* referred to ... seizable by the addressee, and either verbal or capable of being verbalized, a *code* fully, or at least partially, common to the addresser and addressee (or in other words, to the encoder and decoder of the message); and finally, a *contact*, a physical channel and psychological connection between the addresser and the addressee, enabling both of them to stay in communication [Jakobson, 353].

This defines the role of the addressee as limited to the deciphering of cultural, social and linguistic contexts embedded within the message, the successful decoding of which will lead to full comprehension of the addresser's text. Harry E. Shaw notes that, for all practical intents and purposes, the same linear model applies to the conventional cognitive process of consuming narrative:

> The notion of a narrative communication diagram evokes a simple underlying image, the image of someone telling a story to someone else.... Does the story-teller seem to be crafting a version of the story designed to appeal to the particular listener being addressed? Might the storyteller even be attempting to inveigle the listener into adopting a certain kind of role and thereby acquiescing in certain beliefs and values? And what do the story-teller's intentions reveal about his or her own values? [Shaw, 300].

The "image" Shaw describes is traditionally referred to as the implied author, a construct popularized by Wayne C. Booth in 1961 in order to establish a clear separation between the author and the text. Roland Barthes' 1967 essay "Death of the Author" similarly advocates that removing the Author's presence from the act of reading and interpretation has a dramatic effect upon the text's reception: "To give a text an Author is to impose a limit on that text, to furnish it with a final signified, to close the writing.... In the multiplicity of writing, everything is to be *disentangled,* nothing *deciphered*" (Barthes, 147). Thus, the implied author is seen to represent not the physical Author-as-Authority, but rather the aforementioned system of values embedded and expressed by the text itself. Of course, while these theoretical positions suggest that the conceptual assembly of the implied author is the purview of the reader, Booth indicates that the author also participates in this projection: "This implied author is always distinct from the 'real man'—whatever we take him to be—who creates a superior version of himself, a 'second self,' as he creates his work" (Booth, 70). Regardless of its origin, this metaphorical transfer of power—the notion that the *meaning* of a text may be determined by the reader rather than the author—is a precursor to several core attributes of digital storytelling and indicates a certain desire for interactivity and narrative agency on the part of the reader.

How, then, does this view of communication change with the advent of new technologies? The fundamental assumption laid out by Jakobson and carried forth from structuralism into subsequent branches of narrative theory is that the act of transmission is inherently unidirectional. Addressees may compose messages in reply, but this simply reverses the designations of the participants: the receiver becomes a sender, embeds the texts with their own system of codes and values, and transmits the new message. However, a subtle distinction becomes apparent in digital fiction, as the addressee now has certain tools at their disposal which enable assimilation and modification of the source text itself. This may manifest as limited control over the plot, the ability to generate simulacra of existing fictional worlds, or the substitution (partial or total) of the implied author itself, along with the application of a different value system defined by the reader's personal, cultural and psychological background. Moreover, the unprecedented level of access and instantaneous communication afforded by use of the Internet blurs any remaining boundaries between author and reader: feedback to a published text may arrive within mere minutes, and subsequently facilitate immediate real-time dialogue between the two parties. This new form of authorship raises complex questions regarding canonicity, communal reception, textual modification and more, all of which will be discussed forthwith.

The Fictional World and Its Inhabitants

Among its other contributions to the discourse, narratology has also greatly advanced the study of diegetic constructs. In *Fictional Worlds*, Thomas Pavel depicts these constructs as "possible worlds" positioned as alternatives to our own, albeit inherently limited by its own methods of depiction: "How can we define a function that attributes individuals to possible worlds? ... To require from possible worlds an inventory of beings identical to the inventory of the actual one is a position too restrictive for the representation of fictional ontologies" (Pavel, 45–46). In essence, Pavel argues that the process of creating fictional worlds involves transferring familiar objects from consensus reality into said worlds, allowing them to coexist with objects "native" to that fictional reality. Lubomir Dolezel offers a complimentary critical perspective in *Heterocosmica*, focusing on the reader's engagement with specific cognitive processes that form and actualize these diegetic realms: "Actual persons, authors and readers, can access fictional worlds but only by crossing somehow the world boundary between the realms of the actual and the possible. Due to the different ontological status of these realms, physical entry, direct observation and ostension (Rescher 1975, 93) are unthinkable. ...fictional worlds are accessed through semiotic channels and by means of information processing" (Dolezel, 20). Dolezel also draws attention to the significant role the author plays in this process: "The fiction maker is free to roam over the entire universe of possible worlds, to call into fictional existence a world of any type. This is eminently true about the basic types. Physically impossible worlds, called supernatural or fantastic, are as well represented in fiction of all periods as are physically possible worlds, called natural or realistic" (Dolezel, 256). This theoretical paradigm is complicated—but not invalidated—by the possibility of multiple texts making use of the same fictional world; Huckleberry Finn and Tom Sawyer are two early examples of this practice, as protagonists of separate novels who co-exist in Mark Twain's fictional recreation of the American South. Other texts may contain more than one fictional world, per Dolezel's claim that "the set of fictional worlds is unlimited and maximally varied" (Dolezel, 19), as seen in science-fiction and fantasy; the latter regularly produces lengthy sagas that exhaustively portray a particular diegesis, while the former's generic formulae supports (and often encourages) exploration of multiple worlds and layers of reality.

When considering the impact digital technology has had (and continues to have) on the construction, reception and interpretation of fictional worlds and their contents, we must take into account Dolezel's point regarding the one feature common to all such ontological structures, regardless of author, genre or method of production:

> Both fictional and historical worlds are by necessity incomplete. To construct a complete possible world would require writing a text of infinite length—a task that is beyond human capability. If possible worlds of fiction and history are incomplete, then gaps are a universal feature of their macrostructure.... The fiction writer is free to vary the number, the extent and the functions of the gaps; his choices are determined by aesthetic (stylistic) and semantic factors [Dolezel, 257–258].

This notion of lacunae, gaps that are by necessity built into the very fabric of any fictional text, is irrefutable when viewing pre-digital narrative platforms: novels, film, television series and theater performances are all bound by the inherent limitations of their medium with regards to length and/or duration. By contrast, web-based fiction imposes no such restrictions—for example, John McCrae's serialized novel *Worm* totals nearly two million words and was concluded at the author's whim rather than any physical limitations, while Twitch-based roleplaying group *Critical Role* have produced over 900 hours of filmed narrative content since 2015. As a purely digital space, the Internet allows for the possibility of publishing and distributing theoretically infinite texts, precisely the mode of writing Dolezel claimed was beyond human capability. Can digital platforms therefore overcome the universal need for ontological gaps, and produce works which continually address their own lacunae?

Any ontological analysis of a fictional text must also take into consideration the inhabitants of said text: its actants and characters. David Gorman indicates that narrative theory is predisposed towards studying the strategies used to populate fictional worlds, and that the presence and participation of these actants is an essential component in any story:

> First, what does not change is that actions in narratives need agents. Although stories can be told without agents—about the origin of the planets, say, or the extinction of the dinosaurs—these are narratives of events, not actions. What differentiates actions from events, mere happenings, is agency (see Davidson), which in turn opens the door to considerations about intention, motive, and characterization in the broad sense (keeping it in mind, obviously, that action includes reactions to what befalls, since these also manifest agency) [Gorman, 174].

While different narratological approaches inevitably apply different lenses for the examination of characters and their functions, one common conclusion regarding actants is the static nature of their narrative roles. The text itself does not and cannot change, and so interpretations of Tom Sawyer must be contained within the framework of the words Twain uses to describe him. Adaptations may take liberties with these restrictions, as seen most commonly with characters such as James Bond, Dracula or Sherlock Holmes, who have long since escaped the confines of their original cultural and historical contexts; but for all their elasticity, the source material still establishes basic, immutable traits that resist alteration or revision. James Bond's various incarnations will always be womanizers, just as Sherlock Holmes will always shun social interactions and sentiment in favor of intellectual analysis. The extent to which these traits manifest over decades of adaptation varies as well: the first televised adaptation of *Casino Royale* depicted James Bond as an American named Jimmy; BBC television series *Sherlock* implicitly interprets Holmes' antisocial behavior as the product of a neurobiological disorder similar to Asperger's, while its American counterpart *Elementary* posits that Sherlock's affinity for narcotics is a crippling addiction rather than an affectation; 2014 film *Dracula Untold* attempts to paint a sympathetic portrait of Vlad III of Wallachia, despite the historical figure's notoriety. Each of these examples pushes against the prescribed boundaries of what these characters are widely believed to be, yet those aforementioned core traits persist from version to version: Dracula is a narcissistic supernatural predator, Bond a suave and seductive spy, Holmes an exceptionally intelligent detective with an innate compulsion to solve mysteries and explain the inexplicable. These iconic attributes represent lines no adaptation can cross without penalty—specifically, the threat of rejection by audiences familiar with said traits.

But just as digital fiction challenges the theoretical limitations of text as imposed by page counts and reel length, so too does it problematize the assumption of textual permanence with regards to characterization. Digital textuality is not only limitless but transient: the content of a web page may be edited at will, with no easy access to previous versions. A character's initial depiction may be completely overwritten or deleted altogether, leaving no visible sign of revision. The closest analogy to this process would be a reprinted novel or the Director's Cut of a film, which may include updates that change particular aspects of plot or characterization: for example, Ridley Scott's *Blade Runner* has been repackaged multiple times, most recently with variations that significantly alter the audience's perception of protagonist Rick Deckard. The *Star Wars* films have also been rereleased with additional special effects layered onto them, directly impacting the visual representation of its alien landscapes. However, in such cases, the original physical object—whether textual or cinematic—still exists and can be used as a basis for comparative analysis. Retrieving a previous version of a webpage is not nearly as simple or all-inclusive a process, and assumptions of diegetic fidelity may be completely unfounded. Thus, the impermanence and fluidity of digital narratives may have significant impact on existing strategies of characterization and character analysis.

Time, Space and Plot

The positioning of a narrative in time and space is highly relevant to any analysis of its diegetic world. All works of fiction share the basic requirement of taking place "somewhere" and "somewhen"—J.R.R. Tolkien's *The Lord of the Rings*, for example, begins in the year 3018 of the Third Age, in the realm of Middle-Earth. Mikhail Bakhtin refers to this fundamental narrative component as a chronotope, a term meant to ascribe equal importance to both time and space in determining the nature of a given world. This conflation of the spatial and the temporal is further affirmed by

Susan Stanford Friedman, who also emphasizes the inherent narrative significance of these same boundaries being transgressed:

> Space restored to its full partnership with time as a generative force for narrative allows for reading strategies focused on the dialogic interplay of space and time as mediating coconstituents of human thought and experience. In this sense, space is not passive, static, or empty; it is not, as it is in so much narrative theory, the (back)-ground upon which events unfold in time.... Space within the story told—the space through which characters move and in which events happen—is often the site of encounter, of border crossings and cultural mimesis.... Borders of all kinds are forever being crossed; but the experience of crossing depends upon the existence of borders in the first place [Friedman, 195–196].

While the chronotope finds expression in any work of fiction, the manner of this expression changes depending on the type of story being told, and the medium through which it is being transmitted to its audience; Bakhtin states that "the chronotope in literature has an intrinsic *generic* significance. It can even be said that it is precisely the chronotope that defines genre and generic distinctions, for in literature the primary category of the chronotope is time" (Bakhtin, 53). As with other basic components of narrative, the concepts of setting and chronotope have similarly been challenged by technological advances which have led to new methods of representing temporality and spatiality. For example, the virtual worlds displayed in contemporary video games use their platform's capabilities to depict ontological structures no literary or cinematic text can fully emulate. These, in turn, have created new genres and new types of chronotopes, many of which are still being codified today.

Temporality and spatiality also find expression on the level of plot, per E.M. Forster: "We have defined a story as a narrative of events arranged in their time-sequence. A plot is also a narrative of events, the emphasis falling on causality.... The time-sequence is preserved, but the sense of causality overshadows it" (Forster, 45). While pre-digital narratives are capable of manipulating the presentation of diegetic events for artistic and/or thematic purposes (as seen with the film *Memento* or Martin Amis' novel *Time's Arrow*, in which the plot unfolds in reverse chronological order), digital fiction holds an unprecedented capacity for rewriting and rearranging narrative chronotopes. Fan fiction, a prolific mode of online writing, is defined in part by the granting of pseudo-authorial powers (that is to say, the presumed authority of a creator to determine the embedded system of values and the direction of the plot) to any reader; these powers include manipulation of the setting and the causal sequence of story events. Many modern video games work along similar lines, offering the player limited power to determine the order of narrative scenarios, or whether particular events occur at all; likewise, webcomics are able to use the "infinite canvas" provided online to distort, manipulate and elongate the reader's sense of causality and the nominal chronotope. This mutability of plot, contrasted with supposedly iron-clad concepts of spatiality and temporality, is a further example of the ways in which digital storytelling challenges existing paradigms.

The Desire for Agency as a Guiding Principle of Digital Fiction

While new technologies challenge prevailing notions of narrative and their limitations, Abbott insists there is no need to dismiss all existing critical thought as irrelevant or outmoded: "The first general point I want to make, however, is that these diverse experiments in technologically assisted narrative, wonderful and promising as they are, do not represent a revolution or even a minor change in the enduring structures of narrative. Narrative will continue to be narrative, so in this sense the future of narrative is the past of narrative" (Abbott, 531). Indeed, the throughline that becomes apparent upon closer observation is precisely the consistency of the aforementioned key components: even as new tools have been developed to meet an existing desire for interactivity, digital fiction still conforms to the basic requirements of communication, authorial presence, ontological structure, characterization and setting. At the same time, this continuing evolution has had a clear and direct impact on the perceived upper limits of narrative form and function:

> Advances in digitization, connectivity, graphical manipulation, parallel processing, modal interfacing, virtual reality (VR), Flash, and much else have enabled striking transformations of the feel and texture of narrative, whether as hypertext fiction, interactive fiction (IF), text adventures, cybertexts, MUDs (multiuser domains), MOOs (object-oriented MUDs), MMORPGs (massively multiplayer online role-playing games), theme-based amusement park rides built around popular films, or any number of hybrids [Abbott, 529].

This book will focus on three modes of digital fiction, each of which employs a particular platform to satisfy its audience's desire for increased textual and diegetic interactivity with the text. The first section will discuss fan fiction, a form of storytelling which in many ways epitomizes the nature of the Internet itself. The second section will focus on the medium of video games, in which the relationship between technology and narrative experimentation is most abundantly evident. Finally, the third chapter will engage in a comparison between print comics (best exemplified by the globally recognized superhero genre) and their digital equivalents in webcomics, with an eye towards delineating the ways in which both forms of writing express reflexivity and interactivity. Contrary to other scholarly efforts in these fields, this book will demonstrate that the myriad forms of digital writing are not separate, distinct phenomena; rather, they are all products of the same impetus, results of diverse experiments aiming to fulfill a singular goal. As such, they share much more common ground than current theories would suggest, and greater insight concerning their nature and what lies ahead may be gleaned when they are viewed thusly. Exploring the areas in which these media and the fiction they produce intersect and overlap will enable future researchers to take a broader, more inclusive perspective on interactivity and agency in digital narratives; this, in turn, will illuminate how specific tools and techniques transition from one platform to another, further advancing each in turn.

1

Fan Fiction

The Impetus and Methodologies of Fan Fiction

In *Fic: Why Fanfiction Is Taking Over the World,* Anne Jamison attempts to situate the mode of writing known as fan fiction within a larger historical tradition of adaptation and appropriation, claiming that "our understanding of the key relationships—those that exist variously among writer, reader, publisher, object published, and source—changes over time. What doesn't change, or rather, what never disappears, is the writerly habit of writing from sources" (Jamison, 54). While Jamison's comparison does establish certain parallels between common practices in fan fiction and creative processes attributed to Cervantes, Shakespeare and Eliot, a deeper narratological examination of fan fiction's structures and processes reveals a form of writing which has found its ultimate expression in the digital age, and thus differentiates itself entirely from its historical predecessors.

Tisha Turk offers a rudimentary definition of fan fiction as follows: "Fans of a particular source text write stories set in and/or featuring characters from that text's fictional world, usually in order to explore the emotions, motivations, and inner lives of familiar characters; to examine, extend, or create relationships between characters; or to put those characters in new situations" (Turk, 83). More specifically, these exploratory works use accessible media platforms to create and distribute new stories. While fan-texts are, as Turk indicates, explicitly based upon pre-established fictional worlds, each invariably contains a new implied author, representing the fan-author's own embedded system of values. As such, the framing of fan fiction as a reader's rebellion against the Authority of the Author, as put forth by Henry Jenkins' *Textual Poachers*, is especially cogent:

> Unimpressed by institutional authority and expertise, the fans assert their own right to form interpretations, to offer evaluations, and to construct cultural canons. Undaunted by traditional conceptions of literary and intellectual property, fans raid mass culture, claiming its materials for their own use, reworking them as the basis for their own cultural creations and social interactions. Fans

seemingly blur the boundaries between fact and fiction, speaking of characters as if they had an existence apart from their textual manifestations, entering into the realm of the fiction as if it were a tangible place they can inhabit and explore [Jenkins, 18].

Any discussion on the construction, distribution, proliferation and effect of fan fiction first requires context regarding the impetus behind its production. As previously mentioned, Dolezel makes the case for viewing all works of fiction as inherently incomplete: "Since fictional gaps are created in the act of world-making, they are ontological in nature. They are irrecoverable lacunae that cannot be filled by legitimate inference. Statements about fictional gaps are undecidable: it can never be decided whether Emma Bovary did or did not have a birthmark on her left shoulder" (Dolezel, 258). Dolezel argues that these ontological gaps represent an obstacle that cannot be overcome without producing a text of infinite length—by definition, an impossible task. But the deliberate omission of information on the part of the author constitutes the initial point of entry for fan fiction creators: to address and manipulate those lacunae already extant in the ontological fabric of the original text.

The cognitive process which enables and encourages readers to fill these gaps through fan fiction involves what Catherine Gunther Kodat refers to as eidetic variation. In discussing disparate and diverse representations of Spartacus in fiction, Kodat argues that

casting Spartacus as a figure subject to eidetic variation through narrative allows us to view the multiple Spartacus iterations as a connected series of gestures in which what first appears as the strength of a single figure to hold together a crumbling narrative (the fragmentary, incomplete, and contradictory early histories of a slave rebellion in which Spartacus is the common thread) slowly becomes an exploration (really, a test) of the capacities of narrative to contain a single protean figure [Kodat, 486].

This lends credence to Jamison's positioning of fan fiction within a broader literary tradition: the aforementioned examples of Bram Stoker's Dracula, Ian Fleming's James Bond and Arthur Conan Doyle's Sherlock Holmes have all been subjected to extensive eidetic variation for decades, via a multitude of authors and implied authors, and across multiple narrative platforms. According to Kodat, this elasticity has, over time, shaped the minds of contemporary readers to accept multiplicities of meaning when encountering such contradictions, rather than attempt to place them within a hierarchical and authoritative framework:

Viewing the serial iterations of Spartacus as products of just such a process of eidetic variation, one that helps uncover what might, genealogically speaking, be called the "family resemblance" among them, has led me to make several observations. First, it is clear that the many versions of Spartacus both reflect and critique constructions of freedom particular to their given moments of production, and that those constructions are themselves genealogically connected. Second, this approach to the Spartacus narratives shows how difference emerges out of sameness... [Kodat, 487].

Writ large and taken in conjunction with this view of "reader rebellion," Kodat's theory applies as much to ontological gaps as it does to alternative representations of iconic characters such as Spartacus. The same elasticity that permits the modern reader to access and contain divergent interpretations also validates the mindset of the fan-author, allowing for multiple (and potentially oppositional) extrapolations of the same source text, and treating ontological lacunae as narrative catalysts rather than obstacles. It is this perspective that has actualized literary concepts previously limited to the theoretical realm.

Both Jamison and Jenkins assert that fan fiction predates the Internet as a tool of mass communication and publication. Prior to the prevalence of online technologies, the production and distribution of fan works were bound by the inherent limitations of physical media—published in 1992, Jenkins' account of fan production notes that the most significant innovation at the time was the newfound ability to record television episodes using blank video cassettes:

> These viewing strategies, made possible by the technology's potentials, extend the fans' mastery over the narrative and accommodate the community's production of new texts from the series materials. These strategies also create the distance required to perceive the series episodes as subject to direct intervention by the fan and the familiarity with all aspects of the program world required for the creation of new narratives [Jenkins, 74].

Thus, while any individual reader or viewer at the time could use eidetic variation to construct a work of fan fiction, the ability to share that narrative and receive feedback from other fans was constricted by the unilateral nature of communication (following Jakobson's paradigm): having received and decoded the "message" (in this case, the source text), the addressee would compose a new message via fan fiction, encode it using the fan's choice of implied author, and distribute it through specific channels (homemade video cassettes, printed "zines") to other receivers. Jenkins' description of printed fan work collections, shared and distributed via physical means within limited communities, gives some idea as to the finite scope of pre-digital fan production: "A typical issue lists some 258 different current publications (with a number of them having published 30 issues or more) and another 113 publications in planning stages" (Jenkins, 159). By contrast, May 2020 statistics for the website Archive of Our Own (henceforth referred to as AO3), which functions as an online repository for works of fan fiction, indicate that the site currently contains over 6,000,000 texts, published by over 1,600,000 authors. The incomparably vast scale at which fan fiction operates today most clearly delineates the extent to which contemporary technology has been used to bolster the same desire for interactivity in the creation and consumption of narrative which already existed in the age of VHS cassettes and zines. The Internet now functions as a theoretically-infinite, unrestricted publishing space while simultaneously serving as a tool of near-instantaneous communication between members of global fan communities.

To understand how deeply this undermines previous perceptions of narrative limitations, this chapter will further elaborate on the technologies supporting (and encouraging) fan fiction. In *Hypertext 3.0*, George P. Landow claims that "Western culture imagined quasimagical entrances to a networked reality long before the development of computing technology" (Landow, 57). Certainly, there have been many literary and cinematic works which posit "fluidity" in opposition to the "solid" nature of physical textual objects: Michael Ende's 1979 novel *The Neverending Story* features an ontoleptic process in which the boundaries between the diegetic and hypodiegetic dissolve; alongside its peers in the cyberpunk genre, William Gibson's *Neuromancer* describes a realm in which information networks are both ubiquitous and almost-universally accessible. Yet while these texts express, in different ways, the same idealized notion of heightened accessibility to which Landow refers, the advent of the Internet as a tool of near-instantaneous communication actualized this concept and served as a catalyst for the formation of online fan communities and the shift of fan production into digital space. Any presumption of a hierarchical or unilateral binary dissolves in this mode of writing: no work of fan fiction is inherently more authoritative or "canonical" than another, and online archives such as AO3 can (and do) contain a vast array of fan works based on conflicting interpretations of the source text. For all that fan fiction has developed its own literary aesthetics and standards (to be detailed shortly), neither the fan communities themselves nor their archival websites impose any evaluative processes or grading systems upon published fan texts. The prioritization of accessibility finds purchase in the common use of the Internet today, as a widespread utility designed for easy access—a feature Landow explicitly links to the generation of fan-narratives:

> The development of the World Wide Web has stimulated this active reading even more, and one can find all kinds of works by readers who want to write *their versions* of materials commercially published. The presence and productions of very active readers answer the critics of digital information technology who claim it cannot demonstrate any examples of cultural democratization [Landow, 8].

The architecture of the Internet has allowed fan fiction to become one of the most ubiquitous forms of literature in existence. While the medium itself still serves its primary function by facilitating global communication, Graham Allen leaves no doubt that its secondary purpose—its service as a narrative platform—emerged due to desires formulated and explored in pre-digital literary theory:

> Digitalized computing systems such as the World Wide Web, electronic books and hypertexts present a form of intertextuality which seems to many to have finally made manifest the theoretical arguments we have analyzed in this study. Whilst theorists such as Barthes, Kristeva and Derrida attack the traditionally dominant idea of the work's isolation, individuality and authority, the new computer-based systems seem to embody such critiques [Allen, 199].

Indeed, the Internet's unique intertextual and hypertextual mechanisms have allowed fan fiction to realize its full potential, as fan communities once maintained by limited contact between individuals or small groups, and restricted by the capacity of physical media, are now transnational, transcultural spaces open to anyone who meets the qualifying precondition of "being a fan." The constant and persistent communication between fans—be they readers, writers or a combination of both—deeply impacts not only the manner in which fan fiction is consumed, but its stylistic evolution as well, per Ashton Spacey's observation that "engagement with fandom is an interpretive process whereby we explore cultural events and attitudes and the resonances they have with us and with others. Participating within fan communities—and the generation and consumption of fan fiction—remains one of our most prolific forms of active cultural expression" (Spacey, 8).

The near-industrial speed with which creation of fan fiction follows the dissemination of a source text to its target audience is remarkable— fan works addressing ontological lacunae or superimposing a new implied author have at times appeared within 24 hours of the original's release. This has resulted in a cyclical process of readers becoming fan-authors transmitting stories to other readers via what David Ciccoricco calls a network narrative, which "differs not only in its nonhierarchical organization but also in that its narrative emerges gradually through a recombination of elements" (Ciccoricco, 6). The Internet's use of hyperlinks—a quintessential navigational function that enables connectivity between different webpages and sites—has been repurposed by fan communities to form and maintain those connections. These communities further serve as both guides and repositories for new readers, organizing the works of participating fan-authors with links to individual creator profiles, recommendations and so on: "Anyone who stumbles upon any of these writings is likely to find them linked to a personal or group site containing biographies of the site owner, explanations of the imaginative world, and lists of links to similar stories. The link, in other words, makes immediately visible the virtual community created by these active readers" (Landow, 8).

But while the current digital incarnation of fan fiction may be the product and expression of previous desires for interactivity and authorial agency, it has not yet been perfected. On the contrary, the dependency of digital writing upon specific technologies carries with it the potential of its own undoing: "although electronic writing has the multiplicity of print, it does not have the fixity—and hence the reliability and stability—of either written or printed texts" (Landow, 34). For all its near-infinite variety and the lack of internal competition or hierarchical mandates, fan fiction remains reliant on external factors (servers, networks, individual user connectivity) to the extent that a simple power outage, a hardware failure, or a software malfunction of any kind could render an entire library inaccessible at best, permanently lost at worst. Similarly, authors who choose to delete their works are able to ensure a degree of erasure more functionally complete than any parallel in print-based fiction. As such, delving into the literary history of fan fiction can potentially become an exercise in digital archaeology, requiring distant archived "snapshots" of material no longer in circulation, which may not reflect all revisions or alterations made to the text prior to its removal. Accessibility and ease-of-use are both the greatest strength and greatest fallibility of digital writing in general, and fan fiction in particular.

Another potential drawback stems from the free and virtually unrestricted nature of digital space. The sheer uncontrolled quantity of narratives produced and published via this medium makes any comprehensive study of the corpus of fan fiction all but impossible: "Network narratives have boundaries and limits, but they do not offer a reliable way to analyze a structural whole: in an obvious sense readers may or may not encounter all of the nodes that exist in the textual database, but less obvious is the fact that even if they do, it is unlikely that all of the possible permutations of the text will be realized" (Ciccoricco, 28–29). Because digital technology has encouraged and actualized multiplicities of meaning and noncompetitive/nonhierarchical spaces, and given the absence of any supervising body to impose aesthetic standards (below which a work may not be published), attempts to critically engage with fan fiction must by necessity take a narrow and focused approach in the selection of primary texts. The solution proposed herein is to conduct a narratological analysis of ten works along structuralist lines, in an attempt to establish the primary attributes of fan fiction, how said attributes differentiate themselves from their print-based predecessors, and how each feature shares heretofore-unexplored common ground with other expressions of digital writing, bridging the gaps in critical thought between seemingly disparate platforms of interactive fiction.

Competing Authorial Powers, Conflicting Implied Authors

One of the most central concepts in narrative theory to be substantially challenged by the onset of digital writing is authorship. As indicated previously, the act of creating fan fiction presupposes the validity of Booth's theory of the implied author, a theoretical construct designed to stand in for "Authority." Shaw draws attention to the reader's active role in perceiving and interpreting the implied author:

> The implied author is a critical reconstruction of the mind behind the rhetorical purposes informing a work of narrative. It serves to focus the question "What would you have to have believed and valued to have created this work?" by constructing an anthropomorphic agent of belief, and thereby invites those who use it to employ the vast and subtle panoply of techniques, most of them unformulated and hardly conscious, that we draw upon in everyday life when we try to assess the values and intentions of others [Shaw, 301].

Where Booth characterizes the reader as a recipient of the implied author's values—pursuant to Barthes' statement that "the reader is without history, biography, psychology; he is simply that *someone* who holds together in a single field all the traces by which the written text is constituted" (Barthes, 148)—Shaw follows a more active and engaged model of readership. The cognitive processes undertaken by the audience ultimately lead to analysis, interpretation and revelation. But in the hands of fan-authors, these mechanisms are adapted to achieve a transformative effect common to works of fan fiction: using eidetic variation to exploit existing lacunae in the source text, the fan-author is able to reconfigure the implied author and embed a different set of values. Fan fiction may thus be defined as the furthest possible expression of active readership, in which interpretation is no longer personal, individual and self-contained, but rather the foundation of new narrative creation, distributed for consumption by like-minded readers.

Even those critics who espouse the removal of the writer from analytical consideration cannot completely ignore the biographical, social, cultural and political contexts in which the work was produced. Susan S. Lanser states that the author's identity will inevitably play a part in any act of interpretation, regardless of whether the reader accepts or contests the implied author's values:

> Readers may deconstruct this "I," may argue that it utters meanings the author did not "intend," may challenge its assertions, may charge it with various misprisions—for every "I" is ultimately the beholder's "I," by which I mean the "I" that the reader constructs in the process of reading. Readers may of course question the attribution of a text to a certain author, contest the legitimacy of

a particular edition of a text, seek out the truth behind a pseudonym [Lanser, 208].

However, Lanser's proposed solution of "seeking out the truth" becomes a practical impossibility in digital writing. Anonymity—a mere affectation within fan communities in the '90s, when according to Jenkins "the identities of writers are often openly known within the fan community even as they are cloaked on the printed page" (Jenkins, 206)—has become the norm. This depersonalization is expressed in many different ways online, but for narratological purposes, the most significant outcome is an inability to pin down the identity of a fan-author for the purpose of extrapolation. Any attribute that could be used to shed further light on the nature of the text—the author's gender, class, ethnicity, geographical location, cultural upbringing, political ideology, etc.—is not only absent but impossible to reconstruct. Moreover, as Jamison points out, the Internet enables writers to adopt and experiment with multiple authorial personae:

> The option of anonymity led to the possibility of identity play. Plenty of people who would never dream of dressing up as Princess Leia or a Klingon at a fan convention were drawn to create online personae that were themselves a kind of fiction. …they far more often gave people the opportunity to try on new styles, genders, sexualities, and appearances—to live differently, sometimes with more daring, than they did in real life. Today, in female-majority fic communities, a woman writer might take on a male identity to get attention, to experiment with interacting as male, or sometimes to make a political point. A male enthusiast can pass as female and avoid extra attention. People often claim no gender or race or orientation, although many find the same issues and tensions resurfacing in online communities or grow weary of assumptions made about them [Jamison, 141].

Consequently, any sense of the physical entity actively composing and publishing fan-works becomes distorted. For the first time, a form of literature has emerged in which the Author is not only dead but disintegrated beyond hope of reconstitution; only the text remains, and thus scholarly efforts must be directed elsewhere, towards the common values, core tropes and aesthetic standards which have emerged with the consolidation of online fandom as a collective space for reading, writing and rewriting.

A primary aesthetic trait common to all fan works is the balancing act between two paradoxically intertwined necessities: innovation on the one hand, and a particular type of mimesis on the other, expressed as fidelity to the source text. Susan M. Garrett's base guidelines for the evaluation of a fan fiction narrative attempt to firmly establish this principle: "Is the story consistent with what you know of that show? Were the characters and dialogue true to the series or were they false and stilted? … Did the author have some original ideas, was the story just the 'same old thing' or was it 'the same old thing' in a new and vibrant style?" (Jenkins, 164–165). According to Garrett, the value of originality is not absolute, but rather contingent upon a broader consistency with the source material; interpretations which stray too far afield may not be erased outright from the digital space but will certainly be rejected en masse by the community (aptly indicating the upper threshold of eidetic variation). At the same time, fan fiction texts perceived to be "the same old thing" also fall short of Garrett's standards, as they merely regurgitate canonical content. One may therefore conclude that an "ideal" fan fiction narrative (if such a thing might exist) is assembled via a two-step process: first, the ontological structure of the source text—the "original" fictional world—is simulated as accurately as possible, in a form of second-degree mimesis wherein the object being mimicked is itself fictional; innovation is then expressed on the level of plot and character, as the fan-author attempts to recontextualize or directly address gaps in what Ryan refers to as the storyworld, the "complex spatio-temporal totality that undergoes global changes ... an imagined totality that evolves according to the events in the story" (Ryan, 13).

This process is complicated by the wide range of strategies and interpretations produced—and frequently supported—by fan communities, many of which are designed from inception to distort assertions made by the source text regarding its own canonical values, per Spacey's claim that "fan works and fan communities are actively using the genre in order to foreground their concerns. They explore how fan communities continue to generate counternarratives to challenge the forms of hegemonic discourse which traditionally invisibilize and silence them" (Spacey, 13).

Karen Hellekson and Kristina Busse offer further clarification regarding the role of transformative, communicative fandom in this process of production:

> Affirmative fans tend to collect, view, and play, to discuss, analyze, and critique. Transformative fans, however, take a creative step to make the worlds and characters their own, be it by telling stories, cosplaying the characters, creating artworks, or engaging in any of the many other forms active fan participation can take.... Further, transformative fans are often critical of the texts (both of the texts they consume and the texts they create), so they present an active audience that not only disproves the passive-audience models favored in early audience studies but also creates artifacts that can be analyzed and that exist to provide proof of that discontent [Hellekson & Busse 2014, 3–4].

As noted previously, the projection of multiple and variable meanings from a singular text is not in itself an anomalous phenomenon, as it corresponds to existing critical thought regarding the effects of interpretive communities and individual psychological factors on the reading process. But where the interpretations of pre-digital readers could be routinely challenged or threatened by divergent readings, the Internet allows for the spreading of limitless amounts of reconfigurations—a near-endless multiplicity of meanings, all co-existing under the presumption of equal legitimacy and validity. The proliferation of works is practically viral in its speed and efficiency: if, as mentioned previously, a single source narrative in any medium may generate fan fiction responses within 24 hours, hundreds of additional narratives may emerge in subsequent days. Each fan fiction text employs its own stylistic and thematic strategies to project a fictional world superficially identical to the original but designed to enable the fan-author's "usurpation" of the implied author. This, in turn, has a direct and quantifiable impact on the representation of the fan-fictional world itself, as its depiction is informed by this new system of values; canonical ontological details may be modified or removed outright for the purposes of aligning the text with its new meaning. And where Cervantes once found himself in competition with Avellaneda, compelled to produce an "official" sequel to *Don Quixote* in order to contest Avellaneda's inferior derivation, there is no need for any such uniformity in fan fiction, nor would there be any means of enforcing such a thing were it necessary. Garrett's guidelines may inform the popularity of a given work, but failure to meet those aesthetic standards does not prevent any excessively transgressive text from being published and shared. On the contrary, all deviations from the template provided by the source text are equally contained and granted archival space, with no question raised as to which new implied author is more "real" or "authentic." It is this lack of internal hierarchical evaluation, as well as the absence of any particular imperative on the part of fan authors to adhere to Garrett's self-imposed guidelines, which effectively dismantles current applications of the theory of the implied author and differentiates fan fiction from adaptations of source texts. Fan fiction may rewrite Sherlock Holmes as a lesbian alien, James Bond as a neurotic time traveler, Dracula as a vegan high school teacher; and within digital spaces of publication, these vastly divergent representations are capable of going beyond what is "permitted," to the extent that the end product may not be recognizable as an appropriated work at all. Furthermore, as Charity A. Fowler notes, fandom itself is not monolithic, and while all works of fan fiction may deploy the same substitution of implied authors, these new systems of values are not at all singular and homogenous, frequently "splintering" and fragmenting over ongoing ideological debates:

> As a result of this canonical antagonism, many of the works contain emotional and physical violence. For some time now, disagreements over how to handle elements such as these in fan fiction have fractured certain fandom spaces, leading to instances of aggressive policing, bullying and calls for censorship. These debates are not new—to fandom or feminism—but neither are they settled, and they offer a foundation from which to launch the argument about bad bromance slash and female desire [Fowler, 178].

Landow attributes this "splintering" effect to the structure of the Internet itself: "This hypertextual dissolution of centrality, which makes the medium such a potentially democratic one, also makes it a model of society of conversations in which no one conversation, no one discipline or ideology, dominates or founds the others" (Landow, 123). The absence of any dominant organizing principle raises questions as to the specific relationships and dynamics between a source text and its numerous fan fiction offspring. For Turk, the two are inextricably bound: "For readers of fan fiction, immersion in the fantext requires not only engaging in the pretense that the fictional world of the source text is real … but also engaging in the pretense that the fictional world of the fan work is part of the fictional world of the source text and/or that the characters in the fan work are contiguous with those of the source text" (Turk, 99–100). Implicit in Turk's argument is the notion that the template remains an active component in the experience of reading fan fiction, and therefore any access to a fan fiction text is inherently comparative—each implied author is evaluated by the accuracy of its ontological mimesis. This would seem to confirm the validity of Garrett's perspective, reiterating the mandate to maintain some tangible link to the source text; it would also reaffirm Ciccoricco's statement regarding the significance of repetition and subsequent deviation in electronic writing: "Mimesis governs this mode of repetition. In providing obedient copies or representations, it resists distortion or additions. By contrast, masked or disguised repetition derives force by 'knowingly' imparting difference" (Ciccoricco, 16–17). However, the sheer volume of multiplicities available for consumption, and the community's ability to assimilate clashing systems of values without producing internal contradictions, suggests that immersion is possible even with fan fiction narratives that distance themselves—deliberately or unknowingly—from the source work. In essence, this is a practical application of Jean Baudrillard's theory concerning postmodernism's nullification of the need for a "real" original: "The point is not, then, to assert that the real does or does not exist—a ludicrous proposition which well expresses what that reality means to us: a tautological hallucination ('the real exists, I have met it').... For the body of the real was never recovered. In the shroud of the virtual, the corpse of the real is forever unfindable" (Baudrillard, 46). If the boundary between reality and a representation of reality may be blurred, there would no longer be any significant difference between an original and its simulacrum. As with those of his contemporaries, Baudrillard's hypothesis finds material purchase in digital writing: the aesthetic imperative proposed by Garrett calls for an initial simulation of the original, which can (and must) then be altered at will. It is this simulacrum that readers will respond to, and—as will be demonstrated in short order—the canonical original is quickly rendered irrelevant, as fan fiction either subverts or openly violates ontological principles or laws put forth by the source material. In some cases, a work of fan fiction may itself become an "original" in the eyes of its readership, prompting the production of second-order fan fiction from the community in response, and distancing the work even further from any pretense of fidelity and mimesis.

To demonstrate how fan-authors are able to share the same virtual space without the need for competition (and subsequent exclusion), a case study is required. Despite Ciccoricco's valid point that a complete and thorough survey of electronic writing is beyond human capacity, Jenkins reiterates the value of critical analysis and extrapolation in the study of individual works: "No single work of fan literature encompasses the full range of rewriting strategies described above. Yet a closer look at one particular narrative may illustrate the systematic reworking of broadcast texts characteristic of this mode of cultural production" (Jenkins, 182). For the purpose of this specific inquiry, two works of fan fiction will be selected from the same community, the Yuletide Challenge. Rather than base itself on a specific source text or fandom, the Yuletide Challenge is distinguished by its method of generating narrative: "Yuletide is an annual fic exchange for rare and obscure fandoms. Participants sign up to write a story of at least 1,000 words in a fandom someone else has requested, using the selected characters from that fandom. In return, they receive a story of at least 1,000 words in a fandom they have requested, featuring requested character" (The Yuletide FAQ). The Challenge sets its submission deadline near or during Christmas, which contextualizes the creation of narrative as a holiday gift from one fan to another. Galvanized both by the challenge and its lack of restrictive guidelines, the community publishes a large quantity of multi-fandom material on an annual basis, with variable content (and quality of content), providing potential readers with a great many options for perusal; naturally, certain fandoms will appear more often than others based on contemporary popularity. Two Yuletide Challenge texts have been selected for this analysis, written by different authors and based on the same source material, the 1998 Japanese anime *Cowboy Bebop*. Set in a semi-dystopian future, the popular series centers around a pair of hapless bounty hunters named Jet Black and Spike Spiegel, whose solitary existence on the fringes of interplanetary society is occasionally interrupted by attempts (alternatively dramatic and comedic) to apprehend criminals. As a finite, self-contained work, the canonical narrative of *Cowboy Bebop* has a set beginning, middle and end; yet it is precisely the nature of the television medium which creates lacunae, as most of the events depicted in its 26 episodes do not occur in immediate chronological order. The gaps between episodes constitute fertile ground for exploring alternative possibilities.

Two such scenarios were produced by the Yuletide Challenge: *That Night She Dreamt of Stars* by kormantic, and *don't even recognize the stranger* by spock.

The point of departure for both works is the introduction of a homo-erotic component to the relationship between Jet and Spike. As such, both texts are situated in the "slash" genre (to be further detailed in short order) and correspond to common expressions of marginalized sexual identities in fandom, per Samantha Close and Cynthia Wang: "Slash provides a space to explore difference in social organization, in gender, in biology, in politics, and beyond" (Close & Wang, 158). Of course, these expressions are as varied and variable as the corpus of fan fiction itself, and the two Yuletide scenarios will aptly demonstrate Laura Campillo-Arnaiz's view that manifesting these expressions in fiction need not be utopian or quintessentially positive in order to perform their primary function:

> This genre offers the possibility of engaging with sexual fantasies to gain mastery over a host of deep-rooted negative feelings. These feelings of helplessness, humiliation, worthlessness and unlovability—feelings which almost all people have experienced at some point in their lives—are both explored and exploited…. This cathartic experience is anonymously and safely realized in websites around the Internet, where authors and readers can freely express and exorcize their darkest demons through these abusive, brutal and regularly non-consensual scenarios [Campillo Arnaiz, 124].

These variations in expression stem from the fact that the ontological lacuna targeted by the new implied authors is not information absent or withheld from the source text (events that might have occurred "off-screen"), but rather a hypothetical situation which did not or could not manifest in the template—in other words, both stories posit a homosexual attraction between characters who do not express such attraction in the series itself. But despite sharing this common foundation, the implied authors constructed by kormantic and spock exhibit disparate values and priorities, which pull them in diametrically opposed directions.

That Night She Dreamt of Stars is a post-narrative work set after the conclusion of *Cowboy Bebop* and the death of Spike Spiegel. As Jet and fellow deuteragonist Faye Valentine struggle to cope with the loss of their companion, the following conversation takes place:

> "Was he your lover?" She had been waiting to ask that question.
> "No, Faye." His voice sounded softer, ground down.
> "Never? But you wanted him, right?"
> Jet took the question more placidly than she'd expected, and rubbed the bridge of his nose before answering.
> "To tell you the truth, in the early days, I thought about it some." He said finally. "But not because I wanted him. I was just hoping to settle him

down a little. Thought maybe he was looking for an anchor. Turns out **he**
just wanted a ferryman to take him across the river."
Faye tilted her head, fuzzy on the reference but grasping its meaning anyway.
She also spied another helpful little gap she could prize open and poke
around in.
"Bullshit," she said with some satisfaction. "You wanted to nail him because
you wanted to nail him. Don't give me any of that 'for his own good' crap.
Of course you wanted him.... Figures. Cops always have authority kinks"
[*That Night She Dreamt of Stars*, kormantic].

This simulacrum of Jet acknowledges a sexual interest in his companion that was not acted upon; per Jenkins' delineation of the genre's overall objectives, this text evokes a tragic tone in order to recontextualize the
relationship between Spike and Jet as one defined by unrequited desires
(which, with Spike's death, can never be fulfilled). By contrast, *don't even
recognize the stranger*—despite having been based on the same source, featuring the same characters, and being generated within the same community—depicts a scenario in which the protagonists do act upon that same
hypothetical attraction, in a story set prior to the aforementioned finale:

Jet's stamping out his cigarette when Spike walks up to him, pressing their lips
together like it's nothing. When they pull apart, Spike's got that look on his face,
the one that Jet know's [*sic*] means he's flying blind, had made a bet that he isn't
entirely sure will work out, trusting his gut and hoping like hell it doesn't come
back to bite him [*don't even recognize the stranger, spock*].

The fan-author's choice to situate this particular text at a point in time
in which Spike still lives is no coincidence; rather, it allows for the application of a new implied author and a specific reconfiguration of the fictional world so that intimacy between Jet and Spike is not only possible,
but ultimately achieved. As previously noted, this possibility of homosexual
attraction—whether unrequited or mutual, theoretical or realized—steps
far enough outside the established boundaries of existing characterization
that it would not appear (and has not appeared) in any subsequent adaptation with presumptions of canonicity; rather, it is an interpretation that
can only be maintained and perpetuated in a space that does not enforce
any adherence to said canonical perspectives. Furthermore, the authors'
anonymity prevents any meaningful reverse-engineering of their respective implied author, as Close and Wang emphasize the absence of direct
biographical correlation: "Fan fiction is a playful, metaphorical, exploratory space. It would be a grave misreading to suggest that fans desire the
real life enactment of problematic tropes, such as the biological need for
sex that removes characters' abilities to consent to sex in the Omegaverse"
(Close & Wang, 164).
These two stories demonstrate a common occurrence within the field

of fan fiction: a clash between two implied authors, representing a difference of interpretation towards the source text of *Cowboy Bebop*. While both attempt to impose the same broad concept of sexual attraction between the protagonists, one views this possibility as an additional layer of melancholy and loss, while the other takes an enabling approach. Yet these works sit alongside each other, neatly archived upon the Yuletide virtual shelf, with no mechanism to promote any hierarchical preference between them. The only guiding principle to determine which sequence of events an individual reader may find more appealing is simply the personal inclination of said reader. Fan fiction in the digital age calls for a mindset which sets aside traditional notions of canon, monolithic textuality, and unified meanings; such tools are rendered problematic, if not entirely obsolete, by the narrative products of this technological platform, proving that "the migration of digital literature to the Web has created a venue for publication and critique no longer subject to the control of the traditional gatekeepers of the literary establishment" (Ciccoricco, 189). The ubiquity of artistically-inclined social media platforms such as DeviantArt and Tumblr only further enable the dissemination (and possible acceptance) of fan interpretations—the more popular a particular perspective becomes within the global fan community, the more likely it is to supplant the original altogether and become a form of "canon" in itself for subsequent exploration and replication in other fan works.

Ontology, Metalepsis, and Storyworld Manipulation

Ontological analysis—that is to say, critical examinations of the construction, maintenance and nature of fictional worlds—contributes greatly to the overall understanding of narrative works. As mentioned previously, Pavel's *Fictional Worlds* offers a first step by defining these diegetic structures as derivations of consensus reality; for Pavel, the reading process is one of addition and subtraction, resulting in an ontological system comprised of familiar "immigrant" objects imported into the diegetic space by the author, alongside "native" objects which have no physical or tangible counterpart in extradiegetic reality. The number of immigrant versus native objects is dependent upon the genre of the text itself: a realistic narrative set in New York City or London may contain a greater amount of immigrant objects (as these locations exist in consensus reality and are, to varying extents, known to the reader), whereas a science-fictional or fantastic text may feature a large number of native objects as genre rules lean towards defamiliarization and cognitive estrangement. Dolezel supplements this theory with a view of the reader as an active participant in the reading process who uses the text as a basis upon which to mentally project the world contained within. Implicit in both Dolezel's and Pavel's arguments is the assumption that while the text itself is the primary source of the fictional world, every reader's mental reconstruction of said world may vary depending on a multitude of factors ranging from cultural background to age. The fictional world does not exist as a "real" object which can be quantified and evaluated objectively; rather, it is an ephemeral configuration informed both by the implied author of the text and by the reader's own projections.

But just as with authorship and the implied author, digital technologies have raised complicated new questions pertaining to narrative ontology. Dolezel's representation of the reader as a traveler moving from one imaginary realm to the next is a useful starting metaphor in considering the complex network of fictional worlds, simulacra, expanded universes and fan-constructed multiverses which have emerged with the advent of digital media. This is not to suggest that the phenomenon of a fictional world spilling out beyond the confines of its source text began with technological platforms; on the contrary, to expand upon a previous example, one may view Mark Twain's 1876 novel *The Adventures of Tom Sawyer* and the subsequent 1884 novel *The Adventures of Huckleberry Finn* as being two source texts ostensibly set in the same diegetic space, as the novels share characters (including the titular protagonists). Birgit Spengler claims that the texts "blur the discrepancies between the diegetic worlds and the social agendas of the two novels. Although the impression of the congruity of the two books is undermined at least from chapter seven onwards, when Pap's cruelty challenges readerly expectations of a world of childhood adventures that resembles *Tom Sawyer*, the formal continuity of the two worlds remains an underlying interpretatory frame for *Huckleberry Finn* throughout" (Spengler, 315). Of course, the link between these two particular works is relatively self-evident, as they share the same author; questions of ontological congruity become infinitely more complicated when characters such as Dracula or Sherlock Holmes slip the bonds of both their original generic/diegetic framework and their original implied authors. In 2012, Guinness World Records declared Dracula to be the most ubiquitous literary character in the Western world, tallying up a total of 272 separate and distinct representations across over a century of media, in short stories, novels, films and serialized television. More have, of course, emerged in the years since, and this tally does not take into account the many appearances Dracula has made in new media such as video games—the number of which would have increased the count exponentially. In addition, popular franchises such as *Star Trek* and *Star Wars* have developed their own expanded universes, with licensed novels, television shows and films broadening the scope of the core narrative beyond the limitations of the original works. These expansions are filtered through dozens of authors, implied authors and interpretive lenses, though the resulting fragmentation is curtailed by legal, editorial and corporate oversight, all of which impose some measure of uniformity upon the final products. How, then, should such materials be treated in narratological terms? What mechanisms, if any, exist to separate licensed expanded universes from fan fiction, and are those mechanisms capable of significantly differentiating between the two?

One useful approach in applying existing critical thought to licensed expanded universes is to synthesize the positions of Pavel and Baudrillard: if, for Pavel, fictional worlds are extrapolations of our own reality, an expanded universe is therefore an extrapolation of the fictional world depicted in the source text. In this scenario, the "consensus reality" being fictionalized through the addition and removal of immigrant objects is in itself a fictional construct; in essence, every subsequent derivation would fall under Baudrillard's definition of a simulacrum, a copy without a tangible original. While diegetic continuity supposedly remains a high priority, each new contribution to a franchise such as *Star Wars* makes the prospect of total consistency that much more difficult, as the post-narrative timeline is developed further and further, with an increasing number of authors invited to project their values and interpretations onto these replicas of the original ontological structure. Alice Bell provides a framework that can fully encompass these fractured simulacra, categorizing them as Textual Possible Worlds: "Textual Possible Worlds belong to the same Textual Universe as the respective Textual Actual World and represent alternatives to what is given as fact in the narrative. Textual Possible Worlds are generated by characters' mental processes such as wishes, dreams or imaginings and therefore constitute possible alternatives to the actual course of events" (Bell, 25). What Bell attributes to wishes and dreams can just as easily apply to any use of eidetic variation by an author of licensed content to expand a fictional universe in any given direction; furthermore, Bell views the increasing fragmentation of the source text into dozens of ontological simulacra as a helpful factor in further analysis: "Since Possible Worlds Theory is an approach which is primarily concerned with the relationships between ontological domains and their constituents, it provides tools which can be used to analyse the reader's relationship with the text including negotiating, locating and interrogating the borders between the Actual World and the Textual Actual Worlds as well as the ontological structures contained therein" (Bell, 186).

In contrast to the relatively controlled expansion of licensed materials for established fictional worlds, fan fiction adopts the furthest possible extreme of this practice. Speaking to the phenomenon of post-narrative fan fiction (stories set after the chronological endpoint of the source text), Jenkins notes that "the destruction of old narrative situations opens room to explore possibilities that fall beyond the parameters of the original series" (Jenkins, 169). While the hard limitations of most narrative forms are a product of their respective media (the set number of pages in a novel, the runtime of a film or a play, the episode count of a television series) and licensed expanded universes are similarly contained by editorial oversight, fan fiction is able to appropriate the process of ontological simulacra for practically any purpose. Porous though their applications may be, the theories of Pavel, Dolezel and Bell are all in agreement that fictional worlds are inherently singular in their textual representation, whereas the unsupervised and virtually unlimited power given to fan fiction authors is such that they have both the capacity and the ability to manipulate the very ontological fabric and structure of said worlds. Bell attributes this to a natural outcome of technological hypertextuality, noting that "while all texts construct alternatives and thereby always implicitly construct a modal system, hypertext fiction makes that system of reality very explicit by literalising the alternative possibilities" (Bell, 25). Similarly, the repeated splitting-off of simulacra from a fictional original to facilitate the production of fan fiction may also be technologically-motivated according to Ciccoricco: "Network fictions radically foreground repetition. Recursion, reflexivity, and refrain are all specific modes of repetition that are manifest in literary works.... Thus, by way of a metacritical feedback loop, digital fiction encourages us to ask many of the same questions about narrative texts in a different context, as must all readers and writers who can no longer take their medium for granted" (Ciccoricco, 27).

To narrow the scope of this discussion on a specific aspect of fan works, this section will focus on diegetic manipulation as a foundational component of a category called "crossovers." As the name implies, the premise of all crossover stories rests upon a juxtaposition of two or more distinct fictional worlds. These can include (but are not limited to) intersections of texts with similar generic origins; transmedia conjunctions of novels, movies and/or television; transplants of specific characters from one fictional world to another; and convergences of disparate and seemingly incompatible source materials. Erwin Feyersinger compounds this definition by highlighting the specific technique used to compose such stories: "Unique to crossovers are distributed intertextual metalepses. Intertextual metalepses do not transgress boundaries in ascending or descending direction between embedded worlds, but horizontally between distinct fictional worlds" (Feyersinger, 130). Feyersinger also provides a helpful framework for contextualizing the vast number of crossover works by breaking down the different forms of storyworld manipulation into two categories:

"Interdiegetic ontological transgressions (intra- or extrametalepsis, entities fully and physically enter other functional/diegetic level): moving to the target world; [and] Interdiegetic ontological conflations (two ontologically distinct worlds are completely blended)" (Feyersinger, 147). Naturally, these strategies lead to very different ontological configurations, and are influenced in no small part by the nature of the new implied author imposed upon the simulacrum. Indeed, crossovers are a far more common type of narrative in fan fiction than in licensed material, bound as the latter is by copyright laws and logistics.

As with the previous section's practical exploration of implied authorship via particular works of fan fiction, the principles of ontological manipulation within fan communities are best exemplified in a narratological study of works which exhibit these principles. Two crossover stories have been selected which are again based on the same source content: the 2004–2009 Syfy television series *Battlestar Galactica*, which depicts the travels of a refugee fleet carrying the last survivors of an apocalyptic war through unknown space. The protagonists are seeking humanity's long-lost sister colony on Earth, all the while relentlessly pursued by their cyborg enemies the Cylons. Both works of fan fiction chosen for this case study are predicated upon the notion of a crossover occurring during chronological lacunae within the show itself. The first story, *Dreams of Electric Sheep* by thedeadparrot, begins with the premise that the fleet has at last reached Earth, only to discover that it is the Earth depicted in Ridley Scott's film *Blade Runner* (itself an adaptation of Philip K. Dick's short story "Do Androids Dream of Electric Sheep?" hence the fan-author's appropriation of the title):

> Lee finds himself on the streets of Los Angeles. According to what they've been told, this is supposed to be the better part of town, but Lee can't really see it. It's dirty and crowded, too many people in too small a space. There are so many people, they've been forced to go upwards, in buildings taller than even the tallest on Scorpia.
>
> Across the street, he sees a woman amongst the crush of people. She is regal and elegant, back straight, hair neatly pulled back, face pale and smooth. She looks like no one else Lee has ever seen. She looks over her shoulder, only once, and meets Lee's eye. A small smile appears on her face, strange and enigmatic, before she turns and walks into the steam and the shadows.
>
> Lee follows her.
>
> She is waiting for him outside a building, perfectly still. Lee wonders where she gets it from. The smile is still on her face. "My name is Rachel," she says. He watches her lips, because they are the only part of her that moves [*Dreams of Electric Sheep*, thedeadparrot].

This text is an example of an interdiegetic ontological transgression, per Feyersinger's definition: the characters from *Battlestar Galactica* have quite literally entered into the world of *Blade Runner*. Of course, the templates in question are perhaps more compatible than in other crossover fiction, in that both *Battlestar Galactica* and *Blade Runner* are concerned with extrapolated futures in which artificial life (Replicants in the latter, Cylons in the former) attempts to define itself in relation to its human creators while assuming quintessentially human forms. Both narratives bear a tangible undercurrent of fear, and suspicion of infiltration, as it becomes clear that there is no reliable way to distinguish humans from their synthetic adversaries; indeed, both source texts eventually conclude that there is no quantifiable difference at all, and that biological and synthetic life forms are more alike than not—one of the last lines in Scott's film, referring to Replicant protagonist Rachel, is: "It's too bad she won't live! But then again, who does?" (Scott, *Blade Runner*). These thematic similarities serve as the foundation upon which fan-authors have built their own narratives, and the effect of this particular crossover is transformative: *Battlestar Galactica* positions Earth within the imagination of its protagonists as an Edenic place of refuge and salvation, the idealized destination at the end of any difficult journey. Within the context of the series, Earth also represents the last hope of a species dangerously close to the extinction threshold, as each episode begins with a count of the surviving humans, dwindling with every casualty sustained during the course of the series. By welding this configuration onto the Earth portrayed in *Blade Runner*, thedeadparrot deconstructs the most basic premise of the journey narrative: Scott's Earth is already overpopulated, already dystopian, already struggling with its own quandaries concerning artificial life. The completion of the Galactica's odyssey becomes melancholy rather than celebrative:

> She feels alone, as she looks out the window of Colonial One. Below her,
> Earth spins, a sphere of black and blue and white. She should be proud of this
> moment, for taking them this far, for achieving this much on so little. She has
> led them to Earth like she said she would. She should be proud.
> Instead, she finds herself missing home.
> The planet she thinks of is not Earth [*Dreams of Electric Sheep*,
> thedeadparrot].

thedeadparrot also contextualizes the points of encounter between these worlds as moments of alienation and disappointment: the previously cited romantic liaison between Lee Adama of *Battlestar Galactica* and Rachel of *Blade Runner*, and the later meeting between President Laura Roslin and Dr. Eldon Tyrell, serve to reiterate the ultimate outcome of this particular ontological juxtaposition as an utter inversion of premise, theme and plot. The focalizers of *Dreams of Electric Sheep* are exclusively drawn from *Battlestar Galactica*, ensuring that the reader will view Scott's Earth only through defamiliarized perspectives; of the characters native to *Blade*

Runner, only Rachel and Tyrell appear, the former in a passively seductive role echoing her original relationship to protagonist Rick Deckard. Deckard himself is noticeably absent, as are any Replicant actants. These deliberate stylistic choices suggest that the new implied author's aim is to set aside the original thematic center of both works—the question of synthetic life— in favor of subverting the idealized expectations typically associated with the conclusion of a long journey.

Dreams of Electric Sheep also demonstrates the independence of the simulated world due to its retroactive discontinuity. At the time the fan fiction story was being composed, *Battlestar Galactica* had not yet concluded, and thus Earth was still an ontological lacuna that could be appropriated by fans in any way they desired. However, the series finale sees the fleet reach Earth, in a scene that obviously that bears no resemblance whatsoever to thedeadparrot's scenario—consequently, the lacuna initially addressed by fan fiction was filled by the canonical source work itself, changing the context of *Dreams of Electric Sheep* from predictive to alternative. This would be a point of concern for licensed fiction, due to the demand of a uniform, hierarchical canon and the exclusion of works which contradict said canon; however, as Turk indicates, fan-produced simulacra stand independent of changes to the original:

> For fans, the processes of fan participation and creation are important parts of the fantext; what matters is not just the extension of the universe (commercial media tie-in novels may do similar work) but the fact that the fan community, collectively, is doing the extending.... This dedication to communal exploration and expansion of shared canon means that the boundary between canon and fantext is seldom marked within the text itself [Turk, 89].

Dreams of Electric Sheep is still available to read online as of the time of writing, and its reception among its community of readers is similarly unaffected by the later closing of the ontological gap that motivated its creation. The text now presents an alternative interpretation, a "what if?" scenario common to this mode of writing which will be further elaborated upon in the coming sections.

Where thedeadparrot's fan fiction achieves its aesthetic goals by transposing the characters of *Battlestar Galactica* into the world of *Blade Runner*, smercy's *For Our Own Benefit* situates itself in Feyersinger's second category of crossover, the interdiegetic ontological conflation. This term applies to texts in which the boundary between two fictional worlds is dissolved, and the resulting diegesis is defined by hybridity rather than transplanted narrative components. Similar to the Yuletide texts discussed in the previous section, *For Our Own Benefit* is the product of a community encouraging the generation of fan fiction in response to specific challenges—in this case, the "Many Worlds Space Show Crossover Challenge"—and combines

Battlestar Galactica and *Star Wars*. smercy proposes that both narratives are taking place in different locations within the same fictional universe, and depicts a scenario in which the fleet arrives on the sanctuary world of Dagobah, home to popular *Star Wars* character Yoda:

> Yoda walked slowly into the clearing, making sure to step on every squeaking root in his path. The boy startled as he looked down at him. "Racetrack," he said walking backwards from him, "I think there is some sort of indigenous life form here."
>
> "Well," the woman inside of the spacecraft said, "We knew we were bound to find some eventually. I'll get the camera." The boy did not alter his gaze, but continued methodically in his work.
>
> Yoda cleared his throat, used to the assumptions of children, "Trespassing, you are," he squawked, "My home, this is."
>
> "Oh frak," the boy said, "Racetrack, oh frak!" His voice raised to the highest registers and he reached for a firearm. Their names were not likely names, probably a military callsign [*For Our Own Benefit*, smercy].

This encounter represents a deliberate breach of a key thematic imperative in *Battlestar Galactica*: namely, as a work nominally aligned with the "hard" end of the science-fiction generic spectrum, the source text is devoid of any depictions of alien life. It may be inferred from the original implied author that this absence is meant to deepen the human refugees' sense of isolation, as they are only able to interact with members of their own community or with their Cylon enemies. smercy's new implied author espouses different values, choosing Yoda as the first non-human, non–Cylon character to cross the fleet's path. The use of *Star Wars* as the second component in the crossover is as significant a choice here as *Blade Runner* is for *Dreams of Electric Sheep*; where the latter story uses compatible themes and plots to achieve a successful relocation of actants from one text to the other, the juxtaposition of *Battlestar Galactica*'s hard science-fiction and the science-fantasy of *Star Wars* creates an incongruity which smercy explores via focalization:

> The fourth woman was not a woman. Her presence in the Force was all wrong, clustered only around her brain and down the spinal cord. She held no Force in her limbs or torso, her carefully blank face. Yoda had never heard of such a case, such a grievous misplacement of presence. The Force was part of the body as it was with the soul, and no specific bit of either was exempt. But her body was blank, barely visible in the force through the shining of her spine. Yoda had to vigorously shake his head to clear himself of the disturbance [*For Our Own Benefit*, smercy].

The woman in question is identified later in the story, but this scene is designed as a coded cue for readers familiar with both source texts, as it refers to the singular nature of Galactica pilot Sharon Agathon, a Cylon among humans. Viewed through the lens of *Star Wars*, Agathon's outsider status is reinforced by the author's reminder of the active ontological conflation: the *Star Wars* films have never featured androids with human features, thus Yoda is initially unable to deduce Agathon's true nature (whereas the reader can). At the same time, the Jedi Master's supernatural connection to the Force provides an additional lens through which Agathon is seen as "Other" from her human compatriots on an essential, biological level—a lens that would not be available in any other singular ontological configuration.

Another point of comparison between *Dreams of Electric Sheep* and *For Our Own Benefit* concerns the aesthetic objectives of the authors in question. As mentioned previously, thedeadparrot posits a conclusion of sorts to the narrative of *Battlestar Galactica* but inverts the emotional significance of said conclusion through the use of Ridley Scott's Earth as a futile destination for the refugees. In stark contrast, smercy attempts to maintain the plot integrity of both source texts by framing the encounter between Yoda and the Galactica cast as accidental and transient. Dagobah is simply another stop on a long journey, and Yoda intentionally misleads Laura Roslin in order to keep the refugees away from the antagonistic Empire:

> The President leaned towards him, careful to keep her posture open and friendly. "So, Yoda," she said, smiling, "Are we the first humans that you have met?"
>
> "No," he said, "Met others, I have." He sighed, quietly. "A long time ago, it was. Learned their language, I did."
>
> "Do you know any humans now?" A complex question.
>
> Yoda did not fidget or shift his posture. "No," he lied, "I do not. Alone, I have been, for a great number of years." It would not be prudent to share the location of the Empire with them at this time.
>
> "Do you know where they came from?"
>
> "Talked about it, they did not," he said. "A long time ago, it was." They had not encountered any other humans, a bad sign.
>
> "Did they ever talk about Earth?"
>
> Earth was the birthplace of humans, the old birthplace, lost to the Empire.
>
> "The birthplace of humanity, it is. But know more, I do not" [*For Our Own Benefit*, smercy].

This exchange highlights another lacuna in the source text: Earth, the much-hoped-for salvation for the Galactica and its people, has never been mentioned in *Star Wars*, nor has the origin of the human species ever served as a point of reference. Each *Star Wars* film begins with the phrase "A long time ago in a galaxy far, far away," explicitly situating these events as far removed from our own consensus reality; in a galaxy full of alien life, humanity is simply one more sentient species. At the same time, the villainous Empire is comprised almost entirely of humans, and so the intersection of these particular core texts leads to a conflict of value systems wherein the humans of *Battlestar Galactica* are predominantly sympathetic, implied author-approved protagonists, while their *Star Wars* counterparts are greedy, violent and aggressively militaristic, having enslaved millions and annihilated entire worlds. Yoda's deception, though framed as well-meaning, brings this calculated clash of values to the forefront, while serving the implied author's overall goal of preserving the schism within this hybridized ontology. In doing so, the canonical narrative arcs for all characters involved in the crossover are maintained, with the focalizer providing diegetic justification on behalf of the implied author: "The Emperor would find them. The heavy hand of the Empire would fall upon them, stealing their technology, their independence. And the technology to make the cylons would be horrible in the wrong hands, what it might do to the clone technology, to Vader. They would not be able to settle in safety in the new Empire. He would not wish the Emperor upon his worst enemies" (*For Our Own Benefit*, smercy).

When considering the individual merits of the source material, it is clear that extradiegetic factors prevent the linking or conflation of original fictional worlds, as Jenkins notes that Western legal systems have not yet fully come to terms with the ramifications of rapid technological development and its effect on the consumption of narrative: "Nobody is sure whether fan fiction falls under current fair-use protections. Current copyright law simply doesn't have a category for dealing with amateur creative expression.... Our current notion of fair use is an artifact of an era when few people had access to the marketplace of ideas, and those who did fell into certain professional classes" (Jenkins, 189). The scenarios proposed in these works are only possible within the specific milieu of fan fiction, as any canonical merging of fictional works with incompatible implied authors would lead to thematic incongruity. The abundance of life in the *Star Wars* galaxy would clash with the Galactica refugees' single-minded determination to find Earth, owing to the overwhelming absence of other planets capable of supporting life; but these conflicts may be manipulated and resolved when dealing with simulacra, and plausible alternative scenarios may be posited to address not only lacunae in the existing ontological structure, but the perceived boundaries of said structures as well. Indeed, the co-existing multiplicities of meanings and interpretations in digital space allow such thought experiments to be disseminated as narratives of subversion or usurpations of original value systems, a source of pleasure in itself:

> The raw materials of the original story play a crucial role in this process, providing instructions for a preferred reading, but they do not necessarily overpower and subdue the reader. The same narratives (*Dragnet*, say) can be read literally

by one group and as camp by another. Some groups' pleasure comes not in celebrating the values of their chosen works but rather in "reading them against the grain," in expressing their opposition to rather than acceptance of textual ideology [Jenkins, 64].

Both stories discussed in this particular case study exemplify the same aesthetic framework, maintaining a careful balance between mimesis—expressed by both thedeadparrot and smercy in the construction of their simulacra with an eye towards fidelity to the original content—and innovation, a de facto product of the crossover itself, whether transgressive or assimilative in nature. Any incompatibilities between the source texts in terms of theme, genre or ontological law—as well as the fact that neither canonical corpus could support such a crossover to begin with—is firmly dismissed, rendering the imperatives of the source material irrelevant to the production of further splinter-texts. As such, *Dreams of Electric Sheep* and *For Our Own Benefit* provide apt demonstrations of diegetic manipulation made possible via the Internet's unregulated narrative capacity.

New Genres, Sub-Genres, and Metafiction

As a tool of narratological analysis, genre classification provides further insight into the nature of a given text. Bakhtin asserts that chronotopes largely inform genre, to the extent that the choice of when and where a story takes place inevitably creates expectations on the part of the reader: "What is the significance of all these chronotopes? What is most obvious is their meaning for *narrative*. They are the organizing centers for the fundamental narrative events of the novel.... All the novel's abstract elements—philosophical and social generalizations, ideas, analyses of cause and effect—gravitate towards the chronotope and through it take on flesh and blood, permitting the imaging power of art to do its work" (Bakhtin, 57). Of course, these expectations can be manipulated for the purposes of estrangement or defamiliarization; for example, Patrick McHale's *Over the Garden Wall* makes use of a dark forest and bizarre visual cues to trick the audience into believing the story takes place in the distant past, when it is in fact set in an American suburb during the 1980s. The eventual revelation of this deception causes the viewer to revisit and reevaluate the work in a new light.

As with every other component of literary production and reception, digital media has had a significant impact on how genre is understood. Robyn R. Warhol notes that even prior to the advent of unrestricted fan production, genres were defined in part by their inherent boundaries:

Narrative genres are known as much by what they do not or cannot contain as by what they typically do contain: a novel or film belongs to a particular genre as much for what it does not say or do as for what it does. The limits of narratability vary according to nation, period, and audience as well as genre, but they also stretch and change as genres evolve. Indeed, shifts in the category of the unnarratable are, I would say, significant indicators of generic change itself, and they both reflect and constitute their audiences' developing senses of such matters as politics, ethics, and values [Warhol, 221].

Just as the ability to create simulacra of fictional worlds has led to more porous and flexible ontological structures, so too have generic categories emerged which are unique to this particular mode of writing and are in many ways designed to overcome the limitations of their textual and filmic predecessors. The codification of these new genres and sub-genres is as inherently communal as any aspect of fan fiction production and demonstrates the high levels of interactivity and reflexivity between fan-author, fan-text and fan-reader, as "fan-produced works respond to the perceived tastes of their desired audience and reflect the community's generic traditions as much as those originating within commercial culture" (Jenkins, 90). Within this plethora of new generic configurations, several categories stand out as highly relevant to the overall understanding of fan fiction as a narrative form; to establish and explore these categories, the following texts have been selected as representative of their respective trends: *Whole New World* by Roga (transgeneric shift), *Beauty* by Kate Bolin (Alternate Universe/AU), *DILF* by twentysomething (slash) and *I Never (The But Just This Once Remix)* by TheSecondBatgirl (remix). In addition, the collaborative story *Steve Rogers at 100: Celebrating Captain America on Film* will examine properties of emergent online "meta-fan-fiction." These texts are also useful as instances of generic overlap, as they share more commonalities as products of the same communal impulses than might be found in mainstream examples.

The impetus behind the formation of these genres may be viewed as another manifestation of fandom's resistance to authorial authority; Turk frames all forms of fan production as a way for readers to express desires the source text does not (or cannot) address:

> The most significant boundary that is crossed in fan works is not the border of the fictional world but the border of the text itself, the boundary that separates creator and flesh-and-blood (as opposed to implied or authorial) audience: the extratextual reader or viewer inserts herself into the discourse level and becomes the narrator, the director…. Fan works, then, are always metaleptic in the sense that they represent the imposition of extradiegetic desires upon the fictional world and the transformation of a text in the service of those desires [Turk, 90].

It stands to reason, then, that the creation of new genres unique to digital platforms is another expression of that same push against the normative nature of established implied authors. Roga's *Brand New World*, a Yuletide-produced fan fiction text based on 1992 Disney film *Aladdin*, embodies one such method of rebellion, as the text employs a transgeneric shift in order to address an ontological gap that is implicit rather than explicit. In the film, the jovial Genie displays an anachronistic awareness of 20th-century phrases and popular figures, at times imitating Peter Lorre, Rodney Dangerfield, Arnold Schwarzenegger and Jack Nicholson. The question Roga posits is epistemological in nature: how does Genie know what he knows? Extradiegetically, these references are attributed to the late Robin Williams, an actor known for his tendency to improvise and ad-lib his lines to humorous effect; as such, Genie's quirks draw no particular attention from other inhabitants of the fictional world. But by moving this question back into the diegetic sphere, Roga proposes an alternative interpretation very much in line with Jenkins' definition of recontextualization:

> [If] genre represents a cluster of interpretive strategies as much as it constitutes a set of textual features, fans often choose to read the series within alternative generic traditions. Minimally, fan stories shift the balance between plot action and characterization, placing primary emphasis upon moments that define the character relationships rather than using such moments as background or motivation for the dominant plot.... More broadly, fan stories often choose to tell very different stories from those in the original episodes [Jenkins, 173].

The transformative effect of *Whole New World* lies in the shifting of focalization from Aladdin to Genie, whose implied immortality in the film is compounded with transtemporal awareness in the fan fiction text. Where *Aladdin* uses these references purely as a source of comedy, Roga rewrites the premise in order to shift Genie—and, by extension, the simulacrum of *Aladdin* represented in the fan-text—from lighthearted humor to somber tragedy, and into an ontological structure which includes both the fantastic, cartoonish landscape of Agrabah and the far more brutal reality of present-day Iraq:

> He learned it—the Brando impression, that is—from an American soldier who was stationed in the country futurely known as Iraq in the 21st century (or the 14th century, or the 57th, depends on who's counting). Who *will* be stationed, technically. Cute kid named Corpor "Al" Peters, which is what drew Genie to him in the first place, his name, even though he keeps insisting to be called Ryan. He even looks like Al a little, although Al's saber's been replaced with a semiautomatic, and his curly black hair is cut down to regulation [*Whole New World*, Roga].

The story continues in this fashion, as Genie vacillates between various time periods while maintaining friendships with Aladdin, Corporal Peters and a young Iraqi boy he calls "mini-Al." But the protagonist's ability to experience different points in time simultaneously ultimately leads to a sense of grief and loss which is fundamentally incompatible with the tone of the source film:

> In the end, though, it'll be the Brando that'll come in more handy, because after mini-Al will win his lifetime's supply of sweets, he'll get shot by an American soldier and die on the spot. Genie has never and does not and will never want to know who it was who shot the boy, because it won't change anything, and because he's afraid of the answer. He skips over that scene, then, tries to move on, except that's when Cpl. Ryan Peters will be killed, and Genie doesn't have much practice in grieving, so he'll go deep into the desert where no one can hear him but the red rocks and the snakes and fall on his knees, raise his fists to the heavens and scream Stella's name for a few hours until he is empty, devoid of emotions, devoid of purpose now that he has no masters for wish-granting and no lamp to hide in [*Whole New World*, Roga].

Implicit (but never stated outright) is the notion that Corporal Peters was the soldier responsible for the death of the Iraqi child; again, a scenario more conducive to contemporary realistic fiction than to the sanitized ideals featured in typical Disney narratives. The distance between the original implied author and the implied author of *Brave New World* is a product of the decision to place the Genie in a different generic framework; this lends significant credence to the notion that the fan-text's stance towards the source material is one of subversive defiance. The introduction of wartime Iraq into the bloodless, largely non-violent musical comedy/adventure of *Aladdin* creates an inherently estranged ontology, one the reader must then navigate via the story's altered chronotope.

While Roga's transgeneric reconfiguration is a useful example of the transformative effects of fan fiction, the modes *Whole New World* shifts between are among the oldest and most familiar in literary tradition—namely, comedy and tragedy. It is only when that transformative effect is coupled with new generic systems that a clearer picture emerges as to how fan fiction has developed its own unique set of narrative tools, terminologies and functions. One such genre is colloquially referred to as AU (Alternate Universe), which explores simulacra of fictional worlds by rearranging the plot sequence of the original narrative. These texts examine "what might have been," scenarios which could feasibly have come to pass if events in the source text had occurred along a different causal chain. At first glance, this genre bears great similarity to the sub-genre of Alternative History featured in such classic works as Philip K. Dick's *The Man in the High Castle* or Michael Chabon's *The Yiddish Policemen's Union*, in which the author imagines different outcomes to specific historical events, defamiliarizing the "present" in which the story is set. What sets fan fiction AU apart, of course, is that where Alternative History relies upon plausible modifications to the known past of our consensus reality, AU takes the same approach to the intangible history of fictional worlds, allowing for an exponentially broader range of possible extrapolations. According to Bell, this multitude of multiplicities is perfectly appropriate for network fiction, as it represents a clear and direct literalization of the Possible Worlds Theory:

> Fittingly, such an approach, which focuses on the interplay between ontological domains and their internal structures, can ensue without picking definitive reading paths so that lengthy lexia configurations are not necessarily required. Possible Worlds Theory therefore removes the subjectivity associated with first-wave analyses because it is able to accommodate the multi-linear hypertext fiction structure rather than attempting to manipulate it into a pseudo-linear format [Bell, 26].

Kate Bolin's *Beauty*, a work of fan fiction based on J.R.R. Tolkien's *The Lord of the Rings*, is another product of intra-communal writing—specifically, the 2002 "One Ring Challenge," which tasked its members to rewrite Tolkien's source text under the premise that various characters had, in the course of the diegetic sequence of plot events, laid claim to the eponymous One Ring and thus achieved supremacy over Middle-Earth. Bolin chooses Galadriel, the elf queen featured in Tolkien's *The Fellowship of the Ring*, and proposes an AU which splinters off from the canonical scene in which Galadriel is offered the Ring by protagonist Frodo Baggins:

> "You will give me the Ring freely! In place of the Dark Lord you will set up a Queen. And I shall not be dark, but beautiful and terrible as the Morning and the Night! Fair as the Sea and the Sun and the Snow upon the Mountain! Dreadful as the Storm and the Lightning! Stronger than the foundations of the earth. All shall love me and despair!" She lifted up her hand and from the ring that she wore there issued a great light that illumined her alone and left all else dark. She stood before Frodo seeming now tall beyond measurement, and beautiful beyond enduring, terrible and worshipful. Then she let her hand fall, and the light faded, and suddenly she laughed again, and lo! she was shrunken: a slender elf-woman, clad in simple white, whose gentle voice was soft and sad. "I pass the test," she said. "I will diminish, and go into the West, and remain Galadriel" [Tolkien, 400].

Where Tolkien depicts Galadriel's ability to resist temptation as a natural outcome of her inherent benevolence and nobility, Bolin's text subverts these associations by constructing a Textual Possible World in which the same Galadriel becomes the supreme ruler of Middle-Earth, one whose reign is even more insidious and tyrannical than that of designated villain Sauron. The fan fiction text begins with a description which seems to align itself with the same values expressed in Tolkien's work:

> It was a world of beauty.
> Under Her rule, the forest returned, seedlings running over battlefields and

ruins, slowly turning down the symbols of Man and replacing them with peonies, roses, morning glories, delicate willows and sturdy oaks.

Wherever She walked, beauty reigned. The lush green hills and valleys of Middle-earth flourished, and the people responded in kind, growing fair and strong and so beautiful that the elder folk, the ones from before Her rule, would occasionally weep at the sight of the children [*Beauty*, Kate Bolin].

However, as the story progresses it becomes clear that Bolin is using the divergence from canonical events to effect a deeply transgressive inversion of the positive qualities Tolkien's implied author attributes to elves, producing a far darker outcome:

Of the ones who grew old, of the ones who were scarred, nothing was said.....

Of the traitor Boromir, who took a knife to Her consort Celeborn and ravished his beautiful face.... Nothing more was ever said of him or of Celeborn.

Her court knew of these tales, remembered the tang of blood and the cries of despair, and lived in terror of being found ... imperfect. They bartered with wizards and begged with witch-women, their sleeping chambers strewn with salves and powders and oils. They searched for things that would tighten, color, fade, remove, and make them seem young. Young as the day She accepted their Gift.

For all things come with a price, and beauty most of all [*Beauty*, Kate Bolin].

The Middle-Earth depicted in *Beauty* is posited as a logical outcome to a linear, chronological sequence of events, with a single moment altered by authorial fiat; this, in turn, strips the fan-text of the generic traditions of high fantasy and replaces them with elements of dystopian horror. The inhabitants of Bolin's simulacrum are brutalized and terrorized by the demands of a character whose canonical personality has been corrupted by her claiming of the One Ring. As with any alternate history scenario, the end result is a world which cannot be reconciled with the original, as the embedded systems of values are in direct and total conflict.

Rewriting *The Lord of the Rings* via the framework of AU also allows the implied author of *Beauty* to take a critical stance towards Tolkien's alignment of elves with beauty, light and nature, as well as his implied author's explicit approval of these qualities in quintessentially positive terms:

The chamber was filled with a soft light; its walls were green and silver and its roof of gold. Many Elves were seated there. On two chairs beneath the bole of the tree and canopied by a living bough there sat, side by side, Celeborn and Galadriel. They stood up to greet their guests, after the manner of Elves, even those who were accounted mighty kings. Very tall they were, and the Lady no less tall than the Lord; and they were grave and beautiful. They were clad wholly in white; and the hair of the Lady was of deep gold, and the hair of the Lord Celeborn was of silver long and bright; but no sign of age was upon them, unless it were in the depths of their eyes; for these were keen as lances in the starlight, and yet profound, the wells of deep memory [Tolkien, 388].

Conversely, Bolin's implied author takes those same descriptions and inverts their significance: the world in which Galadriel rules is beautiful only by virtue of having violently destroyed anything perceived to be imperfect or ugly. This distorted representation of elves is used to directly challenge the original implied author's use of "beauty" and "good" as synonymous terms; where Tolkien describes the apex of elven rule as a golden age of utopia, Bolin adds a sinister undertone to that idealized perfection. Thus, in stark contrast to the note of renewal and hope that concludes *The Lord of the Rings*, *Beauty* ends with all the novel's protagonists destroyed or subverted to Galadriel's will—a dead-ended dystopia despite its gilded exterior.

This unorthodox extrapolation is made possible by the generic mechanisms of AU, a system capable of achieving what Bell refers to as ontolepsis, "a means of categorising narrative devices which result in incompatible or contradictory versions of a fictional world including embedded narration and alternative version of narrative events" (Bell, 18). It is precisely this ontoleptic effect which allows for significantly diverse variables to present themselves in AU fan fiction, as the lacunae being exploited relate not only to what the source text omits, but to scenarios and values the source text might have contained under a different author. Of course, all fan fiction could technically be classified as AU, given that any deviation from the canonical work would be considered "alternative" by default; but what distinguishes AU within the larger oeuvre is its fidelity to the generic laws of alternative history, namely the narrative prioritization of causality. AU stories such as *Beauty* achieve their aesthetic purpose by altering, with pinpoint accuracy, a particular moment or incident, causing a new chain of events to emerge in response. While the process of constructing these "what if" scenarios does indeed lie at the heart of any fan fiction text, AU's reliance on causality narrows the reader's focus while still offering the same exploratory power to engage with unconventional configurations which would be categorized as implausible or impossible for the source text.

The desire to navigate chronotopes and scenarios relegated to the margins of mainstream fiction also serves as the primary impetus for the production of slash, among the most dominant and ubiquitous forms of fan fiction. No other genre, defined as slash is by the presentation of homoerotic relationships (whether chaste or explicitly sexual) between established characters, more clearly epitomizes narrative creation and consumption as an act of rebellion against perceived norms and conventions:

> Fan writers, freed of the restraints of network censors, often want to explore the erotic dimensions of characters' lives. Their stories transform the relatively chaste, though often suggestive, world of popular television into an erogenous zone of sexual experimentation. …in "Slash" fiction, the homosocial desires of

series characters erupt into homoerotic passion as Kirk and Spock, Riker and Picard, Crockett and Castillo, even Simon and Simon become bedmates and lovers [Jenkins, 179–180].

In point of fact, the positing of a same-sex romantic dynamic is the sole qualifier which determines whether a work of fan fiction is considered slash; in terms of its generic formula, no further authorial modification is required (though, of course, such changes may follow regardless). This may explain the overwhelming abundance of slash fiction, as the absence of any other imperative results in an extremely flexible form of fiction, capable of assimilating attributes or combining traits from any source; one may find slash embedded within horror, detective fiction, science fiction, romantic comedy, AU and other literary categories. The ease with which slash is able to move through the boundaries of established generic formulae echoes Lev Grossman's historical account of the genre's inception in his foreword to Jamison's *Fic*, in which slash fiction is clearly framed as an act of calculated transgression:

> "A Fragment Out of Time," the founding document in slash fanfiction, appeared in 1974 in a zine called Grup (short for "grownup," a reference to a Star Trek episode about feral children). As the first depiction of a love scene between Kirk and Spock, it wasn't just hot; it was a way of making visible the hidden thread of attraction that runs through the complex bond between the two characters. It elevated subtext to text. In doing so it gave rise to an entire writhing, sweating universe of romantic and sexual pairings. But slash isn't just about making porn out of things that weren't already porn. It's also about prosecuting fanfiction's larger project of breaking rules and boundaries and taboos of all kinds [Jamison, 14].

DILF by twentysomething, based on 2011–2017 MTV television series *Teen Wolf*, serves as a clear expression of these transgressive processes, though as with digital writing as a whole, it is practically impossible for any single text to encapsulate the full range of possibilities enabled by the medium and various generic frameworks. Rather, the strategies and techniques employed in this particular work may shed light on the broader principles of slash fiction. As the name implies, *Teen Wolf* is a supernatural drama centered on teenage werewolf Scott McCall, his best friend Stiles Stilinski, aloof mentor figure Derek Hale and an assortment of other characters. However, the introductory paragraphs of *DILF* present a drastically divergent fictional world:

> Derek hadn't worried when he'd sent Jackson to kindergarten. He remembers when Jackson was little, he was sweet and prone to crying, but after the accident, Jackson was harder. Which Derek worries about, but the upshot was that it had meant he'd be fine at school. In fact, Jackson had practically flung himself out of the car to get away from Scott, who had been crying desperately because Jackson got to go to school and he didn't.

> Today is Scott's first day of kindergarten and Derek is terrified. Scott has always been equal parts space cadet and sensitive; Derek wants to go to school with him and throw any kid that looks at Scott wrong out the window [*DILF*, twentysomething].

These lines immediately alert the reader to the extreme ontological reconfiguration on display: protagonist Scott has been de-aged to early childhood and rewritten as Derek's adopted son, along with secondary antagonist Jackson Whittemore. This, in turn, shifts focalization from the main character of the source text to a supporting member of the cast. In itself, this change does not meet the basic requirement of slash but rather facilitates it, as Derek's subsequent encounter with Scott's kindergarten teacher signals the author's introduction of homoeroticism between canonical characters:

> Derek has never been able to imagine what "Mr. S" might look like—between the strange science experiments and teaching gig, all that comes to mind is Beakman and Ms. Frizzle. He knows that's crazy, but that's still sort of what he expects to see when he's greeted at the classroom door.
> What he's not expecting is a guy who looks even younger than him, with dark hair and an evaluating stare, matched with an inviting grin [*DILF*, twentysomething].

The incongruity is immediately apparent, as the original Stiles is meant to be the same age as Scott; by effectively removing Scott from the narrative while making Stiles a peer of Derek, twentysomething rearranges the components of the simulated fictional world in order to create circumstances conducive to homoerotic romance: "The narrative formula of slash involves a series of movements from an initial partnership, through a crisis in communication that threatens to disrupt that union, toward its reconfirmation through sexual intimacy. These conventions represent both the dystopian dimensions of conventional masculinity and the Utopian possibility of a reconstructed masculinity" (Jenkins, 211). *DILF* corresponds to this basic structure by reframing interactions between characters as tropes of romantic comedy; for example, genre conventions necessitate an overlapping of personal spheres which inevitably triggers a series of chance encounters: "He's a little relieved and weirdly disappointed for no reason he can figure out. Derek sends back a quick 'Received,' because it's only polite. He figures that it'll go on the calendar and that'll be that, which is probably why they run into Stiles in the cereal aisle in the grocery store that night" (*DILF*, twentysomething). Naturally, the possibility of an intimate relationship is complicated by the existing dynamic—the single father and his son's teacher—which only intensifies unexpressed desires the longer both actants are in close physical proximity:

It hits Derek like a ton of bricks.

Stiles' cheeks are flushed from cold and his mouth is just a little open and so red. His shirt is clinging to his chest, the v of the collar dragged down by the weight of the water, so far that Stiles' collarbone is visible on one side. Derek can see the surprising definition in his chest and stomach-hugging the shape of his abs, the curve of his shoulders. There's a thread of water running down Stiles' neck, and Derek wants to put his mouth all. over. Stiles.' body [*DILF*, twentysomething].

The narrative ultimately concludes with an explicit sexual encounter between Derek and Stiles, again confirming Jenkins' point regarding the use of eroticism as an expression of resistance to the original implied author's heteronormative values.

DILF is an example of extreme ontological reconfiguration, to the point of casting aside any notion of mimesis altogether: beyond the rearrangement of interpersonal dynamics that comes with aging and de-aging characters, this simulacrum also lacks the supernatural phenomena which define its source text. There are no werewolves, and more broadly, no depictions of violence at all; as a result, twentysomething's characters share names and physical descriptions with their originals, and practically nothing else. Moreover, the absence of canonical female characters such as Scott's love interest Allison Argent or Jackson's girlfriend Lydia Martin allows the author to produce a familial unit which excludes female participants altogether. On the one hand, this certainly corresponds to the subversive impulse common to all works of slash fiction; on the other, this also produces a gap between source and simulacrum which is practically irreconcilable, far moreso than in Roga's *Brave New World*. With slightly different physical descriptions and character names, *DILF* could just as easily be construed as original fiction—save for the fact that the distance between this representation and its template is, in itself, a significant source of meaning for readers of fan fiction. At the time of writing, the copy of *DILF* archived on AO3 has received over 24,000 kudos (anonymous notes of praise), has garnered over 1,000 comments (consisting almost entirely of compliments), and has been accessed by over 578,000 readers; these statistics would seem to challenge Tisha Turk's assertion that "that source— the media text on which a given story is based—still exerts influence on fan works, even though it cannot define them: it acts as a sort of center of textual gravity around which a given fan work orbits more or less distantly and elliptically" (Turk, 88). Rather, the prioritization of same-sex romance in slash seems to permit near-total omission of the original—indeed, *DILF* has become an original in its own right, inspiring a sizeable amount of tribute artwork by members of the same fan-community. While these illustrations use visual cues provided by the original actors, they exclusively depict the characters as twentysomething represents them; thus, Turk's point that "fans consuming fan works are perfectly well aware that there is in fact a boundary between the original text and the fantext" (Turk, 89) may require further scrutiny, as the level of awareness clearly varies and does not necessarily favor the original in any overt way.

That the publication of *DILF* has led to further intra-communal production in response should come as no surprise: "Fan reception cannot and does not exist in isolation, but is always shaped through input from other fans and motivated, at least partially, by a desire for further interaction with a larger social and cultural community" (Jenkins, 77). The potential for reactivity and interactivity has existed in fan fiction since its earliest iterations—in fact, one may view pre-digital texts such as Neil Gaiman's short story "Snow, Glass, Apples" (originally published in 1994) as a precursor to the practice, in that it deliberately applies a new deconstructive implied author to the tale of Snow White. However, the shift to online digital writing has considerably refined and actualized this potential. The capacity for near-instantaneous feedback accelerates the speed at which fan fiction is distributed, consumed and processed; thus, fan fiction texts may generate responses within a much shorter time span, and are often instigated by direct contact between fan-authors and readers: "However similar to past forms of collective storytelling, this is something new. This newness has to do with technology, speed, format, and the conventions and forms these changes enable. Fanfiction communities collect people who may be very far apart in physical space and connects them, in 'close' proximity in virtual space, through near-simultaneous activities of authoring, editing, responding, and illustrating" (Jamison, 28).

This accelerated rate of reception and response has led to the creation of a fan fiction trend known as the "remix," which bears a simplified genre formula similar to the single qualifying feature required for slash: remixes must be in direct dialogue within an existing work of fan fiction—in essence, fan fiction of the second order. The impetus for the creation of a remix is identical in cause and purpose to the impetus for the creation of all fan fiction: just as the latter exists to address ontological gaps and apply different value systems to source texts, remixes attempt to do the same to works of fan fiction. As with AUs, a cursory examination might lead to the conclusion that all fan fiction falls within the purview of remixes, as the mechanisms of appropriation and reinterpretation are the same. But this conclusion misconstrues the end result, in that a remix produces a second-generation simulacrum—a copy of a copy—which in turn frames the intra-communal production of text and response as an interactive network. In theory, a practically infinite system of fan-fictional ontologies may emerge, with each derivation defining itself in relation to an earlier simulacrum.

Comparing *I Never* by harmonyangel and *I Never (The But Just This Once Remix)* by TheSecondBatgirl clarifies the practical application of the remix's generic mandate and formula. Both works are based on popular superhero franchise *X-Men*; *I Never* lists its publication date as March 11, 2009, while its remix was published on December 18 that same year, the product of a communal challenge titled "remixredux09." The first text—to be viewed henceforth as "original" despite being a reconfiguration of a pre-existing fictional world—is set in the early days of the X-Men team, with its familiar characters written as hormonal teenagers. A social drinking game leads to the revelation that Scott Summers, the group's leader (more commonly known as Cyclops), has never been kissed; the subsequent event situates *I Never* within the generic tradition of slash:

> "It appears that young Mr. Summers is the most prudish of the group," Hank noted, with an air of objective observation.
>
> Scott looked downcast, the tips of his ears turning almost as red as his glasses. "I just … haven't had the chance."
>
> "Well," Warren said, from his spot next to Scott, "I can fix that." Without giving him a chance to react, Warren slid a hand up and over Scott's jaw, resting his fingers near his ear, and pulled him in for a kiss that was anything but tentative.
>
> Scott pulled back after a frozen moment, sputtering. "I'm done," he muttered. "I didn't want to do this in the first place." He grabbed his orange juice and stalked off to the staircase to the dorms.
>
> Warren rolled his eyes again. "I'll go talk to him." He stood up, leaving his own bottle on an end table, and followed Scott's path from the room, his step only slightly wobbly [*I Never*, harmonyangel].

As with twentysomething and *DILF*, harmonyangel alters the established ontological structure of *X-Men* (albeit not in as drastic a fashion as the former) for the express purpose of introducing homoerotic tension between Scott and Warren Worthington, the mutant superhero Angel. But the focus of the story is not on these characters; when they exit the scene, the author continues to dramatize the game, leading to a subsequent romantic encounter between Jean Grey and her sometime-rival Wanda Maximoff. The outcome of the first pairing is only revealed at the end of the story, and is focalized through Jean:

> An hour later, Hank and Bobby had fallen asleep on the couch with their X-Box controllers still in their hands, Hank's character towering over Bobby's in a triumphant pose. In the common room, Wanda had fallen asleep, too, in Jean's lap, her fingers still entwined with those of the girl she'd spent the last hour kissing and touching and whispering to. Jean, however, was still awake, and, after taking a few contented moments to play with Wanda's curls, she disentangled herself, letting her friend fall to a more comfortable position on the love seat. Upstairs, on the way to her own dorm room, she happened to pass Scott's, where Scott

and Warren were splayed in a tangle of limbs on the bed, their shirts thrown on the floor and red blotches evident on Scott's neck and chest, and she smiled [*I Never*, harmonyangel].

Here, then, is evidence that Dolezel's assertion regarding textual lacunae is indeed universal: just as *I Never* purports to present its narrative as a possible sequence of events omitted by the original implied author, the simulacrum is itself incomplete due to the fan-author limiting the reader's awareness to Jean's perspective, relegating any further exchange between the male characters to the same type of ontological gap. TheSecondBatgirl's remix fiction, *I Never (The But Just This Once Remix)*, responds to this missing information by recreating the world of *I Never* in order to shift the focus back to Scott and Warren:

> Scott was shaking as he made his way up the stairs and into his room. He shouldn't be so affected by this. It was just a kiss. Actually, it was just his first kiss. From his teammate. Who was male. And who up until this exact minute Scott was pretty sure he hadn't actually been attracted to.
>
> Of course, there were all sorts of logical and rational reasons for why he'd be feeling something now. It was his first kiss, after all. Anyone would feel something after that. And Warren was experienced, after all. He knew that Warren had kissed plenty of girls. Apparently he'd also kissed a few guys as well. He was good at it. Really good at it [TheSecondBatgirl].

The remix goes on to detail the "missing" encounter from Scott's point of view, with the requisite erotic component central to Jenkins' definition of slash. However, this creates an immediate conflict of values between the implied authors of the two fan works: harmonyangel's text prioritizes female experience over male, given the exclusion of Scott and Warren in favor of exploring a similar homoerotic dynamic between Jean and Wanda. In itself, this is not unusual, as both Jenkins and Jamison agree that fan fiction is a predominantly female-led creative space, which Jamison frames within the greater discourse of fan fiction as resistance to existing paradigms: "About those gender binaries that still govern the world most of us live in: it's important that in fanfiction, women are largely running the show. Where else is that true?" (Jamison, 34–35). However, the implied author of the remix omits any female presence altogether, choosing instead to focus on the perceived "absence" featured in the original (in this case referring to *I Never* rather than *X-Men*). The possibility of ideological dissonance within a given fan community lends substantial credibility to Allen's argument that "the new hypertextuality unarguably fulfils the textual and intertextual vision of poststructuralists such as Barthes, Kristeva and Derrida, along with the theoretical stress on dialogism inherited from the work of Bakhtin" (Allen, 205). Fan fiction texts may be at odds not only with their respective source works but with each other, subsequently marginalizing said source texts to the point of near-nullification. Technological innovation has, in effect, promoted a form of interactivity that is not threatened by internal schisms between creators, and is capable of containing contradictory viewpoints without necessitating the preference or prioritization of one over another.

Further innovations in genre conventions and practices have emerged in recent years, each designed to take advantage of the freedom offered by this particular digital platform: "Songfic" refers to fan fiction texts which incorporate song lyrics into the diegetic plot (as with most hypertexts, the reader is often able to open an embedded link and play the song in question while reading the story); "PWP" (Plot What Plot?), an offshoot of slash, involves eroticization sans any narrative framework that typically foregrounds and justifies the same-sex pairing; "Crackfic" and "Badfic" are forms of parody, deliberate attempts to warp the ontological simulacrum beyond any logical or generic boundaries for the purpose of humor. One commonly recurring phenomenon in the early days of fan fiction (subject to much criticism following the practice's entry into the digital realm) is authorial self-insertion, what Jenkins refers to as personalization:

> Fan writers also work to efface the gap that separates the realm of their own experience and the fictional space of their favorite programs. "Mary Sue" stories, which fit idealized images of the writers as young, pretty, intelligent recruits aboard the Enterprise, the TARDIS, or the Liberator, constitute one of the most disputed subgenres of fan fiction. So strong is the fan taboo against such crude personalization that original female characters are often scrutinized for any signs of autobiographical intent, though there is at least one zine which proudly publishes nothing but "Mary Sue" stories. Other attempts to integrate program materials into fan's own experience have been better received [Jenkins, 176].

Indeed, the Mary Sue is nearly as widespread a tradition in fan fiction as slash, though to some extent the two operate at cross purposes: where slash purports to depict a romantic dynamic between pre-established fictional characters, the Mary Sue is typically meant to appropriate any such dynamic by inserting itself into the network of existing relationships. While this narrative device employs the same metaleptical techniques used in crossovers—essentially allowing authors to fictionalize themselves and project these idealized forms into any ontological framework—Turk notes that this particular transgression of boundaries is often criticized within fan communities themselves:

> In the broadest sense, we might say that *any* fan-created characters (usually called original characters, or OCs, to distinguish them from characters established by the source text) are metaleptic whether or not they are authorial self-insertions: they are fan additions both to the story and to the discourse—the storytelling strategy—of the fantext, elements introduced from outside the

source text. And indeed, in some cases, fans' preference for reading about familiar characters prompts resistance to any fan-created character: if we wanted to read about other characters, the argument goes, we'd read professionally published fiction [Turk, 98].

However, the rejection of the author-turned-character phenomenon does not constitute a rejection of metafiction in general; in fact, self-reflexivity and literary awareness are often active components of fan fiction, and authors frequently choose to draw attention to the artificiality of their own conventions. *Steve Rogers at 100: Celebrating Captain America on Film* is an example of the type of metafiction which has evolved in response to the aesthetics and traditions of fan fiction: a collaborative multimedia project from six fan-authors (eleveninches, Febricant, hellotailor, M_Leigh, neenya and tigrrmilk), the story is based on Marvel superhero Captain America and film adaptations *Captain America: The First Avenger* and *The Winter Soldier*. In the source material, titular superhero Steve Rogers and his childhood friend Bucky Barnes are World War II soldiers who are temporally displaced by way of cryogenics and awaken separately in the 21st century. The fan-fictional text offers a direct (and at times self-referential) commentary on the nature of the mode itself: as Rogers and Barnes are war heroes in their world, their presumed demise has been marked by a plethora of fictionalized cinematic biographies, each representing a particular film genre and historical/cultural era from 1946 to 2014 (the "present day" of the story). The narrative consists of Steve and Bucky viewing a marathon of films purporting to tell their life stories (with obvious artistic license leading to comedic liberties with the "true" events). These viewings are interspersed with doctored film posters, hyperlinks leading to profiles of popular actors (as a way of providing visual cues for the multiple castings and recastings of the primary actants), and faux-academic essays critiquing these hypodiegetic films. The preface to the narrative is presented as an excerpt from a fictional monograph titled *Steve Rogers: A Hauntology: A History of Captain America On-Screen, 1946–2011*, written by Morgan Leigh Davies (a projection of co-author M_Leigh) and published by Oxford University Press:

> It would be fair, then, to say that Steve Rogers is a ghost haunting the American people—or, rather, haunting the twentieth century, for the question we should be asking ourselves is not who he is but rather what he means to us. The man Steve Rogers was has been lost forever to the ice of the Arctic Ocean and to the passage of time—and yet Captain America lingers in the American consciousness, a shadow of the greatest generation that hangs over our national psyche and that continues to chase us into the twenty-first century. We are not the nation we were when the likes of Steve Rogers walked the streets of Brooklyn—but wouldn't we like to imagine ourselves as purely good as he seemed to

have been? Wouldn't we like to think that our war efforts, our foreign policy, our government were as "good" as they were in the pre–Nixon era? And so our fascination with—and glorification of—his ghost continues [*Steve Rogers at 100: Celebrating Captain America on Film*, eleveninches et al].

The multiple layers of commentary—from academic institutions, critical reviews of these non-existent films, and the reactions of Steve and Bucky themselves to these dramatizations of their own history—allow the authors to create a miniature series of hypodiegetic constructs which draw attention to their own fictionality. As Liviu Lutas notes, "such techniques are metafictional because of the way they reveal the artificiality of the text, risking thus to break the mimetic illusion" (Lutas, 44). Each film serves as a metaphor for different methods of adaptive reconfiguration, while positing Captain America himself as a Spartacus-like figure subject to eidetic variation. These include the 1974 melodramatic romance *Heartbreak on the Western Front* (starring David Soul and Farrah Fawcett), the 1995 action movie *Maximum Retribution* (featuring Sylvester Stallone, Bruce Willis and Nazi dinosaurs) and the 1998 French film *Enfants de la patrie*, notable among the other examples in that it stars Chris Evans and Sebastian Stan—the actors who play Rogers and Barnes in the source material—while providing a self-reflexive commentary on slash by alluding to a sex scene between the hypodiegetic actants. While the end result is humorous in tone, the text as a whole is framed as a meta-discussion on adaptation, genre reassignment, conflicting implied authors and popular practices across all forms of fan fiction:

> "Dinosaurs," Steve says faintly. "I—dinosaurs. I died fighting dinosaurs."
> "Why does anybody want to watch any of them?" Bucky says, baffled. "They were—they were so bad, Steve."
> "They were *so awful*," Steve says. "Well, I mean—the one with Matt Damon was all right, I suppose, if you pretend it wasn't about us—"
> "Half of it was you monologuing about America," Bucky says, side-eyeing him.
> "Yes, well, better that than—than—well!" Steve huffs, going red at the ears. "All of that—we didn't ever have sex, Bucky. That wasn't what we—I don't know why anybody would ever have thought that!"
> Bucky blinks at him, once, slow. "I liked that one," he says. "That was the only one that was good."
> "I," Steve starts, jerked out of his (incoherent) monologuing. "What?"
> "It was good," Bucky says. "I liked it. It was artistic" [*Steve Rogers at 100: Celebrating Captain America on Film*, eleveninches et al].

The codification, development and proliferation of these unique literary categories demonstrate the prolonged effects of unrestricted access to a publishing platform, the ongoing aesthetic schism between individual

mimetic aspect by incorporating canonical events into its own fan-fictional narrative, while providing sufficient visual and audio parallels to maintain an internal sense of continuity.

As *Revelations* was released prior to the canonical film *Star Wars: Revenge of the Sith*, its attempt to address a specific chronological gap is retroactively rendered moot, similar to how *Dreams of Electric Sheep* posits an endpoint to the Galactica's journey only to later be contradicted by the core narrative's final episode. However, where this inevitably leads to a shift in the fan-text's generic categorization, the mimetic effect of fan films is not diminished by this canonical intrusion, serving instead as the creators' statement of fidelity to the source material. Keyvan Sarkhosh provides a possible explanation for the prominence of this associative process:

> The concealing of a film's artificiality and factitiousness by means of conventionality is vital for the creation of a seemingly sound, complete, transparent and thus (supposedly) realistic diegesis. All the examples given so far break this convention by metaleptically laying bare certain aspects of the artificiality, textuality and assembly of the respective films, illustrating, moreover, their dependence on a superior extradiegetic world from which they originate by means of production and narration. This exposure nearly always comes about in terms of the story and may thus be characterised as metafictional [Sarkhosh, 184].

Sarkhosh's argument relates to metalepsis in comedic films, but it is clearly applicable to the production of *Revelations* as well. The use of audio-visual cues drawn from the source material (the distinctive sounds of Darth Vader's breathing apparatus, the ignition of a lightsaber, etc.) are meant to create associative links in the minds of the viewers, and narrow the gap between original and simulacrum; at the same time, fan film productions simply cannot compete with the vast resources of studios such as Lucasfilm, and any imperfections in the fan work draw attention to the existence of an aesthetically "superior" canonical template. Sarkhosh uses this hierarchical evaluative term to refer to consensus reality, but in the context of the dynamic relationship between fiction and fan fiction, this could just as easily be construed as homage to the original work.

As *Revelations* is comparable to *Dreams of Electric Sheep* in its attempt to fill chronological lacunae and subvert underlying values associated with their respective original implied authors, Sandy Collora's 2003 fan film *Batman: Dead End* follows the same schematic of the interdiegetic ontologically transgressive crossover as *For Our Own Benefit*. Unlike *Revelations*, *Dead End* does not target any particular ontological gap in the *Batman* oeuvre; indeed, as a character whose serialized adventures have been in continuous publication since 1939, one might argue there is very little in Batman's narrative timeline which has not been explored at one point or another. For the purposes of analyzing *Dead End*, Batman himself is less significant than the ontological structure in which this iteration is assumed to reside. As with any crossover text, it is the conjunction of two (or more) fictional worlds which exhibits the fan-creator's ability to cross boundaries thought to be immutable. *Dead End* begins with a sequence similar in purpose to the Senate scene in *Revelations*: Batman chases, captures and converses with his insane archnemesis the Joker, in a manner that visually and textually evokes similar exchanges the characters have shared over their decades-long conflict. However, the familiar scenario goes awry when the Joker is carried away by a Xenomorph—the monstrous adversary from the *Alien* film franchise. The Xenomorph's violent entry into this simulacrum is punctuated by the swift abduction and off-screen dispatching of the Joker, a deliberate echo of a scene from James Cameron's 1988 film *Aliens*; similarly, the Xenomorph's subsequent obliteration at the hands of a Predator reiterates the latter's assassination of a human soldier in the 1987 film of the same name. Thus the ontological structure of *Dead End* is revealed to be a point of intersection between three separate and distinct fictional worlds.

Of note here is the fact that these properties have a history of authorized collaboration: a comic book miniseries titled *Batman Versus Predator* was jointly published by DC Comics and Dark Horse Comics in 1991, followed by *Batman/Aliens* in 1998. The creatures themselves have been portrayed as natural adversaries in 2004 film *Alien vs. Predator*, a rare example of a mainstream crossover which subsequently spawned its own multimedia franchise of films, comics and novels. What *Dead End* contributes to this network of interconnected texts is a speculative configuration in which Batman, Xenomorphs and Predators all converge in the same space to do battle. With a runtime of eight minutes, *Dead End* is less concerned with plot than it is with spectacle: its value as a work of fan fiction is rooted exclusively in its visual representation of three iconic entities inhabiting the same chronotope and interacting (violently) on the same screen. While this hybrid world contains an irreconcilable internal schism, as its three participants follow very different and somewhat incompatible genre rules, Karin Kukkonen argues that this is of no significance, as the clash itself serves as a catalyst for the film's metaleptic effect: "Metalepsis seems to be essentially anti-illusionist because it destroys the coherence of the fictional world by transgressing its boundary. Contributing to the persuasive power of this assumption is certainly the perceived rise of metalepsis (and other means of metareference) in the disruptive and deconstructive narratives of postmodernism" (Kukkonen, 10). Furthermore, the reenactment and repetition of distinctly memorable scenes from the source works, such as a brief focalization through the Predator's augmented vision, are a product of the medium through which *Dead End* was produced and distributed:

Network fictions, therefore, consist of not only a representation of material but also a representation of structure. Readers must orient themselves "in" or in relation to the structural topology of a network fiction, which is technically adimensional. One of the most common and effective ways to do so involves repetition and recurrence, an experience that can be mistaken by readers and critics as a vice, a malfunction, or at the very least, a frustration [Ciccoricco, 49].

Thus Collora's fan film exhibits the same authorial fiat as twentysomething's *DILF*, as a more extreme demonstration of the extent to which fan works may reshape and redefine their simulacra. The incongruities which arise as a result are ultimately irrelevant in the eyes of the viewer, as the new ontological structure is self-sustaining and does not require further correlation with any of its originals.

In stark contrast to the disruptive effect of *Dead End*'s intertextual transgressions, fan film series *Star Trek: New Voyages* displays its desire for ontological mimesis at every opportunity. A serialized project which purports to continue the ongoing narrative of 1966's *Star Trek* (later referred to as *Star Trek: The Original Series*), *New Voyages* features actors cast in the familiar roles of Captain James T. Kirk, Commander Spock and Doctor Leonard McCoy among others, on a film set which recreates the bridge of the USS Enterprise down to minute detail. As of the time of writing, the web series' homepage declares that since *Star Trek* was cancelled after its third season, *New Voyages* presents a simulated fourth year of that ongoing narrative. Since *Star Trek* is widely credited with launching the first wave of fan fiction, its presence in the medium of fan films is to be expected, as is *New Voyages*' mission statement of expanding the timeline past the aired conclusion of the canonical narrative. What distinguishes *New Voyages* from most fan films is the relatively high number of participants who were also involved in the production of *The Original Series*: thus far, episodes of *New Voyages* have included guest appearances by key actors such as George Takei, Walter Koenig and Grace Lee Whitney, and have featured scripts by longtime *Star Trek* writers David Gerrold and D.C. Fontana among others. Episodes 4 and 5, *Blood and Fire*, are particularly noteworthy as fan-produced content with a direct line of descent from the source material: in an interview with StarTrek.com, Gerrold notes that the script was originally meant to be produced as an episode of 1987–1994 television series *Star Trek: The Next Generation*:

There were two characters who were not very important to the story, but they were the kind of background characters you need. At one point Riker says to one of them, "How long have you two been together?" That was it. The guy replies, "Since the Academy." That's it. That's all you need to know about their relationship. If you were a kid, you'd think they were just good buddies. If you were an adult, you'd get it. But I turned in the script and that's when the excrement hit the rotating blades of the electric air circulation device ["Trek Writer David Gerrold Looks Back–Part 2," StarTrek.com].

Nearly twenty years later, the script was revised and directed by Gerrold himself for *New Voyages*, taking full advantage of the web series' marginal media presence in relation to canonical authorities (thus avoiding entanglement with copyright laws by defining itself as a transformative work), as well as the *Star Trek* fan community's predisposition towards acceptance of minority representation—this being the same community that originated many of the tropes and conventions that have come to define the slash genre. However, *New Voyages* therefore finds itself in a singular position relative to its fan film peers, and to fan works in general: if the Internet eschews a stratified vertical evaluative structure, and fan works are not meant to compete with each other in terms of authenticity, what does the active presence of recognizable figures from the source material signify? Can the ontological structure of this particular fan work still be considered a simulacrum when it is to some extent shaped by individuals who took part in the original work? These questions are relevant due to the collaborative nature of any cinematic project, including those produced by fans; for all that textual fan fiction transgresses ontological and authorial boundaries, it remains by its very nature a medium which favors singular creators. By contrast, *New Voyages* and similar fan films which incorporate components of their respective originals are dependent upon a combination of directors, writers, actors, technicians and a multitude of other contributors, any of whom may have a direct impact on how these works are meant to be viewed and interpreted. Questions of perceived legitimacy, recognition and authenticity are still being raised, resolved and challenged today; as the relevant technology continues to advance, and such projects become increasingly commonplace and widely distributed, further complications will certainly arise. But according to Philip Rosen, these developments may also lead the way towards radical innovation for the cinematic medium as a whole:

> The digital utopia seems to call on the interplay of three fundamental characterizations of the novelty of digital imaging, which one repeatedly finds in discourses of theorists and practitioners. These three ideals taken together provide a provisional sketch for a utopia of the digital. They are (1) the *practically infinite manipulability* of digital images; (2) *convergence* among diverse image media; and (3) *interactivity*.... Speaking roughly, each may be predominantly associated with one phase of the orthodox breakdown of mainstream film production practices: production (practically infinite manipulability), distribution (convergence), and exhibition/reception (interactivity). Full implementation of these digital ideals would mean the realization of the claim for radical novelty [Rosen, 817].

As with textual fan fiction, digital platforms have enabled fan films to be more easily produced, easily shared, and easily accessed than ever before. This, in conjunction with the continuing absence of any qualifying entity to impose standardized frameworks of "quality" or "authenticity" regarding competing implied authors, ensures that the phenomenon will continue to provide multiplicities of ontological simulacra made visually manifest.

The Meaning(s) of Fan Fiction

In tracing the literary and technological development of fan fiction towards its current state, it is clear that widespread use of the Internet to generate and share fiction constitutes a challenge to existing paradigms and has led to the creation of new practical systems for consuming narrative. Yet narratology itself is a constant process of adaptation to emerging discourses, per Monica Fludernik:

> One way to map the history of narratology is therefore to see it as adopting linguistic paradigms one by one as they arose in the twentieth century—structuralism (classical narratology); generativist linguistics (text grammars); semantics and pragmatics (speech act theory, politeness issues, etc.); text linguistics (conversation analysis and critical discourse analysis); and now cognitive linguistics (cognitivist narratology) [Fludernik, 48].

It follows, then, that the fan-author's desire for self-expression, diegetic agency and interactivity—forces which, in fan fiction, manifest in the act of authorial usurpation and the proliferation of non-competing multiplicities—calls for a reassessment of the narratological toolbox, rooted as its principles are in reactions (whether positive or negative) to structuralism as it pertains to the written, printed, singular textual object. Fan fiction constitutes a vast narrative laboratory, its multitude of online works lacking any limitation on experimentation with form, genre and content. Thus, a technology designed from inception to avoid centrality and arbitrary blocks on accessibility has produced a form of textuality that fully expresses those same ideals, as noted by George P. Landow: "What is perhaps most interesting about hypertext … is not that it may fulfill certain claims of structuralist and poststructuralist criticism but that it provides a rich means of testing them" (Landow, 56). Furthermore, the fan-creator now stands as an antecedent to the development of social media products such as Tumblr, Facebook and Twitter, which are themselves significantly transformative in the field of interpersonal global communication—a network dynamic first expressed by those nascent fan communities: "Anyone who has ever fantasized about an alternate ending to a favorite book or imagined the back story of a minor character in a favorite film has engaged in creating a form of fan fiction. Anyone who has ever recommended a You-Tube mash-up, shared a cat macro, or reposted a GIF set has participated in the online culture of audience-generated texts" (Hellekson & Busse 2014, 1). It is fandom, and fan-authors, who stand at the threshold of narratology's future, and whose ideals continue to inform both the way stories are told in the 21st century and the channels through which those stories are distributed and received. Fan fiction authors such as Sarah Rees Brennan, Paul Cornell, Melissa Good and Naomi Novik have found success and acceptance as professional writers, indicating a trend towards the destigmatization of online writing; additionally, the growing popularity of transmedia publishing as a desirable franchising tactic only further dissolves notions of "authentic" authorship, as the canonicity of "the real thing" is no longer necessarily perceived as inherently superior. As the Internet and related online technologies (e.g., new social media websites, smartphone applications, and so on) continue to be repurposed for the creation and distribution of fan productions, it is a certainty that additional innovations and unique narrative forms will emerge.

Subsequent chapters will demonstrate the extent to which the core features of fan fiction discussed herein find remarkably similar expression in other digital media—from textual modification to the proliferation of new sub-genres, from communal narrative generation to metaleptic crossovers and substitutions of implied authors. Viewing the points of intersection between these disparate media platforms will provide greater insight into their structural, narratological and ontological makeup, as well as the various processes through which they generate reactive and interactive fiction.

2

Video Game Narratology

Technological Refinement Throughout the History of Video Games

As one of the newest media to emerge during the digital age, video games have been the subject of intense critical focus over the past two decades. In their introduction to *The Video Game Theory Reader*, Mark J.P. Wolf and Bernard Perron note that for all their inherently unique properties, even a cursory glance at video games reveals the ease with which they can be situated within existing critical paradigms while lending themselves to a vast multiplicity of theoretical approaches:

> The emerging field of video game theory is itself a convergence of a wide variety of approaches including film and television theory, semiotics, performance theory, game studies, literary theory, computer science, theories of hypertext, cybertext, interactivity, identity, postmodernism, ludology, media theory, narratology, aesthetics and art theory, psychology, theories of simulacra, and others.... The medium itself is a moving target, changing and morphing even as we try to theorize and define it. But its trajectory can be traced through the writings of the past three decades that set the groundwork for video game theory [Wolf/ Perron, 23].

While different disciplines may shed light on various aspects of the medium, the central critical schism involves a perceived conflict between narratology and ludology as primary lenses for the evaluation and analysis of video games. Grant Tavinor's *The Art of Videogames* categorizes these approaches thusly: "Three such approaches are salient in the literature: the *narratological* approach, where videogames are characterized as new forms of narratives or texts; the *ludological* approach, where they are seen as being principally games though in a new digital medium; and the *interactive fiction* theory of videogames that emphasizes their fictive qualities" (Tavinor, 15). Naturally, each approach has its defenders: critics such as Jesper Juul and Espen Aarseth have argued in favor of viewing the mechanics of "play" as a priority in achieving any deep understanding of the medium, arguing that video games should be thought of as systems of rules rather than narrative platforms; others, such as David Ciccoricco, discredit the value of an exclusively gameplay-based approach by pointing to a substantial blind spot:

> Ludology is problematic, however, whenever it falls prey to a needless insistence on a mutually exclusive approach: either a video game is read and interpreted as a text (which is the wrong way according to the ludologist), or it is treated as a rule-based simulation (which is the right way according to the ludologist). Such a view leads to a circular polemic that fails to acknowledge the role of narrative in both shaping game structure and motivating game play; more broadly, it fails to consider how creative works can make use of narration *and* interaction, representation *and* simulation, reading *and* play [Ciccoricco, 10].

Indeed, while ludology has been (and continues to be) vital in distinguishing video games from other media, it is in narratology that the foundation this medium shares with other technologically supported platforms is revealed: specifically, that it treads similar ground with regards to provisions of authorial agency, interactivity and subversive variations of the familiar author/reader dynamic. It is also highly significant that a large percentage of video games today follow the broad patterns and requirements of literary storytelling: they are organized into genres, they project fictional worlds, they are set in specific places and times, the experience of play is arranged within a nominal plot, and they contain at least one actant who serves as protagonist. This validates Jenkins' stated position in *Convergence Culture* that, regardless of how new technologies are implemented and how new media may vary in form and function, they are all ultimately shaped and determined by the same core human impulses, and should therefore be viewed as part of a continuum rather than isolated, self-contained phenomena:

> A medium's content may shift (as occurred when television displaced radio as a storytelling medium, freeing radio to become the primary showcase for rock and roll), its audience may change (as occurs when comics move from a mainstream medium in the 1950s to a niche medium today), and its social status may rise or fall (as occurs when theater moves from a popular form to an elite one), but once a medium establishes itself as satisfying some core human demand, it continues to function within the larger system of communication options.... Old media are not being displaced. Rather, their functions and status are shifted by the introduction of new technologies [Jenkins, 14].

As this book is geared towards uncovering the commonalities between different digital media, elaborate discussions of gameplay and its technical implications will be eschewed in favor of exploring the medium's history of narrative presentation. The goal, as in the previous chapter, is to delineate how new technologies have influenced and actualized those same desires Jenkins describes; how, in turn, the need to attain pseudo-authorial power has affected the platform's development over time; and those same areas where video game narratology intersects and overlaps with other forms of digital literature.

When reviewing historical accounts of video games' introduction into popular culture, a pattern of directed development becomes apparent. Each new development in hardware and software is credited to a set of priorities that predate the medium itself, with Janet Murray attributing the eventual materialization of virtual technologies to a similar impetus: "The age-old desire to live out a fantasy aroused by a fictional world has been intensified by a participatory, immersive medium that promises to satisfy it more completely than has ever before been possible. With encyclopedic detail and navigable spaces, the computer can provide a specific location for places we long to visit" (Murray, 98). This may explain why many histories of the medium characterize the earliest days of video game development as a clash between an irresistible force (game designers' wish to satisfy that same desire) and an immovable object (the upper limits of what available technology could do to achieve that goal). Matt Barton summarizes this conflict by noting that "the first CRPGs for home computers are quite crude compared to later games. Programmers had to work with extreme restrictions on memory, and graphics technology was severely limited in terms of resolution and the number of colors that could be displayed on screen. Unlike modern programmers, who have a deep well of previous triumphs and proven routines to draw from, the first CRPG developers had to find their own solutions" (Barton, 47). In other words, the monolithic desire among players for a measure of diegetic agency existed at the medium's most primordial stage and has not changed significantly in the interim; but as with any narrative platform, technological developments have enabled greater complexity of composition and design, in turn allowing a wider range of possible responses to that desire.

While the history of the medium constitutes an intricate, multifaceted epic in its own right, certain key moments are highly relevant when tracing the development of video game narratology. For example, while games were already commercial products in the late 1970s, Tristan Donovan highlights the point at which personal computing became first plausible, then possible, then utterly commonplace, beginning with a brief period of confusion as to what purposes these new tools might serve:

> The arrival of the Apple II, TRS-80 and PET brought a swift end to days when computers were only found in large institutions. Now anyone could potentially have a computer in their home. But while most people agreed computers were the future, few had any idea what households would do with them. Would they

calculate their tax returns or catalogue record collections? Would they teach their children to program the machines in the hope that they would have the skills that would be needed in the workplace of the future? Or would they store family recipes or address books on a cassette tape? It turned out that early home computers would be used almost exclusively for one purpose alone: playing video games. And many of the games they played were versions of those once locked away on the computers of academia, government and business [Donovan, 59].

Donovan's account explicitly frames the introduction of home computers as an assimilation and subsequent adaptation of new technology—a process practically identical to Jenkins' description of printed text, video cassettes, and online archives successively utilized as tools for the further refinement of fan production. However, where the creation of fan fiction follows the same basic conditions for access as its parent medium—reading comprehension for written text, visual comprehension for fan films—video games carry an additional requirement: constant input on the part of the player. The amount and quality of a game's narrative content may change depending on its design (and, as Aarseth and Juul point out, many games are entirely ludological experiences with no story to offer at all), but all games—from the ur-examples of *Pong* and *Space Invaders* to the uncannily lifelike simulations seen today—establish a deep and innate link with the player, displaying immediate reactivity at all times. Furthermore, as different games may require different skill sets, the player's activity has no uniform manifestation, per Clive Fencott: "Different genres and activity profiles require significant differences in terms of agency. The pleasure to be had from slaughtering psychotic alien beasts in *shoot-'em-ups* is presumably quite different from solving the puzzles in Myst or Riven. However, they both arise from agency. Some games are all about agency and presence. In some narrative potential assumes a major role. Games are pleasurable in different ways" (Fencott, 57).

The tools used to create, distribute and participate in games play a significantly larger part in determining the nature of the narrative experience than any cinematic precedent. According to Eric Zimmerman, diegetic agency here is a direct product of the technology being deployed: "Games are, in fact, essentially systemic. Every game has a mathematical substratum, a set of rules that lies under its surface.... To play, understand, and—especially—design games, one ends up having to understand them as systems. Any game is a kind of miniature artificial system, bounded and defined by the game rules that create the game's magic circle" (Zimmerman, 26). Thus, while "video games" are here discussed as a singular medium, it must be understood that this platform is comprised of a multitude of devices—the screen, the keyboard, the controller, the audio speakers, etc.—and is arguably the most dependent not only upon a certain level of advanced technological aptitude, but upon continual innovation for the sake of its own development. The more refined the technology, the more sophisticated the game experience:

> An understanding of technology and its development is needed to understand why games look and play as they do, and have developed as they have. Graphics, sound, algorithms, processing speed, storage capability, accessing speed, peripherals, and so forth all exert an influence on both hardware and software design, which in turn limit programming and shape game design and gameplay experiences. How artistic decisions are shaped by technological compromises needs to be understood by game researchers before assumptions regarding game design can be made [Perron/Wolf, 12].

To demonstrate the medium's progress along historical lines, while taking note of specific attributes which have gradually developed to permit ever-increasing amounts of narrative agency and interactivity, specific games may serve as waypoints. For example, Barton's account focuses on the particular genre of the RPG (Role-Playing Game), and highlights an eight-year period in which many new techniques came to define both the unique traits and shortcomings of video games:

> What we'll see happening between 1985 and 1993 is an explosion of innovation and diversity, with hundreds of titles and a great deal of experimentation. Although many of the triumphs will be in the realm of graphics and sound, others have more to do with the art of storytelling, world building, and character development. We'll also see developers struggling to stay ahead of the latest advances in hardware, for we'll soon see how graphical considerations rise in prominence and, at least for some gamers, eventually trump all else [Barton, 86].

Of course, if any coherent throughline is to emerge, the overwhelmingly vast corpus of games that would qualify for discussion in the context of new technologies—especially towards the turn of the century—must be streamlined. Therefore the games selected for this study contain a clear ontological structure with distinct stories and plots (thus excluding historically-significant but narratively-vacuous products such as *Pac-Man*), and all include at least one instance in which the player's diegetic agency manifests not as competence in a required skill (for example, honed reflexes allowing the player to dodge traps and progress without dying/restarting), but rather as pseudo-authorial manipulation of the plot itself. Tracing these developments, and the techniques used to sustain and evolve them, will aptly demonstrate Ren Reynolds' argument that "today's virtual worlds grew out of a combination of single-player computer games and multiuser computer systems, which in turn grew out of the playful use of computing and electronic that stretches back at least to the 1950's" (Reynolds, 399).

As with fan fiction in the previous chapter, a structural approach here will allow for a clear vantage point with which to discuss common attributes featured in video game narratives, followed by a focused examination of how each trait has changed over time through the incorporation and refinement of new technologies. The first such attribute is the often-cited "garden of forking paths" which frequently transforms video games into unique multitextual objects, empowering the player to navigate divergent scenarios in a manner strongly reminiscent of the pseudo-authorial functions assumed by creators of fan fiction. An analysis of the avatar—the player's diegetic representative—will follow, with an eye towards discussing how elements such as death and sexuality are depicted in video games while simultaneously serving familiar, archetypal narrative functions. The virtual diegesis itself will then be viewed in the context of reactive spaces and authorial fiat writ large, exploring instances where the player is able to affect not only the plot and the arc of their fictional representative, but the entire ontological system itself. Lastly, game metafiction and "modding"— the practice of players reconfiguring the actual programming code of the game to suit their own ends—will clarify points of intersection shared by these new media, with the end goal of discerning how these juxtapositions can be framed within critical theory while new tools are continually being added to the repertoire.

Ryan's introduction to *Cyberspace Textuality* argues for distinct and separate categories of technological functions: "The new forms of discourse and literary genres born out of computer technology can be classified into three categories, depending on the role of the computer. The machine can function as author or co-author, as medium of transmission or as space of performance" (Ryan, 2). However, just as the reflexive cycles of communal fan production have blurred the boundaries between reality, diegesis and simulacra, so too have video games conflated and collapsed Ryan's categories. The machines in question are now capable of fulfilling all three functions simultaneously via audiovisual transmission of an ontological framework, within which the player can exert pseudo-authorial power to craft a singular performance tailored to said player's individual system of values. Thus, Tavinor's claim of an inextricable bond between technological progress and artistic complexity foregrounds narratology's increasing interest in video games:

> Why are videogames displaying this trend toward artistic sophistication? A large part of this artistic growth has been driven by technology: the present is an age of next generation consoles and powerful personal computers—gaming devices that are able to create sophisticated, responsive, and increasingly beautiful fictional worlds into which players step in order to play games.... This technology is a prerequisite for most modern gaming, and though other artworks

such as popular film have felt the influence of the recent technological developments, none is so closely tied to digital technology as videogames [Tavinor, 6].

Manipulation, Morality, and Multitextuality

The previous chapter discusses fan fiction as a potentially infinite succession of ontological simulacra, a multiplicity of possible worlds derived from pre-existing narratives and arranged in nonhierarchical space. As described earlier, these works are characterized in part by a form of authorial usurpation: the original implied author is replaced by a new value system assembled and embedded by the fan-author, a process typically achieved via reconfiguration of plot, genre or diegetic ontology. Video games exhibit a similar dynamic, albeit with a more direct and immediate means for constructing and containing variant plots: the medium is innately multitextual, in that the physical object—be it a game cartridge, a CD-ROM, or whatever other package houses the game software—contains not a singular, linear text but an array of possibilities, to be navigated by the player. This is best encapsulated in Ryan's use of the metaphor popularized by Jorge Luis Borges: "A simulation is not a static representation of a specific state of affairs, but a 'garden of forking paths' (to paraphrase the title of a short story by Borges), containing *in potentia* many different narrative lines threading together many states of affairs. Through the choices of the user, every session in the simulative system will send the history of the virtual world on a different trajectory" (Ryan, 117).

An important distinction must be made regarding the navigation and actualization of variable potentialities in games: on the most basic level, any engagement with a game produces a divergent narrative, as the player's actions may lead to different results depending on reflexes and technical skills. For example, two players of 1989 platformer *Prince of Persia* stand before the same difficult jump—one is able to make the jump and continue on to the next part of the story, while the other miscalculates and their avatar plummets to his doom, causing the sequence to restart. While the concept of virtual death will be explored in much greater detail shortly, this is nevertheless a feature that sets the medium apart from its digital contemporaries: where other narrative formats may exhaust the audience's patience and cause them to cease engagement with a particular text, games actively block progress via progressively increasing challenge and difficulty. A player who lacks aptitude cannot move forward to the next link in the narrative chain of events, irrespective of said player's desire to proceed. While this technically fulfills the prerequisites for consideration as a branching ontological structure, it is an argument that favors ludology over narratology; in the case of *Prince of Persia* and its peers, failure is not diegetic but extradiegetic, as the game does not acknowledge the player's defeat as a plot point. Evan Skolnick makes note of this duality of narrative and experience:

> Most games that incorporate any kind of storytelling include, to one degree or another, two narratives running in parallel. There is the *game story*—predefined by the developers to be the same for every player who experiences it. And there is the *player story*—the narrative unique to each player based on choices she's made or things that just happened to occur via the various interactions of game systems with each other and the player's actions [Skolnick, 130].

Much like "Choose Your Own Adventure" books, the aforementioned scenarios offer only one "true" linear path to traverse, with all "incorrect" variables leading to death or failure, in turn causing the experienced story to reset to reset until the correct sequence is discovered and carried out.

But it is in diegetic choice—agency the player is able to express within the framework of the fictional world—that a pattern of gradual, teleological progress becomes apparent. One of the earliest examples (and, not coincidentally, an apt demonstration of "false" choice) is Enix's 1989 role-playing game *Dragon Warrior*. A simplistic, medieval-themed fantasy tale, *Dragon Warrior* reveals its plot in prompt, unremarkably linear fashion until the final act. When confronting the evil Dragonlord in his lair, the hero receives the following offer: "I give thee now a chance to share this world and to rule half of it if thou will now stand beside me. What sayest thou? Will the great warrior stand with me?" (*Dragon Warrior*). If the player accepts the Dragonlord's bargain, the game immediately ends; this is not appropriate behavior for the protagonist of a heroic narrative, and the player is punished with a form of "Game Over" that acknowledges their failure to successfully decode the implied author's meaning. Upon rejecting the offer and subsequently defeating the Dragonlord, the player stands before King Lorik and his daughter, the beautiful Princess Gwaelin (whom the player had rescued from captivity at an earlier point in the game). As the King congratulates the hero on a job well-done, Gwaelin steps forward and says: "I wish to go with thee on thy journey. May I travel as thy companion?" (*Dragon Warrior*). At this point, the player is offered a choice of two responses, a binary Yes/No. If the player chooses No, Gwaelin will respond "But thou must!" and repeat her previous question. Continuing to deny her request locks the player into an endless dialogue loop until consent is given, at which point the avatar sweeps Gwaelin into his arms and walks away with her. Both scenarios—the Dragonlord's offer and Gwaelin's request—represent the same clash between technological limitations and designer intent to which Barton refers. The developers of *Dragon Warrior* invoke the specter of agency in the game's final moments, so that players may complete their Campbellian Hero's Journey with its traditional values intact: the villain overthrown, the hero married and returning to domesticity. However, the hardware available at the time the game was designed and published—in this case, the Nintendo Entertainment System or NES—lacked the necessary sophistication to accommodate players who might choose to deviate from the scripted path, for any variety of reasons. Thus, pseudo-authorial agency in *Dragon Warrior* is merely illusory, as the player cannot betray the kingdom, or refuse Gwaelin's request, despite the presentation of alternative potential responses.

These restrictions on expressions of agency would gradually erode as the tools used to build and play games became more sophisticated. The first significant step forward from a narratological perspective was the inclusion of multiple endings, as with Silicon Knights' 1996 action game *Blood Omen: Legacy of Kain*. Like *Dragon Warrior,* the game's narrative is utterly linear, concerning the murder of the nobleman Kain, his return as a vampire, and his bloody quest for revenge. The player's control is purely extradiegetic, limited to the various gruesome manners in which Kain may dispatch his foes. However, upon defeating the final enemy, Kain discovers that there are two possible resolutions to his tale: "I am the last Pillar, the only survivor of the Circle of Nine. At my whim, the world will be healed ... or damned. At my whim" (*Blood Omen: Legacy of Kain*). In-game, this choice is presented to the player in the form of two floating cards positioned opposite each other. The player must select one or the other, each triggering a different ending to the game. If Kain chooses to destroy the world, he rules over the broken ruins as a vampiric tyrant; if he chooses to heal it, he sacrifices his own life to do so. Here we have a pre-existing principle finding fruition once technology has caught up: if, in *Dragon Warrior*, the NES was unable to actually present separate outcomes to a binary choice, *Blood Omen* (which debuted on the more advanced PlayStation console) achieves precisely that by momentarily ceding control of the plot to the player. This scene, according to Brian Richardson, corresponds to the "forking path" structure:

> The "forking paths" principle articulated by (though not really embodied within) Borges's story "The Garden of Forking Paths" can lead us directly to a genuinely new kind of multiple, mutually exclusive, orderings of a text. ...the suggested *sjuzhet* is largely linear; the different possible trajectories do not result in radically different *fabulas*, though the interpretation of the basic fabula will alter depending on which version is followed. More radical in this regard are the popular children's "pick your own adventure" books, where different readerly choices result in quite different sequences [Richardson, 175].

Indeed, the player's choice at the end of *Blood Omen* is largely dependent upon their personal interpretation of the narrative as a whole, since the game does not display a marked preference towards either conclusion. Both scenarios are contextually plausible: Kain has been waging war against the villains responsible for corrupting the land, but his motivations have been consistently shown to be those of a self-centered antihero, rather than the kind of protagonist who would sacrifice themselves for the greater good. Later installments of the *Legacy of Kain* series would capitalize on this by retroactively decreeing that Kain had, in fact, chosen to destroy the world—a controversial decision given the nullification of past agency, but a necessary step in extending the narrative beyond the ontological and chronological limitations of the first entry.

The notion of mutual exclusivity is key to understanding the ramifications of the branching plot, defined by Ciccoricco as a modification of the Borges paradigm:

> An arborescent fiction … can refer to a narrative with branches but specifically those that contain mutually exclusive story events or outcomes; a reader of an arborescent narrative makes choices at bifurcating points in the text *and continues on until the end of one of the branches is reached.* Returning to a previous bifurcation in an arborescent narrative is equivalent to rewinding a temporal frame; that is, readers undo and redo the story whenever they decide to go back [Ciccoricco, 6].

A player who reaches the conclusion of *Blood Omen* cannot view both endings simultaneously: the choice must be made, the corresponding consequence revealed, and the final battle replayed in order to reach that branching point again and make a different decision. This increases the level of potential engagement with any multitextual game, as the player is compelled to spend more time in the fictional world despite the supposed completion of its narrative content. To explore alternative branches, the story must be revisited, and the ending rewritten at the whim of the diegetically-empowered player. The function of mutual exclusivity is its inherent increase of diegetic agency: the ability to return to a previous point in the narrative, make different story choices, and experience different outcomes is a direct expression—however underdeveloped at this point in the medium's history—of the desire for authorial control.

Along similar lines, the "multiple endings" technique is not the only possible configuration which allows for such multiplicities of plot branches. If *Blood Omen* presents its narrative as a linear path which forks only at the very end, the reverse scenario—in which the player is given an initial choice that splinters the plot into multiple parallel tracks that never intersect—expresses the same principles. According to Barton, Sierra Entertainment's *Quest for Glory* series (consisting of five games from 1989 to 1998) is noteworthy because "class selection plays a stronger role in the narrative than it does in most CRPGs. Its influence is most clearly seen in the puzzles, which offer solutions unique to each class. For instance, fighters and thieves can climb a tree to fetch a ring in a bird's nest, but magic-users must cast a spell" (Barton, 229–230). Moreover, while variable endings are still a factor in the player's experience, as "each class also gets a different final scene, a fact that no doubt improves the game's replay value" (Barton, 231), all five games also contain entire areas that are class-specific. A Thief will visit locations a Wizard will never see, and vice-versa; neither will share the gladiatorial sequences which are part of the Fighter's storyline. The key events remain the same—all avatars face the same enemies, complete the same narrative trajectory, and share the same overall goals—but the situational presence of particular minutiae allows for some level of variation during the player's engagement with the game. Thus, just as *Blood Omen* attempts interactivity by allowing the player a single choice at the end, *Quest for Glory* attempts the same with its pre-narrative choice of class for the player avatar.

These points of divergence represent the first step in the process of granting diegetic agency within predominantly-linear narrative structures, but the inherent limitation of the above examples is self-evident: the hardware and software available at the time only allowed for the insertion of single branching points, expressed in decisions the player could either make at the start of the game (at which point there is minimal diegetic context to foreground any particular option) or at its very end (by which point the player is unable to explore further ramifications of their decisions). The next step in the evolution of game multitextuality is the introduction of modularity, best epitomized in games such as Interplay's *Fallout 2* (1998). The *Fallout* series takes as its premise and pre-narrative background an alternative version of America, highly influenced by an exaggerated, sanitized interpretation of 1950s aesthetics; the player character comes to inhabit this world generations after a nuclear war has reduced the country to a post-apocalyptic wasteland. Navigating this doubly-defamiliarized space—the irradiated ruins of an America that never existed to begin with—is a major factor in the game's ontological structure and narrative experience. Chiefly relevant to the subject of agency is the fact that all *Fallout* games use modular story structures to offer the player not one but multiple decision points. Kate Berens and Geoff Howard note that "*Fallout's* greatest achievement is its implementation of the concept of free will in a game, attaching significance to almost everything that can be done. ... the results of conversations and actions cannot be easily undone, permanently changing the course of the game and thereby forcing the player to constantly re-orient their 'what if' compass" (Berens/Howard, 82).

At various points throughout the game, the player confronts obstacles which may be dealt with in a variety of ways; some choices depend on the assigned skills and aptitudes of the customized avatar, while others are aligned on a moral spectrum meant to reinforce role-playing mechanisms (for example, offering a Good solution requires more effort, while an Evil solution increases the player's power at the cost of innocent lives). The repercussions are not immediately apparent—the short-term result is simply the player's ability to progress further. However, where *Blood Omen* presents different epilogues based on one instance of agency in its final scene, the endings of *Fallout* games typically consist of a sequence of modular outcomes corresponding to specific decisions the player may or may not have made throughout the course of the entire narrative. For example, in *Fallout 2* the player visits the town of Modoc, a settlement besieged by a hostile faction known as the Slags. The people of Modoc ask for the player's assistance in resolving their crisis, and several options are presented: the player can aid Modoc in destroying the Slags, make peace between the opposing forces, or simply do nothing and continue onwards. Each course of action will lead to a different conclusion presented during the ending sequence (many, many hours after said decision was made); if the player sides with Modoc, the narrator will present the following: "Armed with flares and clubs, the people of Modoc invade the Slags' underground city. The Slags are quickly defeated, and the Modoc residents slaughter every man, woman, and child they find. Rumor of this vicious attack spreads far and wide, and fear motivates Modoc's neighbors to attack and destroy the town" (*Fallout 2*). If the player chooses to pursue a truce, the town greatly benefits: "Relations between the Slags and residents of Modoc flourished. Between the two peoples, Modoc prospers and becomes a major farming community, supplying all the outlying regions with food" (*Fallout 2*). Choosing not to aid Modoc at all sees the town reduced to dust by a drought the Slags could have averted.

As with earlier attempts, this method of choice and consequence has innate ludological value, in that it encourages the player to prolong their engagement with the game. On a narrative level, however, the appeal is the same as that which spurs the creation of fan fiction: with every choice the player makes, an ontological simulacrum is constructed and shaped largely by the sum total of said choices. It is impossible for players to simultaneously contribute to Modoc's destruction and save its people—thus, replaying *Fallout 2* with different avatars, different strategies and different authorial decisions may lead to any combination of potential resolutions. Of course, unlike fan fiction, the number of simulacra is by necessity limited—as Skolnick notes, the software that comprises the virtual diegesis must contain within it a script for each variant:

> Perhaps the most significant and challenging feature games of this ilk sometimes attempt is to incorporate player choices that *do* affect the overarching, pre-crafted narrative in some way. These branched structures are tricky since,

with multiple levels of branching, they have the potential to set up a combinatorial explosion of possibilities, each of which may require custom content—most of which will never be experienced by a given player during a playthrough [Skolnick, 132].

The more sophisticated a game's code, the more branches it can contain, and the better it can accommodate variables which increase its multitextual value. Where *Quest for Glory* contains five potential narratives (corresponding to the five character classes), a *Fallout* game may contain a dozen different storylines which emerge through the pursuit of specific paths, and which provide a greater allotment of diegetic agency to the player. Just as with fan fiction, there is no imposed uniformity—a player may choose to save Modoc, but later condemn a different town to destruction for reasons specific to that enacted story. Whatever modular sequence emerges at the end of each engagement, it is always the aggregate sum of decisions made by the player during that particular run through the game.

These examples share a common drawback in terms of how they are presented: for all that decision points may be dispersed throughout the game's narrative timeline, consequences are deferred to the ending, past the point of active participation on the part of the player. The narratives of *Fallout* and its contemporaries are shaped by agency, but the player is only able to view the results of their actions as a passive spectator. Again, this is a technological limitation rather than an intentional creative decision: the tools of the time were unable to accommodate the possibility of a diegetic space that could change while the player was still active within it. However, given mechanical advances shaped specifically by the pursuit of that ideal, new paradigms inevitably presented themselves:

> One solution to this dilemma is to restrict the ramifications of player choices to settings that are quietly tracked by the game itself. Invisible to the player, these "flags" don't usually change the big-ticket aspects of the narrative—where you go, what you must do—but instead alter more minor aspects of the experience along the way. For example, if you are rude to an NPC in Mission 1, the game may silently set a flag that is referenced and reflected when you run into that character again in Mission 3. (Perhaps he's much less friendly.) [Skolnick, 132].

Skolnick's proposal does in fact represent the next phase of authorial empowerment in video games: rather than delay the outcomes of player agency to the final moments of the narrative, contemporary attempts such as Telltale Games' 2012–2018 adventure series *The Walking Dead* and Stoic Studio's 2014–2018 strategy trilogy *The Banner Saga* exhibit branching structures which directly express player agency while the narratives are still ongoing. When decisions are made, short-term consequences will emerge as the player continues on their chosen path—these variables serve to further differentiate individualized narratives within the array of possibilities. Chris

Crawford confirms that this mode of storytelling is a more complex iteration of the pre-existing narrative strategy: "an interactive storyworld consists of a core plot with some variations. The designer defines an initial state for the storyworld, then defines each of the dramatic branchpoints in the storyworld. Each branchpoint in turn leads to a number of different dramatic states, which have their own branchpoints, and so on" (Crawford, 323).

The proliferation of decision points (with varying amounts of dramatic weight) represents another substantial increase in the player's pseudo-authorial power and allows further exploration of diegetic spaces that are being actively molded rather than passively viewed. According to Miroslaw Filiciak, this particular narrative structure has a powerful psychological impact on the player:

> There is also one important fact—that the user plays an active role in modulating the transmissions that reach him, and has control over them. Of course to some extent, what he watches on the screen depends on his actions and the choices he makes. Obviously it is easier to identify ourselves with something that is partly created by us than with pictures imposed on us by somebody else. The possibility of transmission modulation (through influencing the game appearance in real time) enhances the game comfort to a large extent; it allows the user to adapt the game to his or her own preferences [Filiciak, 123].

The Walking Dead, based on the popular comic and its subsequent television adaptation, begins with the player cast as Lee Everett, a former professor of history who has been convicted of murder and is being transported to prison. The inciting event of the overarching *Walking Dead* narrative—a global zombie outbreak—leads to Lee's escape and his befriending of a young girl named Clementine, who serves as the player's companion throughout the story. As is typical of transmedia adaptations, the game is designed to mirror its antecedent texts both structurally and thematically: society breaks down, technology fails, and familial units (such as the bond formed between Lee and Clementine) are the only interpersonal dynamic that can sustain itself in the long term. Where the game distinguishes itself in opposition to its source material is the player's ability to eschew the character arc of the typical *Walking Dead* protagonist in several ways. The first, and most prominent, involves conversations: when speaking with Clementine or other members of their small group, Lee is given several possible dialogue options ranging from friendly to confrontational to utterly silent. The game notifies the player when characters are affected by what has been said—for example, if the player chooses to lie to Clementine in an effort to shield her from the harsh reality around her, the words "Clementine will remember that" will appear in the upper left corner of the screen, and in a later exchange she may be slower to take Lee at his word where another player's honest approach will be rewarded with immediate trust.

While this form of malleable interpersonal dynamic corresponds to Skolnick's notion of "smaller-scale" interactivity (as, similar to *Quest for Glory,* most key events in the overarching plot of *The Walking Dead* occur in every variant), the game also presents certain branching points with a far more tangible impact on the narrative experience. At the end of the first chapter, the protagonists are besieged by a zombie horde; two of their new allies, Carley and Doug, simultaneously fall into peril. As time slows to a crawl, the player must choose which of the two to save, condemning the other to death—not the inconsequential "video game death" so common to the medium, but a diegetic event treated as genuine and irreversible. Naturally, this has a visible effect on the following chapter: some players will rescue Carley, others may rescue Doug. Moreover, these are not interchangeable characters, as Carley's skill with handguns allows her to assist Lee during a later combat sequence, while Doug lends his engineering talents to the creation of a primitive alarm system for the group's base of operations. Each also develops different relationships with the rest of the cast: Carley is presented as a possible romantic interest for Lee, while Doug shows a strong dislike for the rude and abrasive Larry. As the game progresses, more characters are introduced, followed by more decision points and a corresponding increase in the number of possible outcomes. The presence of these "determinant characters" produces substantial variability in the individual player's experience of the plot, as particular subplots may or may not occur depending on whether certain characters survived or died—a factor wholly subject to player agency.

The Banner Saga takes a similar approach but demonstrates a further evolution of this technique. At the start of the first game, the player is presented with a Nordic-inspired fantasy world teetering on the brink of apocalyptic collapse. Two refugee caravans are attempting to reach the same safe zone from different directions, and the player alternates between focalizers from each caravan: the human hunter Rook and the Varl warrior Hakon. Each chapter of the story constitutes a section of a particular caravan's journey, and at regular intervals the player is confronted with scenarios that have immediate consequences for that particular group. As with *The Walking Dead,* one of the most visible expressions of agency involves the presence of determinant characters: by taking (or refusing to take) certain actions, the player can set in motion a chain of events that may lead to the death of prominent cast members. However, *The Banner Saga* features two additional elements which contribute further depth and complexity to the process. The first is ludological in nature, as the surviving characters are also active participants in the game's strategic combat sections—thus, causing the death of a useful fighter may have direct repercussions not only within the diegetic space but extradiegetically as well, as the player must then adjust their tactics to compensate for the loss. The second and far more significant factor is the temporal extension of the causal chain. As befits the tone of its source text, *The Walking Dead* frames decision points in an atmosphere of immediacy: the dilemma to save Carley or Doug is presented in real-time, as both characters are in extreme danger and the player is distinctly aware that only one can survive. *The Banner Saga*, by contrast, creates cause-and-effect sequences which unfold over multiple chapters. This is best demonstrated with the character of Egil, a companion of Rook's daughter Alette, who has a total of three possible scenarios in which player agency may lead to his death. However, one of these scenarios places a considerable distance between choice and consequence: allowing a certain character to join Rook's caravan in chapter 4 will lead to a mutiny in chapter 6, during which Egil is killed. This prevents the player from easily reversing their actions, as backtracking to the decision point would require undoing a considerable amount of progress. Egil's demise becomes an incontrovertible fact of that specific variant plot, but as with all instances of multitextuality, foreknowledge and a second (or third) re-engagement will allow the player to explore alternative routes in which Egil survives to the very end of the trilogy.

The constant, consistent reinforcement and reflection of player input makes these games exemplars of the contemporary branching path structure. Earlier attempts were only capable of casting the player in the role of a passive spectator while viewing the ultimate outcomes of any agency expressed within the diegetic space; modern games, by contrast, place substantial points of divergence within the body of the narrative itself. *The Walking Dead* and *The Banner Saga* are multitextual in the most accurate sense of the term, constrained only by the upper limit of possible scenarios each game can contain—a number that increases as the technological capabilities of game platforms continue to be refined for that specific purpose. One result of this process is the ability to establish diegetic continuity between successive entries in a game series, where the player's decisions can be collected into a single file and then "imported" into the next game. This feature is critical for both *The Banner Saga* and *The Walking Dead*, as they are both multi-part series; choices made in previous installments will continue to be referenced and may provide even more texture, context and definition to the individual player's constructed narrative. For example, the final battle of *The Banner Saga* results in the death of either Rook or Alette, depending once again on what course of action the player chooses to take; in an interview with gaming website Rock Paper Shotgun, Stoic Studio writer Drew McGee highlights the causal chain resulting from this particular fork:

> "Rook has just gone through something devastating or Alette has also gone through something devastating," adds McGee. Which of the two you're playing as changes the challenge a little and alters the expectations of other characters.

If it's Alette it's almost like starting over with a new game, needing to prove your worth solo and convince people to follow you. If you're Rook it's more about dealing with grief while living in a society which doesn't have space for that process. "How do you cope with grieving in a society where you should shrug it off but he doesn't? His whole reason for living was to save his daughter," says McGee [Warr, Rock Paper Shotgun].

This use of inter-game continuity creates divergent texts before the second game's narrative even commences—from its outset, players of *The Banner Saga 2* will experience the story differently depending on whether their embodied protagonist is Rook or Alette. The same principle holds true in the transition from the second game to the third, where the sum and impact of aggregated choices is even greater.

Viewed historically and/or chronologically, the examples provided herein all indicate that the teleological evolution of the branching plot structure has been incremental over an extended period of time and has yet to reach an endpoint or plateau. It is nevertheless important to note that older structural models continue to be in use; games produced today may still offer a linear narrative with multiple endings, or a modular structure that gives more weight to choices made at specific plot junctions. However, most multitext games share a particular catalyst designed to compel players along certain paths: a morality system which situates possible courses of action along a Good/Evil (or corresponding binary) spectrum. Derived from tabletop game franchise *Dungeons & Dragons*, morality systems serve as the contextual foundation for the player's decisions, largely due to the fact that, as Tavinor points out, "the player takes a part in the moral situations presented there, and whether or not the evil occurs is often up to them—the potential of games for the exploration of moral issues seems somehow more vivid: and perhaps more dangerous, where the game does not provide opportunities to put the content in a thoughtful or realistic context" (Tavinor, 9). Every game discussed thus far has, at its core, moral imperatives which define the different paths players can take. Some, such as *Dragon Warrior* and *Quest for Glory*, are either unable or unwilling to accommodate "evil" scenarios even as these scenarios are presented, punishing the player for acting contrary to the implicit heroic standards of the fictional world. Others such as *Blood Omen* and *Fallout* impose no penalty upon players who choose to act immorally, viewing such decisions as products of role-play (in other words, as an affectation of clear separation between diegesis and extradiegesis, wherein the player may perform the part of an evil protagonist without necessarily sharing or endorsing that mindset). Products of more contemporary technologies such as *The Walking Dead* and *The Banner Saga* will often complicate the moral quandary by situating such choices in an ambiguous context; in a world on the brink of collapse, moral standards may shift out of necessity rather than whimsy. At the end of chapter 2 of *The Walking Dead*, Lee and his starving companions stumble upon an abandoned car loaded with food and supplies; as the other members of the group eagerly descend upon the vehicle, the player-as-Lee must decide whether or not to partake in a possible act of theft. This choice is made difficult by the extant conditions of this particular fictional world, in which resources are scarce due to the zombie epidemic and the comforts of the modern world have long been rendered null and void. Clementine staunchly refuses to steal from others, but when she is offered a hoodie (with the threat of a difficult winter ahead), the player cannot evade the mitigating factors that might not have otherwise affected this clear moral decision.

For Murray, these points of player agency are illusory, as the sum of all possible variations in a multitextual game are pre-established, having been programmed and implemented by the original developers:

> There is a distinction between playing a creative role within an authored environment and having authorship of the environment itself. Certainly interactors can create aspects of digital stories in all these formats, with the greatest degree of creative authorship being over those environments that reflect the least amount of prescripting. But interactors can only act within the possibilities that have been established by the writing and programming. They may build simulated cities, try out combat strategies, trace a unique path through a labyrinthine web, or even prevent a murder, but unless the imaginary world is nothing more than a costume trunk of empty avatars, all of the interactor's possible performances will have been called into being by the original author [Murray, 152].

However, this perspective is the product of viewing video games in isolation, rather than as one platform of several which have been shaped by pre-existing desires; as such, it overlooks the narrative effect of player choice and the broader significance of diegetic control. Just as fan fiction enables the assembly of ontological simulacra informed by the fan's own system of values, the ability to make moral choices in games results in the player embedding their own implied author into the text as it is being experienced. Murray is correct in that this process is inherently limited due to the constraints of the medium—it may be more accurate to say that the player is choosing from among several possible implied authors. But that choice in and of itself expresses a measure of pseudo-authorial control that determines how the narrative as a whole is perceived. *Blood Omen* is either the uplifting tale of a murdered man redeeming the world, or a dark journey undertaken by a sociopathic antihero who is granted supreme power. The player determines which of these is directly experienced, and which exist only as unrealized alternatives. Where Richard Bartle suggests the prototypical Hero's Journey is key to any video game experience, as "virtual worlds are unique among fictional constructs in that they enable players actually to *undertake* their own, personal hero's journey directly" (Bartle, 105), this notion can be utterly subverted by players choosing to play the role of an antihero or an outright villain. The constructed plot may be formed out of the same sum of components contained within the game, but it will correspond to a particular set of values aligned with the player's actions.

This degree of authorial agency is situated beyond the framework of mechanical performativity as proposed by ludology. Rather, it more closely resembles the cognitive impetus for the creation of ontological simulacra seen in fan fiction, with the qualifying caveat that fan-authors must first engage a source text and assimilate it in order to produce the required mimetic effect. Conversely, games provide opportunities for diegetic agency while the player is actively immersed in and experiencing said source work. The end result is a particular arrangement of pre-scripted blocks of text—and while this arrangement does not and cannot exceed the boundaries of existing code (just as fan works cannot directly affect their canonical templates), what emerges is still a configuration determined by the individual pseudo-author.

Love, Death, and the Avatar

The use of avatars—diegetic figures that embody the player and serve as conduits for potential actions in the game world—is another feature that distinguishes video games from other narrative media. Indeed, the inextricable connection between player and character blurs the boundaries between the real and the virtual, as all avatars are programmed to immediately execute any inputted command. Depending on the genre of a given game, the manner of execution may vary: action-oriented games such as platformers or first-person shooters may require split-second reflexes, while adventure and role-playing games allow lengthier interims between actions so the player may calculate and strategize. Regardless of the ludological principles which govern play as an active process, however, the narratological implications of the avatar are highly relevant to any examination of video games as a form of interactive fiction. Much like plot structure, the methods and conventions of avatar depiction have been also honed by directed technological progression, as noted by Martti Lahti: "One of the characteristics of video games throughout their history has been an attempt, with the help of various technologies, to erase the boundary separating the player from the game world and to play up tactile involvement. Indeed, much of the development of video games has been driven by a desire for a corporeal immersion with technology, a will to envelop the player in technology and the environment of the game space" (Lahti, 200).

Before delving into the varied narratological functions the avatar may serve in different types of games, a brief overview of its evolution may provide useful historical context. Much like the primitive attempts at multitextuality in early games, the first avatars were almost abstract in form and function, due to the limitations of the medium. Beginning with ASCII symbols such as asterisks or pound signs, these symbolic projections of player agency then took the forms of iconic sprites like Pac-Man and Mario, and today typically appear as fully rendered digital humans; thus, the virtual body has become increasingly mimetic even in forms designed to evoke alienation (as is often the case with inhuman, subhuman or superhuman protagonists). But according to Bob Rehak, the purpose of the avatar remains the same regardless of its endlessly variable appearances: "The avatar's navigation of 'contested spaces' and its often violent interactions with other avatars (either human- or computer-controlled) generate the narrative-strategic pleasures of the video game experience.... Players experience games through the exclusive intermediary of another—the avatar—the 'eyes,' 'ears,' and 'body' of which are components of a complex technological and psychological apparatus" (Rehak, 139). Indeed, the psychological processes enabled by this deep connection between player and protagonist are unparalleled, creating a sense of immersion no other medium can easily replicate. Filiciak uses the term "hyperidentity" to define the effects of the player's dual role as actant and spectator, author and audience: "While using an electronic medium in which subject and object, and what is real and imagined, are not clearly separated, the player loses his identity, projecting himself inward, becoming the 'other,' and identifies with the character in the game. During the game, the player's identity ends in disintegration, and the merger of user's and character's consciousness ensues" (Filiciak, 124). Ironically, the qualities which typically define the avatar—hypercompetence, uniqueness, a singular nature within the fictional world—are traits that would qualify them for the much-derided title of Mary Sue in fan fiction (discussed previously), as the narrative mechanics are indeed identical: both are produced via a projection of the fan-author or player into the diegetic layer of the text. The difference is one of purpose: the Mary Sue is viewed as having a distortive effect upon the attempted mimesis of the source material, whereas the avatar is positioned as a protagonist in its own right. More significantly, as Brendan Keogh points out, the avatar's function as both agent and actant creates a figure that uniquely bridges the gap between diegetic and extradiegetic engagement:

To account for embodied textuality, then, is to be *reflexive*; it is to account not only for how the player instantiates videogame play but also for how the player is incorporated into, becomes part of, and is ultimately made by the system of videogame play they instantiate. This accounting ultimately points toward locating the videogame experience as a *coming-together* of the player and the videogame not as preexisting, separate, distinct subjects or objects but as a cybernetic assemblage of human body and nonhuman body across actual and virtual worlds [Keogh, 22].

Three features provide key insight into the avatar as a constructed aspect of virtual narrative, and its essential contribution to the mechanics of play in any video game: customization, death and romance. These tools, like the forking path structure, have been repeatedly deployed, improved, and redeployed over decades of progress, and their evolution parallels new developments in the medium's overall narrative capabilities. Additionally, the lack of uniform application allows different factors to be used in tandem, producing a very broad spectrum of possible combinations. This section will focus on a pair of video game trilogies—*Mass Effect* and *Dragon Age*, both developed by Canadian company BioWare—as examples of specific innovations in the aforementioned fields, with the reiterated caveat that these do not represent widespread cessation of older formulae.

Customization has a long and storied tradition which predates the digital age by a sizeable margin: as with the implementation of morality systems, this process of foundational character design is attributed to *Dungeons & Dragons,* which indeed allows players to configure their diegetic Player Characters' gender, race, skills, profession and more prior to starting the game. One of the first applications of this principle in video games, according to Barton, is 1988's *Pool of Radiance*:

> Critics made much of the fact that players could customize the portraits and icons of their characters. The system for the portraits reminds me of playing with paper dolls; it's basically a collection of heads and torsos that are interchangeable. The icons are a bit more dynamic, with lots of options for colors and parts, such as the weapon, head, cap, and so on (later "Gold Box" games facilitate this process with customizable templates). These icons can be altered during the course of the game, such as when a character starts using a new weapon or acquires new armor. Though we might look at this system today and chuckle, it was nothing short of remarkable in an age when every other CRPG offered noncustomizable icons and, if they had them at all, standardized portraits [Barton, 147].

Of course, Barton's description highlights both the possibilities on display and, implicitly, the fact that the player is restricted to those same options, confirming Murray's point regarding the inevitable upper limit of potentialities contained in a game's code. In 2001, Marie-Laure Ryan further asserted the inability of existing hardware to take character customization further: "In the present state of development of VR technology, virtual identities must be selected from a menu of ready-made avatars. Playing a role, in these systems, is not a matter of becoming whomever you want to be but a matter of stepping into what Brenda Laurel has called a 'smart costume'—smart because it does not merely alter appearance but implements a change of body dynamics" (Ryan, 62). However, just as the basic structure of the forking path has grown more complex and sophisticated with the creation and implementation of advanced tools, so too have customization options increased in both number and type. Many current games allow players to modify their avatars' skin tone, ear and nose shape, eye color, hair color, and cheekbone height, among other variables. As such, the likelihood of different players having physically identical avatars is drastically reduced, further ensuring a stronger connection between pseudo-author and the individualized creation.

At the start of science fiction action–RPG *Mass Effect*, the player is cast in the role of Commander Shepard, an officer of the human Systems Alliance. The first installment of the trilogy begins with a diegetic conceit to enable avatar customization: attempting to access the character's personnel records reveals that the files have been corrupted, and thus the player must reconstruct the data, tailoring Shepard to their specifications. However, where past incarnations of Player Characters might be seen as little more than *tabula rasa* slates for the execution of the player's will, Hanna-Riikka Roine draws attention to the manner in which Commander Shepard straddles the line between avatar and actant:

> As an avatar, Shepard is an audio-visually represented manifestation that, in a sense, embodies the player's agency—that is, the player's means to act in the game world and interact with it. For example, the avatar-Shepard belongs to a certain character class that enables the player to access certain active powers in combat, to increase health, shield and melee damage (measured in points), and to influence Shepard's reputation or morality. Actor-Shepard, however, can be perceived as an imagined, fictional character with a past, present, and a potential directed toward the future, but as such, Shepard is still dependent on player input [Roine, 76].

In addition to gender and appearance (which are, in themselves, highly significant categories to be discussed shortly), and profession (the sum total of the avatar's abilities as chosen by the player), Shepard's pre-narrative background and psychological profile are also variable and at the player's discretion. The game's official guide stresses the significance of these decisions: "This is not just text you'll never see again, however; your choices here affect the storyline by accessing exclusive assignments (side quests) and Shepard's dialogue with various NPCs [non-player characters]"

(Anthony, 6). If Shepard is given a personal history in which they were the sole survivor of an alien attack, the avatar may then express a prejudicial mistrust towards that particular species throughout all three games. Alternately, Shepard may be a celebrated war hero who went beyond the call of duty to save lives—a history with its own effects on the character's narrative arc and their interactions with other inhabitants of the fictional world. While the number of possible combinations remains limited, each creates a version of Shepard unique to the player's subsequent experience with the game; and just as forking paths require re-engagement to explore routes not taken, new Shepards must be produced for the player to view alternative combinations of history and personality. At the same time, certain facts about Shepard are immutable, as they constitute the foundation upon which the protagonist's character arc is built. At the start of the game, Shepard is executive officer of the starship Normandy, and has been nominated to join an interspecies organization known as the Spectres, agents of the galaxy's ruling Council (to which Earth is on the cusp of admission). The player, as Shepard, must investigate a conspiracy relating to an ancient precursor race while hunting down criminals, rogue artificial intelligences, mercenaries and other threats to galactic stability.

Key to Shepard's development as both diegetic protagonist and avatar for the player is their journey along the game's branching paths—as previously described, morality serves as the basis upon which the player makes most of their decisions in the game: "The choice is yours, but here is the simplest generalization: Paragons do the right thing in the right way. Renegades get the job done by whatever means necessary.... You could be talking to a demeaning Alliance Fleet Officer and have a dialogue option to respond in a polite and respectful manner or you could unholster your sidearm and shoot him in the knee" (Anthony, 13–14). The more choices the player makes, the clearer the image of the player-as-Shepard emerges; and unlike *The Banner Saga* or *The Walking Dead* (which change protagonists between installments, even as decisions are imported from one game to the next), the player of *Mass Effect* remains in the same role throughout the trilogy. As such, Shepard becomes not only a symbol of the player's control, but the embodied sum of all decisions made within the multitextual array. Thus the character is modular, similar in design to the epilogues of *Fallout 2*: "In the *Mass Effect Trilogy*, the story of Commander Shepard is not monolithic; it is a result of many small fragments used in the performance of the character as a part of the communication or dialogue between the player and the system" (Roine, 83).

Medieval fantasy trilogy *Dragon Age*, consisting of *Dragon Age: Origins* (2009), *Dragon Age II* (2011) and *Dragon Age: Inquisition* (2014), takes a different approach in the construction and deployment of the avatar, while maintaining the high degree of interactivity found in its science-fictional counterpart. Each game has its own protagonist—the Warden, the Champion and the Inquisitor, respectively—and each narrative is broadly self-contained, as opposed to the consistent arc the player experiences as Commander Shepard. However, where *Mass Effect* distinguishes itself in carrying the outcomes of Shepard's choices from one chapter to the next (thus prioritizing consistency and continuity within the diegetic space across all three games), *Dragon Age* presents a world in which the presence and decisions of each actant affects the next. In *Origins*, the player is offered a choice of race (human, elf, dwarf), profession (warrior, thief, mage) and six possible backgrounds—similar to Shepard, these backgrounds represent variant pre-narrative histories which inform the story's initial chapter. Each selected combination of features results in different narrative experiences, as the world of *Dragon Age* is designed in such a way that an elf avatar will experience racism, victimization and prejudice where a human might not, and a visit to the underground dwarf kingdom of Orzammar will be contextualized in an entirely different light if the player's diegetic agent is a dwarf as well. This set of choices is narrower in the second game, as the plot requires the avatar's role to be more defined—a human with the surname Hawke—but options are expanded again in *Inquisition*. The end result is a trilogy in which the player's multiple protagonists set in motion events which affect each other, creating an intertwined narrative nexus which projects a dynamic fictional world, one increasingly made singular by the aggregate outcomes of player control.

While these factors correspond to the choice system described earlier, and lead to the same types of narrative differentiation within the totality of the multitext, *Dragon Age* shares a common element with *Mass Effect* which further blurs the diegetic and extradiegetic spheres: their representation of death. Rehak points out that the prospect of virtual demise has been present for as long as the medium itself has existed, noting that "most significant (and often overlooked thanks to the event's ubiquity), avatars differ from us through their ability to *live, die, and live again*. Their bodies dissolve in radioactive slime or explode into a mist of blood and bone fragments, only to reappear, unscathed, at the click of a mouse" (Rehak, 142). He further notes that this long-standing tradition is directly linked to technological progress enabling gradually realistic avatars: "This aspect of gameplay—the simulated experience of death and resurrection—is a key function of the avatar, one that would become more explicit as avatarial forms metamorphosed from the crosshairs, spaceships, and missile bases of the late 1970s to the 'living' bodies of the early 1980s" (Rehak, 151). Of course, this argument refers specifically to extradiegetic considerations asserting themselves through gameplay; as previously mentioned, the avatar's death signifies an error on the part of the player, with the nature of that error depending on the type of game being played. In an action game, a mistimed jump or a poorly aimed shot is all that is required for the avatar to "die," whereas role-playing games may punish a player's failure to mentally prepare for a particular encounter, or to develop a certain skill required to complete a challenge. Greg Costikyan defines this as a quintessential element of uncertainty which, in large part, defines our engagement with games at any given moment: "in *Super Mario Bros.*, the uncertainty is in *your performance*—in your ability to master the skills of handeye coordination demanded by the game and apply them to overcome its challenges. You can—and typically do—fail many, many times before 'beating' the game. Mastering, and overcoming, the uncertainty posed by your uncertain skills, and your uncertain ability to maintain concentration and focus, is the heart of the appeal of the game" (Costikyan, 20). In these cases, the avatar's destruction is immediately followed by a reset, allowing the player opportunities to learn from past mistakes and strive for success. At the same time, the perpetual cycle of death and resets reinforces Skolnick's argument that while the boundary between the real and the virtual may be blurred, it is neither porous nor truly flexible: "In games, of course, the heroic elements of risk and sacrifice are seen through a different lens: the player's. It is rare that the player has any true fear of forging ahead in a game, because ultimately his own life is not really on the line. This is another example of ludonarrative dissonance, and one that is difficult to completely overcome. It's the reason why in games you rarely see the Refusal of the Call—Heroes can be reluctant, but players rarely are" (Skolnick, 51).

One consequence of this dissonance within the overall structure of video game narratives is the relegation of death to non-diegetic status: the plot does not acknowledge player failure, and should an avatar die, reset and succeed, only the success will be considered a valid narrative event. Both *Mass Effect* and *Dragon Age* subvert this by shifting the possibility of permanent, irreversible avatar death fully into the diegetic level; rather than result from gameplay failure, Commander Shepard, the Warden and Hawke may all meet their demise at the climax of a causal chain. Chronologically, the first of these instances occurs in *Dragon Age: Origins*, during the final confrontation with the draconic Archdemon: "A Grey Warden must launch the final blow against the archdemon to kill it. If you or a fellow Grey Warden had a child with Morrigan, no Grey Warden will die with the final blow. If you refused Morrigan's ritual, you must choose to slay the archdemon yourself (in which case, you sacrifice yourself) or allow your fellow Grey Warden (Alistair or Loghain) to slay the archdemon and perish in the process" (Searle, 296). The potential death of the player's avatar is treated as a variable story branch like any other, and if the player imports this particular ontological configuration forward, their Warden will remain dead, and acknowledged as such in subsequent installments.

Mass Effect 2 (2010) takes this a step further: the game begins with Shepard's death, as the Normandy is ambushed and destroyed by an unknown enemy. The narrative then jumps ahead two years, and in a cinematic cutscene the protagonist is painstakingly resurrected through nanotechnology and cybernetic implants, concluding with a facial reconstruction program that allows the player to further customize their avatar's appearance to their satisfaction. This entire introductory sequence is a plot event the player can neither prevent nor overcome through skill, as it represents the next step of Commander Shepard's overall narrative; moreover, the traumatic events leave visible scars on the avatar's face, a phenomenon practically unheard of in a medium where virtual bodies are rarely (if ever) visibly impacted by injury or "temporary" death. Shepard's scars will either deepen or fade depending on the player's moral choices: "If you walk the path of the Renegade, expect to see the effects of these decisions physically manifest on Shepard's face. Deep scars and red eyes are the marks of Renegades" (Hodgson, 20). The prospect of death again becomes a variable component of the forking path at the end of the game, in which Shepard's carefully assembled squad must launch a final mission to rescue the Normandy's abducted crew. Referred to in-game as "The Suicide Mission," every aspect of the endgame is informed by actions the player may or may not have taken over the course of the story: "If the Normandy's shields were not upgraded, another team member is killed in the explosion. If you did not upgrade the Normandy's armor, you lose another team member during the crash landing" (Hodgson, 276). Death is diegetic and permanent in this context: if the player leads these squadmates to their demise, they will not reappear in the trilogy's final installment.

Moreover, the mission itself requires that the player select Specialists within the squad to accomplish specific tasks; while there are several correct options mixed in with incorrect possibilities (the latter of which will lead to more deaths), of note is the game's emphasis on narrative over gameplay to guide those decisions. The squadmates have their own unique skills and personalities, and these are more relevant to their success as Specialists than any gameplay element the player has mastered thus far. For example, when a Tech Specialist is needed to hack a security system, chief engineer Tali is described as "a mechanical genius even among the advanced engineers of the quarians … most effective when faced with technical problems that can be solved with the application of intelligence rather than brute force" while another option, Dr. Mordin Solus, notes that "Although his knowledge is extensive on a variety of subjects, his true genius is for all matters biological" (*Mass Effect 2*). Selecting Mordin for the task will directly lead to his death, where Tali will succeed and survive. Making the correct choices requires that the player know their squadmates as characters rather than embodiments of mechanical systems, and failing to accommodate the narrative demands of *Mass Effect 2* will result in the most disastrous outcome: if too few of Shepard's companions survive the final battle, Shepard will also perish. Unlike the opening act of the game, this death is both permanent and a consequence of the player's failure as a pseudo-author rather than an expression of poor gameplay skills. Failing the Suicide Mission will render that particular Shepard's save file inoperable, as it cannot be then transferred to *Mass Effect 3*; as with Rook and Alette at the end of *The Banner Saga*, this constitutes an exceedingly rare—but increasingly prevalent— example of a virtual death granted narrative permanence which is carried across multiple games, tangibly impacting the resulting constructed plot.

Dragon Age: Inquisition presents further innovation in its depiction of diegetic death: midway through the story, the player's avatar (the Inquisitor) encounters Hawke, the protagonist of the previous game: "If you imported a world state from *Dragon Age Keep*, you can customize Hawke's gender, appearance, and key decisions to match your gameplay experience from *Dragon Age II*" (Knight/Musa, 42). Hawke serves as a temporary companion to the Inquisitor, a scenario which places the player in the unique position of witnessing a previous avatar speak and act autonomously. Each version of Hawke makes explicit references to events the player caused, through choice and consequence, in the previous installment, further solidifying the notion that this is indeed the same character produced by past ontological and narrative configurations. Shortly thereafter, the player must decide Hawke's fate: "Following the defeat of the fear demon, the massive spider-like demon reappears. Hawke volunteers to stay behind and distract the demon while the rest of you escape through the rift. But Stroud feels it's his responsibility as a Warden to stay behind. You must make the decision, choosing whether Hawke or Stroud remains in the Fade" (Knight/Musa, 52). In essence, the player-as-Inquisitor is forced into a situation where they may potentially bring about the death of their own character once-removed. As with the aforementioned Suicide Mission, Hawke's death signifies a diegetic event that is subsequently carried forward. Moreover, if the Warden (the player's protagonist in *Origins*) is also dead, this will be similarly referenced at various points as historical fact: "The Archdemon clashed with the allied forces at the city of Denerim and was eventually slain, but at terrible cost. Much of the city lay in ruin and the Warden who rallied the armies—later known as the Hero of Ferelden—perished in battle" (*Dragon Age: Inquisition*).

While these trilogies are the products of the same studio, and therefore share certain philosophies of game design by default, they nevertheless represent a broader trend of reconceptualizing ludological mechanisms as narratological components: these deaths, should they occur, are inscribed into the diegetic space by the player in their function as pseudo-author. While they exist as potentialities within the games' code, their actualization is not the product of unrefined skill or poor hand-eye coordination, but rather the outcomes of decisions made by the players themselves. Of course, the ability to backtrack and manipulate outcomes with greater awareness is inherent to any participant in the medium—a player may inadvertently condemn Hawke to death, then reset and replay the sequence again so that circumstances favor that former avatar's survival—but the end product is an act of authorial fiat, per Roine's application of this principle to *Mass Effect*: "the player who recognises the shape can very consciously 'tweak' the stories to her liking while playing the game. This attitude is both gamist and narrativist in nature because it can be used simultaneously to beat the game and to perform as a certain kind of fictional character" (Roine, 83). Each emergent text becomes both canonized and personalized, and—just as with fan fiction—competing accounts of diegetic events may co-exist without conflict. Players may construct multiple Wardens, Hawkes, Inquisitors and Shepards, each corresponding to different implied authors and specific to particular ontological configurations, with no inherent or imposed need to arrange them hierarchically in terms of canon or significance. Furthermore, as each character occupies a different "save file," it is hypothetically possible to direct multiple protagonists through the game simultaneously, making different choices at each junction in order to diversify the process of narrative experience. This form of story consumption would most closely resemble the process of navigating fan fiction archives and confronting dozens (if not thousands) of branching paths and competing interpretations for the reader's selection. Thus the constellation of actualized fictional worlds emerging from the multitext may be preserved in the same space (in this case, the memory of the hardware platform used to play the games), reaffirming Landow's view of digital media as designed from its inception to contain multiplicities of meaning:

> One of the greatest strengths of hypertext lies in its capacity of permitting users to find, create, and follow multiple conceptual structures in the same body of information. Essentially, they describe the technological means of achieving Derrida's concept of decentering. In contrast to the rigidity and difficulty of access produced by present means of managing information based on print and other physical records, one needs an information medium that better accommodates the way the mind works [Landow, 10].

Navigating the potential experiences of diegetic avatar death is not the only way players can assert authorial fiat upon the virtual text. Perhaps the purest expression of narrative agency in video games involves depictions of romance and sexuality, particularly in scenarios where the avatar is able to pursue a love interest. In this, *Mass Effect* and *Dragon Age* are products of a long-running teleological process, one that requires additional historical context to fully grasp its current-day implications. Skolnick's assessment of the avatar as an embodiment of archetypal protagonists is essential: "In games, the player almost always takes on the role of Hero. Because of this, identification with the Hero is even more crucial than in other storytelling media. After all, you aren't just watching or following the Hero; you inhabit the character's body, controlling him not unlike the way you control a car" (Skolnick, 45). Consequently, romantic and sexual themes in video games serve the same purpose as in the classic monomythical Hero's Journey: Odysseus has Penelope, Arthur has Guinevere, and so on. What changes in video game narratives, beginning in the early '90s, is the player's ability to choose their hero's love interest, where the aforementioned *Dragon Warrior* offered no choice in the matter of accepting Gwaelin's proposal. According to Barton, one of the earliest manifestations of this form of agency occurs in the 1991 role-playing game *Treasures of the Savage Frontier*:

> Essentially, it boils down to two nonplayer characters, or characters that are controlled by the computer rather than the player. These characters are a female named Siulajia and a male named Jabarkas, one of whom may fall in love with the active character at a certain point in the game (the choice of Siulajia or Jabarkas depends on the active character's gender; only heterosexual relationships are possible). However, love is not assured—romance will only bloom if the lead character has conducted him or herself so as to attract a partner, helping out the weak and standing bravely in battle [Barton, 157].

Key to this description is the word "if"—despite the game's relative simplicity (again owing to its age and the hardware limitations of the time), the decision to engage in a romantic subplot is entirely at the player's discretion. It is equally possible to experience a version of the game's narrative that contains neither courtship nor sexual interest as emergent themes. However, Barton indicates that beyond additional story content, there are also gameplay benefits to exploring this possibility:

> Assuming that all goes well and love does flourish, the loved one can join the party, and the two lovers will receive combat bonuses. However, if the lover is injured, the partner will fly into a berserker rage, charging recklessly into the fray. If the lover dies or is dropped from the party, the partner will become depressed and suffer penalties. At some point the lovers will admit their feelings to the rest of the party, who will then be asked to approve or condemn it. If the other members disapprove, the nonplayer character leaves the party, and the forlorn lover will thereafter fight with much less zeal and effectiveness [Barton, 158].

The conflation of story and gameplay rewards for successful completion of a romantic subplot is not universal; rather, individual games may favor one over the other, depending on the relative centrality of potential love stories to the core narrative in question.

Just as the quantity and quality of branching points increase exponentially as new technologies become available which are able to sustain them, the narrative implementation of romance subplots grows more complex over time, with BioWare spearheading the trend even prior to the release of *Mass Effect*: in 2000's *Baldur's Gate II*, male avatars could court one of three mutually exclusive female companions, while female avatars were limited to the somewhat-abrasive knight-in-training Anomen Delryn; 2005's *Jade Empire* allowed players to configure not only their avatar's appearance but their sexuality as well, permitting male characters to pursue the rogue Sky while female characters could establish a romantic rapport with Princess Sun Lian. According to Mia Consalvo, the addition of same-sex romance options allowed for greater arrays of possible role-playing experiences within the diegetic space: "That might be the case for some players, if when people engage in play, they put on various 'masks' of identity and experiment with alternate rules (and discard social conventions), if only temporarily" (Consalvo, 191). *Mass Effect* and later *Dragon Age* would take this paradigm forward by adding a greater number of romantically inclined companions, substantially increasing the variables which shape narrative experiences. The growing presence of same-sex romance also correlates to the centrality of the slash genre in fan fiction, for largely the same reason: the desire to depict narrative possibilities that, within a conventionally heteronormative tradition, would be marginalized or excluded altogether. What differentiates BioWare's optional romantic subplots from its contemporaries is that any "reward," in stark contrast to Barton's 1991 example, is entirely narrative-based. From a mechanical standpoint—in terms of increasing the avatar's power (and thus the player's own capacity to overcome obstacles)—there is no inherent reason to prefer one love interest over another. The function is wholly story-driven, dependent on a complex network of dynamics between the player, the character they have constructed, and the scripted companion they feel is best suited to that particular protagonist. The choice to engage in (or avoid) romantic entanglements is a tool used to further personalize the story, another diegetic fragment to be aligned with the pseudo-author's personal system of values. As *Mass Effect* carries the same character across three entries, it is possible for a player to steer Commander Shepard towards a different love interest in each game or remain loyal to the same character throughout. The romantic subplot built into archetypal heroic narratives becomes an additional catalyst for expressing diegetic agency within the ontological simulacra. As with the subject of death, this is not to suggest that all contemporary games characterize diegetic romances as purely narrative, optional content; on the contrary, 2018's *Pillars of Eternity II: Deadfire* grants the players temporary boosts to physical and/or mental skills after engaging with courtesans of either gender; 2017's *Wolfenstein II: The New Colossus* continues a scripted, centralized romance between protagonist BJ Blazkowicz and resistance fighter Anya Oliwa (a relationship that the player cannot opt out of, despite controlling BJ's actions directly); and dating simulators such as 2017's *Dream Daddy* express the process of romantic pursuit through ludological activities (e.g., puzzle-solving, multiple-choice questionnaires, and so on). These variations have also evolved considerably over time, taking advantage of modern platforms' abilities to run more sophisticated programs in order to diversify and subvert the experience of virtual romance in both narrative and gameplay terms.

What these examples effectively demonstrate is the manner in which universal concepts pertaining to the prototypical heroic narrative—such as death and love—are applied to virtual entities who straddle the intersection of diegetic actant and extradiegetic vessel. Even the most storied protagonist is still under the player's control at all times, and must be so for the medium to achieve its immersive effect; otherwise, there would be no functional difference in presentation between a video game and a cinematic film, a correlation Wolf explicitly points out: "The player-character surrogate in the video game is, in a very concrete sense, the external object into which the player is absorbed, which received the player's will to activity. This may help explain why the majority of player-character surrogates in video games are character-based" (Wolf, 89–90). Commander Shepard, the Warden, Hawke and the Inquisitor are characters who signify the principle of incremental complexity along technological lines: their respective games are able to increase pseudo-authorial potential either by moving mechanical functions (such as "death" due to player failure) into emergent narrative, or by implementing a system of potential romantic subplots which enable more role-play and projection into "alternative selves." Per Filiciak's claims, the avatar is therefore an apt demonstration of a broader trend of the digital age: "Thus, in the era of electronic media we should rather talk about hyperidentity, which is related to identity as a hypertext to a text. It is, rather, more a process than a finished formation, a complex structure that we update incessantly by choosing from the multitudes of solutions. Any moment, we actively create ourselves" (Filiciak, 130).

Navigating Reactive Spaces in Persistent Digital Worlds

In his discussion of new forms of contemporary narrative, Uri Margolin makes note of a paradigm shift in terms of constructed experiences:

Being viewed from within, and in the midst of the action, the narrated domain is inevitably represented as a succession of unconfigured particulars, while narration itself becomes the gradual figuring out of what is the case as it evolves.... The fact that numerous events are of necessity presented as still being in progress at narration time has far-reaching implications for the factive dimension, that is, for what and how much can be reported as fact with certainty or full knowledge.... Their results or outcomes simply do not exist as yet [Margolin, 151–152].

This definition is certainly appropriate for video game narratives, given the emphasis on experiential storytelling; the player's navigation of forking paths occurs in real time, with a direct impact on how the story is assembled and consumed: "As for the alternatives and possibilities that may exist at any given moment, the narrator cannot as yet tell which of them will be actualized, and even their very existence may merely be possible from his epistemic perspective" (Margolin, 153). Where other platforms assume physical passivity on the part of the recipient, video games require that the player actively move their avatars through diegetic space. This traversal of the virtual ontological structure is both similar to other forms of digital fiction and singular in its specific attributes: on the one hand, these worlds are based on the same foundational principles as their textual and cinematic counterparts, governed by a set of laws determined by their generic formulae. On the other, the avatar's interaction with the virtual world far exceeds the level of ontological access possible in other media: minute details may be observed, objects may be moved around and manipulated, hypodiegetic books may be read—and on a far greater scale, entire continents may move or change at the player's whim. This manipulability of the game world is, quite deliberately, highly reminiscent of the process fan fiction authors deploy to alter and reconfigure ontological structures for the purpose of assembling and distributing alternative scenarios; in both cases, the empowered reader/player asserts pseudo-authorial agency directly upon the ontological configuration of the text.

The prospect of manipulating ontological systems adds an exploratory dimension to the narrative reception of games: "The cybertext reader *is* a player, a gambler; the cybertext *is* a game-world or world-game; it *is* possible to explore, get lost, and discover secret paths in these texts, not metaphorically, but through the topological structures of the textual machinery" (Aarseth, 4). To recall an earlier example, *Dragon Warrior* permits the player full and unrestricted access to the world of Alefgard in its entirety: it is possible, from the very start of the game, to walk in any direction until reaching impassable oceans (beyond which there are no lands to explore). Of course, gameplay conventions allow developers to direct the player along specific routes by placing increasingly difficult enemies in key locations, necessitating a gradual increase in the avatar's power before attempting to brave those challenges. But Murray suggests that active movement is, in itself, a source of narrative pleasure for the player: "Computer-based journey stories offer a new way of savoring exactly this pleasure, a pleasure that is intensified by uniting the problem solving with the active process of navigation" (Murray, 139). Tavinor concurs with Murray's claim, putting forth the argument that even the most basic and linear representation of navigable space constitutes a potential multitext, in that one player turning right where another turns left may already be considered a point of narrative divergence which produce different experiences: "Videogames provide a prop that not only depicts vivid imaginative worlds and narratives, but worlds that respond in various ways to the interaction of the player, so that if I manipulate the controller in such and such a way, a new fictional event is depicted in the world of the game: the slash of a sword, the casting of a spell, or the grappling of a mutant humanoid" (Tavinor, 53).

Recent games have taken steps towards advancing this concept of malleability by embedding a measure of reflexivity within the diegetic space itself. These worlds are mutable and impermanent, with geographical and topological alterations set to match certain actions or changes within the game itself. An apt example of this process can be found in Arkane Studios' 2012 game *Dishonored* and its 2016 sequel. These implement a binary morality system greatly similar to those found in older games: "*Dishonored* is uniquely designed so that its actual gameplay changes depending on how lethal or nonlethal you choose to play. As you progress through each mission, the game tallies a 'Chaos' score based on your actions—in general, the more NPCs you kill (instead of choking them unconscious or simply avoiding them), the higher your 'Chaos' score" (Lumis et al., 24). But where earlier versions of this system limited variability to specific plot events (e.g., "Good" or "Evil" resolutions to certain quandaries, and the consequences which follow), decisions made in *Dishonored* affect the world itself. For example, in an early segment of the first game, the player—in their role as Corvo Attano, disgraced bodyguard to a murdered empress—is tasked with infecting a distillery with samples of the deadly rat plague. Should the player fulfill this task, the area will be utterly devastated upon their later return, with a dramatic increase in infected victims wandering the streets. Alternatively, a stealthier and pacifistic approach will result in lighter guard patrols, and fewer ravenous swarms of rats (as the player has left fewer corpses in Corvo's wake). These changes extend to the very landscape itself: at the climax of the first game, the player visits Kingsparrow Island for a final confrontation with Corvo's enemies. If Chaos is low (by way of avoiding excessive bloodshed and immoral actions), the island will be calm and relatively peaceful; conversely, high Chaos will have Corvo arriving in the midst of a violent storm, befitting the grim and bloody tone the player has established for this iteration of the narrative.

It is highly significant that these variables cannot be openly manipulated by the player: "Keep in mind that this Chaos tally is a hidden mechanic that happens 'under the hood'—you don't see your Chaos score in-game" (Lumis et al., 24). Rather, they are an aggregated effect of choices made throughout the entire course of the game. This mode of participation, in which the fictional world's physical appearance is itself shaped by expressions of agency, highlights the responsive nature of the platform and the unique aspects of ontological structures built on reflexivity and interactivity. The metaleptic effect of being (and acting) within the diegetic space is key to enabling the pseudo-authorial powers of the player: "Video games' ability to provide that experience to the player—to allow him to really feel like he is *in* the environment, as opposed to just observing it—is one of the unique and compelling storytelling elements that separate games from other entertainment forms. From the macro of a city's layout to the subtle clues laid out in a single room, settings are characters with their own tales to tell" (Skolnick, 160). Thus, the world itself continually reflects the player's choices in their enacted role.

Skolnick's emphasis on the use of virtual diegesis as a storytelling channel presents another possible narrative function of the game world: "Conveying narrative backstory and exposition by embedding it in the environment itself—without using a cutscene, character dialogue, or even UI text—is a highly efficient method of storytelling, and one of the best ways to create a player-pleasing amalgam of gameplay and narrative" (Skolnick, 164). Rather than rely solely on language, visual cues such as paintings or the virtual landscape may transmit information to the audience while maintaining the pleasure of exploration, as the player must first locate these cues and assemble the fragments of information into a coherent whole. In Annapurna Interactive's 2017 game *What Remains of Edith Finch*, the player is cast in the titular role of the last surviving member of the Finch family, returning to her long-abandoned home in search of answers. The player's objective is to scour the house, unlocking hidden passageways, and uncovering objects that help Edith piece together her family tree and the fates of her relatives. Moving from room to room, other subplots begin to appear, having been carefully threaded throughout the virtual space: the legend of the Finch family's "curse," the many tragic losses suffered by family matriarch Edie, the mysterious disappearance of Edith's brother Milton, and more. Of course, the notion that inanimate objects can contribute to storytelling is not new or unique to video games (as evidenced by any story involving forensic investigation or the deductive reasoning epitomized by Sherlock Holmes), but games such as *What Remains of Edith Finch* are able to take this concept a step further by eliminating all other sources of information that would traditionally accompany forensic investigation. There are no other characters in the house for Edith to talk to, no way for her to fully verify any of the evidence she uncovers, and Edith herself is no detective: her limited experience becomes a hindrance the further back into the past she tries to reach. Only the house, its objects and Edith's narration are capable of conveying any information to the player at all. There are, of course, upper limits to the player's ontological access—once she enters, Edith cannot leave the house, or take any course of action that would allow her to break through the established boundaries of the game code—but within the framework of the narrative itself, the freedom of exploration and the coupling of "physical" navigation with exposition is unparalleled.

Another point of interest concerning the ongoing evolution of video game ontology is the introduction and widespread popularity of the Massively Multiplayer Online Role-playing Game (MMORPG), perhaps best epitomized by Blizzard Entertainment's *World of Warcraft* (2004–present). This game, and those like it, represent a technological innovation that deviates substantially from the normative functions and designs of virtual worlds thus far; for all that the single-player experiences described previously are built on techniques and practices drawn and evolved from their non-digital predecessors, the recipient remains as capable of "pausing" the narrative's progression by choosing to cease reading, watching or playing at any time. In stark contrast, *World of Warcraft* projects a persistent diegetic world that continues to exist and change even when the player is not actively engaged. Maintained by a global network of online servers, *World of Warcraft* has the capacity to sustain thousands (if not millions) of simultaneous participants, producing a densely populated virtual realm. Skolnick provides a useful breakdown of the genre while pointing out its inherent narrative drawbacks:

> MMOs feature persistent worlds that don't stop or "pause" when you decide to suspend or end your play session. In an MMO you don't play as the main character; you are one of thousands of players simultaneously interacting with the virtual space. And there is no main conflict that you try to resolve to end the game. The game doesn't even *have* an ending—it theoretically goes on forever (or at least as long as it's profitable or feasible). In an MMO, you're just another adventurer among many. There might be world-altering "events" that are staged by the game designers from time to time in which you can participate in some small way, but you will never be the central character of that world, nor the individual who resolves that world's singular conflict. So how can you be the Hero? [Skolnick, 31].

World of Warcraft does indeed contain a loose overarching narrative: the player's avatar is an inhabitant of the fantasy realm of Azeroth, currently besieged by numerous malevolent forces. By joining factions, participating in quests, gaining strength and earning prestige, the avatar becomes a hero, challenging corrupt deities, murderous zealots and demonic overlords in an effort to save the land. However, Barton bolsters Skolnick's analysis by noting that the open, persistent, always-online world comes with its own significant limitations:

> There are some things that a MMORPG can't do as well a CRPG. The most important of these limitations concerns story and plot. Although *World of Warcraft* and other MMORPGs offer quests, sometimes strung together in long sequences, the nature of the persistent gameworld inhibits the carefully contrived plot structuring we see in *Baldur's Gate* or *Betrayal at Krondor.* An MMORPG or MUD developer simply cannot tell a story the way a CPRG developer can. Unlike MMORPGs with their teeming persistent worlds, the gameworld of a single-player CRPG should be totally focused on the individual player, who has an all-important role to play. The characters one meets, the places one visits, and the events that unfold in a CRPG should all contribute to creating and sustaining a dramatic intensity [Barton, 432].

While Azeroth's narrative cohesion may be weaker than the standard single-player experience, its ontological structure is singular—the player has full geographical access, including the ability to cross oceans and visit other continents. Moreover, the developers have released a constant stream of expansion packs over the years which add new territories and inhabitants to the virtual world, at times altering the very topology itself. This produces a fictional world that is dynamic, shifting, and subject to constant, irrevocable change in real-time, even as the player is immersed within it.

As might be expected of such a world, Azeroth is host to a mixed population of programmed characters (such as monsters and quest-givers) and a massive quantity of human-controlled avatars navigating its cities, dungeons and fields. These concurrent narrative experiences have led to the formation of clusters and communities similar in shape and function to fan-communities, with the caveat that membership in such organizations is typically hierarchical. Brad King elaborates on the inevitability of these groupings, given the genres *World of Warcraft* emulates:

> The spread of D&D-like games onto computers and computer networks changed the boundaries of the paper game. It opened up geographic borders, linking people from around the world in ways barely imaginable before. It gave storytellers, now in the form of programmers and game designers, a much wider palette on which to paint their universes, changing the dynamics of narrative fiction. It gave the players themselves the opportunity to interact with the story, changing the games in ways developers never intended.... It may seem strange to think of computer game communities in the same lights as sports teams ... but for gamers, those virtual worlds are now just an extension of the real world [King, 6–8].

Indeed, the persistence of the virtual world in the absence of the player complicates the very notion of simulacrum as an ontological attribute: the game does not create copies of itself that correspond to the whims of individual players, but rather establishes a consistent communal realm whose inhabitants may come and go as they please, with very little capacity for pseudo-authorial power. This entangling of the diegetic and extradiegetic levels has led to heretofore-unseen levels of mimesis within the fictional world; for example, Scott Rettberg notes that *World of Warcraft* has produced its own economic system: "The spirit of capital in *World of Warcraft* is not simply reducible to more gold = greater achievement. Money is not a meaningless abstraction; gold is more often a means to an end.... Even honor, earned through battle, is ultimately rewarded in a materialist way—certain 'epic' items are only available for purchase by players who achieve a particular rank" (Rettberg, 24). The rise of a capitalistic system, further complicated by the subsequent possibility of exchanging real money for fictional gold, contributes to immersion while distancing the game even further from traditional narrative formats. MMORPG avatars similarly exist outside the aforementioned framework of single-player experiences. Character growth is entirely ludic, with no possibility for expressions of diegetic agency that affect the world—by its very nature as a shared ontology, the game can offer no path for individual participants to impose their will on other players. In-game accomplishments manifest visually, with different outfits purchased or earned through combat; avatars journeying through Azeroth need not fear the loss of a limb or facial scarring, where such visual indicators are key to expressing outcomes of player agency with characters such as Shepard, Hawke and other single-player protagonists. As of the time of writing, MMORPGs at large have yet to achieve such an effect.

Of course, this is not to suggest that online games are incapable of producing interactive fiction in their own right. In fact, these dynamically shifting virtual environments are a key factor in the creation and dissemination of emergent narratives, a method of storytelling unique to video games which consist of stories put together in retrospect, using techniques comparable to narrativized history (for example, positioning events in a set sequence which imposes causality rather than contingency). One of the most infamous examples took place in the early years of *World of Warcraft* and is referred to as the "Corrupted Blood Incident." Tavinor highlights the significance of this event both in relation to the game itself and the medium as a whole: "The *corrupted blood* incident occurred when new content was introduced to the game through an update patch.... The ancient Blood God Hakkar the Soul Flayer inhabited the cave acting as a *boss* for the level, and was able to cast a spell—or *debuff*—against the players called the *corrupted blood* spell. The effect of the spell was to damage the player's life points, while infecting anyone standing nearby" (Tavinor, 36–37). This establishes the most fundamental principle of emergent narrative: a lack of authorial intent. What followed the introduction of Hakkar the Soul Flayer was not at the behest of the game's designers, but rather the product of an almost-random confluence of player action, errant programming, and the game world itself:

> Very shortly after the release of the Zul'Gurub content, on September 13, 2005, the virus spread to the main game world, apparently through non-player-characters and the pets of player-characters, causing a virtual epidemic. The corrupted blood curse spread especially quickly in the densely populated cities such as Ironforge and Ogrimmar, killing many characters with low hit points.... The game's epidemic does seem to have interesting parallels with real-world behavior, in particular the malicious spreading of the virus observed in the game that involved an *exploit* (a manner in which players might take advantage of the unforeseen design consequences of a game to have an effect on the game world) in which players intentionally spread the disease by summoning their infected pets into the main game world [Tavinor, 37].

For players active while these events were unfolding, the result was a world thrown into utter chaos: entire swaths of the virtual environment were quarantined as the plague spread, infecting and killing hundreds of avatars. Some players chose to participate in the emergent narrative by spreading the virtual disease further, performing the villainous roles of Typhoid Mary-esque figures in a typical "plague narrative." The highly disruptive event forced the developers to actively intervene by resetting the contaminated areas and reprogramming the Corrupted Blood code so that it operated correctly. Despite not having been planned in advance, the incident has since become a part of Azeroth's diegetic history and has led to a mass narrativization of digital space: *World of Warcraft* and MMORPGs in its vein have become nearly-autonomous fiction generators in their own right, introducing an element of randomness and spontaneity into ontological structures that were, until recently, perceived as being rigidly programmed and bound by exact specifications. Indeed, the lack of a strict narrative framework ensures that there is no set endpoint to the player's adventures: "Complex interactions between the various in-game systems produce interesting and highly unpredictable results that, with the benefit of hindsight, should mesh with what the player knows of the world and the choices he's made. With no specific victory condition, the player's story can go on indefinitely" (Skolnick, 136).

Viewed as a whole, these diverse ontological configurations reveal the deep and continual influence of technology on the creation and reception of game worlds; narrative-driven experiences such as *Dishonored* permit player agency to affect not only the avatar or the plot but the landscape itself, while MMORPGs produce interactive and interacting systems that remove directed authorial expression and personal ontological simulacra in exchange for a nominally "level" playing field, which allows stories to randomly emerge in response to actions taken by its inhabitants. The sheer scale of these online worlds produces new phenomena on an almost-daily basis:

> The Internet has also proved to be a significant technological impetus to gaming, both in allowing people to come together to play online, and in bringing gamers together to discuss games and to criticize them on the many gaming forums scattered around the net. These discussion boards have led to a level of gaming criticism and connoisseurship not previously seen. The Internet has led to the development of videogames with simply huge fictional worlds.... Millions of players interacting in a virtual fantasy world is a stunning fact of both technological and artistic significance [Tavinor, 7].

Thus, just as fan fiction utilizes technology to challenge existing preconceptions of authorial power, video games continue to adapt and refine new tools to produce increasingly sophisticated paradigms for representations of fictional worlds, positioning the medium at the forefront of narrative experimentation.

Metafiction and Fan Fiction Apparatuses in Video Games

As previously stated, the textuality of fan fiction is limited only by the relative aptitude of the fan-creator in establishing ontological simulacra which correspond to new implied authors. In theory, any deviation—however outlandish—may still be published, shared, and accepted by a given community. By contrast, Murray's claim that agency in games is limited to choosing from a predetermined array of potential storylines is accurate, as the average player cannot select a variable or impose an implied author that does not exist within the defined parameters of the software. The exception to this is the phenomenon colloquially referred to as modding, in which players with high technical aptitude use third-party programs to modify the most foundational codes of a given virtual world. This allows for insertions, alterations and permutations beyond the scope established by the original designers; from a practical standpoint, these mods are perhaps the ultimate expression of authorial usurpation for its specific medium and constitute a key point of overlap between the media of video games and online fan fiction.

Lahti's contextualization of video game evolution as a gradual unification of player and avatar raises the specter of the same impetus Jenkins attributes to the creation of fan work, noting that "video game history is characterized by a significant shift in perspective relations between the player and the field of play, from the vertical omniscience of the God's-eye-view, through a ground-level, third-person perspective along the horizontal axis, to a fully subjective perspective where character and player are unified into a first-person movement through the virtual space" (Lahti, 202). Zimmerman similarly supports the notion that contemporary games encourage immersion and active participation, inevitably leading to the formation of communities specifically designed to pierce established boundaries of the virtual environment and effectively reprogram them: "Players do not just play games; they mod them, engage in metaplay between games, and develop cultures around games. Games are not just about following rules, but also about breaking them" (Zimmerman, 27). Just as fan fiction exists to address lacunae and present alternative scenarios which may or may not be consistent with the expressed values of the source text, mods present an ever-growing array of fan-created possibilities which are freely available and, for the most part, easily implemented by other players. This section will discuss two popular mods in relation to their original games, with an eye towards analyzing how these programs affect the player's narrative experience of "virtual fan fiction": "Ascension" for BioWare's *Baldur's Gate II: Throne of Bhaal* (2001) and "Zelda Starring Zelda" for Nintendo's *The Legend of Zelda* (1986).

Given the status of *Baldur's Gate* as one of the most highly regarded role-playing games in the medium's history, it should come as no surprise that multiple modding communities continue to produce new content to this day. Based on a specific fictional setting drawn from *Dungeons & Dragons*, there is a case to be made for the games themselves being a form of fan fiction, albeit licensed (and therefore "authorized"): the player designs a character which is then inserted into a virtual realization of the Forgotten Realms, a D&D fictional world first established in 1987. The effect is pseudo-metaleptical per Kukkonen's definition: for all intents and purposes, the player is projecting their avatar into a pre-existing ontological structure, one which has served as the template for countless novels and tabletop narratives. The game itself offers an additional visual and exploratory dimension to the experience, allowing players to navigate forests and bustling cities that had previously existed only in textual or abstract forms. A survey of the games' dominant modding groups reveals that the most common type of modification is the "NPC mod," which adds one or more new characters to the game as potential companions to the player. As the technical design of *Baldur's Gate* makes the introduction of such characters a relatively simple process, over fifty such mods are actively being circulated within the game's fandom as of the time of writing. While many of these may fit into the classic mold of the Mary Sue in terms of their incongruity with the source material, others have clearly been designed to supplement the existing array of canonical characters. Statistically, at least a quarter of these mods include the possibility of same-sex liaisons, further substantiating points made by both Consalvo and Jenkins regarding the use of fan-created content to express marginalized alternative scenarios pertaining to sexuality and defiance of enforced heteronormativity.

Within this broad spectrum of potential modifications, one in particular calls for further elaboration: "Ascension," first released in 2001 and continually updated until 2009. Designed to expand the climactic act of the series' overarching narrative, "Ascension" distinguishes itself from other fan-made content by virtue of containing input provided by David Gaider, one of the game's original designers. Per Gaider's own description:

> Some people like the ending to Throne of Bhaal well enough, I guess. I liked it well enough (I did a lot of the work on it, after all), but I remember wishing that we had had the time to tinker with it more. At Bioware we never seemed to have enough time to tinker with the Infinity Engine scripting language as much as I might have liked. With better AI and some leisurely time spent considering various options, the ending might have been more fully realized. That's a game designer's fantasy, obviously, especially when you're working within the time-frame of an expansion (which must come out while the game's still on peoples' hard-drives) ... but seeing as a mod like this can be done in one's spare time, it doesn't have to be. Consider this my offering of what might have been. You might not necessarily like it better ... heck, you might not even like it at all ... but I think it shows off what the Infinity Engine can do when stretched to its limit and offers a bit more bite to Throne of Bhaal's climax for those who think that's not a bad idea ["Ascension" README].

Gaider makes explicit reference to several principles which govern the overall reception of fan fiction in relation to their source texts, particularly the desire to expand upon inadvertent gaps in the material—here attributed to financial and time-related constraints linked to the marketing and publication of the game. Indeed, when installed onto *Baldur's Gate II*, "Ascension" creates a sense of emotional intensification by pitting the player against past antagonists, a challenging final battle meant to evoke the character's heroic journey in its entirety. Gaider is quick to note that despite his position within the company that produced the game, "Ascension" is not to be considered a canonical contribution: "this is NOT an official Bioware product and Bioware does not support it. I work for Bioware, but I've done this on my own time" ("Ascension" README). Nevertheless, the involvement of an individual who participated in the creation of the source text complicates existing paradigms of fan-authorship—does the implied author of "Ascension" hew closer to the original due to Gaider's involvement? Should the mod's content be considered canonical from an evaluative standpoint, despite Gaider's own statement to the contrary? Regardless, the presentation of a free component that can be installed or removed at will demonstrates the same ease of access and lack of hierarchical imposition that governs navigation of fan-constructed spaces; the diegetic realm can become modular, configurable and malleable beyond the rigid definitions of the program itself, placing further prioritization upon the individual (and individualized) narrative experience, which has been customized to suit the recipient's desires.

A similar desire to break the supposedly immutable framework lies at the heart of the "total conversion" mod, as defined by Berens and Howard:

> Modding (modifying), or customizing games, was also becoming a large part of the online PC gaming experience. It's a simple enough concept, involving independent coders taking a developer's commercial release and extending its gameplay, perhaps through the creation of extra levels and character models, and then posting them online for public consumption: this is referred to as partial conversion. More extreme, and potentially more exciting, is total conversion, in which the game in question is so thoroughly made-over that it becomes its own entity [Berens/Howard, 38].

One such total conversion is "Zelda Starring Zelda," a program that makes a single—but highly significant—modification to one of the earliest console games, Nintendo's *The Legend of Zelda*. Released the same year as the prototypical *Dragon Warrior*, *The Legend of Zelda* depicts a similarly classical adventure narrative in which the hero Link braves a monster-infested world to recover the fragments of the mystical Triforce, and rescue Princess Zelda from the evil Ganon. In 2013, blogger Kenna W described her experience with the game and her subsequent desire to change its meaning:

> For me, I played my first Zelda game when I was pretty young, and at the time, I thought the game *did* star Princess Zelda. I figured I'd get to play as a magical battle princess that saved her kingdom. The game was fun, but I was bummed out that I never got to play as Zelda. But like I said, I'm an adult now. There's no one to stop me from eating candy before bed and there's nothing standing in the way of me creating the games I want to play [Kenna W, "Zelda Starring Zelda: The Story"].

Taking it upon herself to redefine the game's canonical focus, Kenna W constructed a program that would swap the digital avatars of Princess Zelda and Link. Consequently, the player controls not Link but Zelda herself, wielding a magic sword and shield, on a quest to save her kingdom and rescue her captured "protector" Link. Mechanically, the gameplay is identical: Zelda has no special powers of her own, but rather acts precisely as

Link does in the original game, with access to the same mystical artifacts and combat aptitude. Just as with *Star Wars: Revelations*, "Zelda Starring Zelda" addresses a perception of female underrepresentation; even as Nintendo continues to release *Legend of Zelda* games today which feature Link as the player's avatar, Kenna W's project is a clear demonstration of technology used in the pursuit of individual agency and subversion of authorial intent: "It makes me happy too. It feels really good to play as Zelda. I feel like I connect with her character better and it makes me feel like a big damn hero. It's so nice to be swinging around a sword as Zelda. I can't describe it. You really should try it for yourself" (Kenna W, "Zelda Starring Zelda: The Story"). Thus, while the ludological qualities of "Zelda Starring Zelda" are identical to its template, the mod may nevertheless be viewed as a total conversion in that it completely inverts the original implied author—the captive princess becomes the hero and the hero becomes the captive, and *The Legend of Zelda* thus becomes Zelda's story rather than Link's.

The subversive impetus expressed by modders has been embraced and adopted by game developers as well—over the past five years, an increasing number of independently-produced games have contained direct challenges and critique of broadly accepted trends in mainstream gaming. Just as fan fiction has evolved to produce its own metafiction, so too have games progressed to the point of generating self-reflexive parody, commentary and subversion. To demonstrate these processes, three games can be discussed in terms of their metafictional properties: *Deltarune*, *Doki Doki Literature Club* and *ICEY*, all of which have been released between 2016 and 2018.

Deltarune (2018), a sequel to popular (and similarly metafictional) role-playing game *Undertale*, begins with a clear statement of purpose regarding conceits of character design and authorship: the game starts with a typical "character creator" sequence in which the player chooses their avatar's appearance, blood type, emotional status and more. Upon completing this initial process, the following message is relayed by the unnamed narrator who has guided the player through the sequence: "Your wonderful creation will now be discarded. No one can choose who they are in this world" (*Deltarune*). This blunt statement is meant to come as a complete surprise to the player, as it exists in complete opposition to the principles of avatar customization as previously delineated. By suggesting this agency only to deny it moments later, creator Toby Fox sends a clear message as to the limitations deliberately placed upon the player's pseudo-authorial power, no doubt confounding expectations established by *Undertale* (which treated the act of resetting as a diegetic power to "undo" past mistakes and contained several branching paths). The narrative then reflects this imposed linearity by nullifying player choice at every opportunity, while suggesting the player's control over the protagonist is suppressing said character's own free will.

Doki Doki Literature Club, released in 2017, takes a similarly deconstructive approach to the concept of diegetic game romances. Superficially, the game mimics the appearance and general narrative thrust of a Japanese dating simulator: the player's faceless avatar is a boy surrounded by four beautiful yet stereotypical teenagers seeking his attention: childhood friend Sayori, energetic waif Natsuki, shy bookworm Yuri, and confident club president Monika. However, only the first three are options for romantic pursuit. Though initially following its prescribed genre trappings, *Doki Doki Literature Club* takes a dark turn when Monika, aware of her status as a scripted computer-generated entity, begins tampering with the codes of the other girls, warping their personalities so as to make them unappealing or unavailable to the player. Obsessed with achieving the player's love despite not being programmed as a viable romance option, Monika goes so far as to become an extradiegetic actant, deleting the other girls altogether and crashing the game so that the player is compelled to stay with her. The only way the player can "defeat" her is by following suit and deleting Monika's own character file, causing her to disappear from the game. By inverting the implication that objects of romantic pursuit in games are essentially tools for the player to express authorial power, *Doki Doki Literature Club* delivers a pronounced critique of how easily the medium can accidentally portray obsessive love and superficiality in positive terms, as products of agency.

ICEY (2016) goes as far as to declare war on one of the most basic features of storytelling: the narrator. The player controls an android girl named ICEY, who is tasked with destroying a dangerous artificial lifeform known as Judas. As might be expected, the narrator recounts ICEY's story in the past tense while the player navigates diegetic space; however, because the narrator speaks before the avatar takes action, the player is able to contradict the story being told. If the narrator says, "ICEY proceeded right," the player may then turn left. The narrator then reacts with frustration, breaking the fourth wall to suggest that the player has made an error and must return to the course of the story. However, if ICEY persistently goes against the narrator's commands (phrased as simple storytelling imperatives), the diegetic space becomes more and more porous and disrupted, as the narrator grows increasingly disenchanted and furious with the player's refusal to "play the game." Finally, if the player has opposed the narrator consistently throughout the course of the game, a special final sequence is triggered in which the narrator realizes that he himself is merely a fictional character with no actual control over the player's choices; seeking to destroy ICEY, he disables the player's controller to render the avatar helpless. And then, in an ultimate rejection of authorial fiat, ICEY becomes autonomous, defeating her enemies and shaming the narrator for his misdeeds without any input at all from the player. The emphasis of this resolution on the removal of player control—another foundational component of this particular narrative platform—only further highlights the degree to which metafictional approaches in games have progressed, and the extent to which technological sophistication enables complex commentary of both the medium and its most closely associated tropes.

Just as fan fiction has advanced as a mode of writing to the point where its metafiction is capable of both depicting and critiquing its own conventions (as seen with *Steve Rogers at 100*, which both satirizes and expresses tropes of the slash genre), the aforementioned examples are just a few of the ways in which video game metafiction can problematize and question its codified traditions. Initially the province of individual players seeking to modify games to their own liking, developers have come to embrace this process, producing games in direct dialogue with the medium's own history. And where fan fiction can only go so far in its manipulation of hypertext and static imagery, these metafictional games are able to dissect, experiment with and reassemble their component parts in unparalleled ways. Even a concept as universal to the medium as the player's avatar can be utilized to disrupt existing paradigms and raise questions as to the future of video game narrative.

The Continuing Evolution of Diegetic Agency

In discussing plot structure, characterization and ontology, it is clear that video games and fan fiction share common traits as narrative platforms: each employs extant technologies to transfer a measure of pseudo-authorial power to the reader/player, creating an entity whose active participation in the consumption of story content goes beyond cognitive processes of interpretation and projection. But fan fiction has relied on digital media almost exclusively for purposes of distribution: the creative processes remain largely the same whether the platform is textual, filmic or online/communal, as evidenced by the fact that the generic strategies and techniques used to create mimetic simulacra have largely remained the same over decades of production. Conversely, video games are much more deeply and intrinsically tied to technological development for every aspect of their narrative capabilities—as new tools are produced and appropriated, the subsequent leap forward in game engine capacities invariably produces storytelling innovations ranging from deeper explorations of detailed virtual worlds to a proliferation of multitextual systems designed to enable and bolster player agency. This is not to say that game-play mechanics do not factor into the developmental process, but rather that there is a clear connection between different digital media in how they are refined by a consistent desire to achieve greater levels of interactivity and ontological flexibility. The end result is a second digital medium which prioritizes interactivity and agency—a fact that, according to Chris Crawford, will come to define the digital era as a whole:

> Interactivity is not some secondary attribute like color balance or stereo imaging quality. Interactivity is the sum and substance of the entire revolution that has been shaking our society for the last few decades. We don't refer to the Industrial Revolution as the "Steam Engine Revolution" and we don't refer to the Agricultural Revolution as the "Plow Revolution," and two hundred years from now they won't call this the "Computer Revolution"—it will be known as the Interactivity Revolution [Crawford, 325].

These attributes continue to be refined today, coalescing as parts of an ever-developing "toolbox" which produces new paradigms for theoretical approaches with unmatched speed and variety. A thorough understanding of this toolbox can only be achieved and expanded upon by acknowledging that while the technological components of the medium have played an incontrovertibly significant part in defining its features, the capacity of game narratives to contain divergent canonical texts, encourage transfers of authorial power, and experiment with heretofore-unseen chronotopes and ontological configurations share common ground with the creative impetus, tropes and mechanisms of fan fiction and webcomics.

3

Webcomics

Defining Webcomics in Opposition to Print

In *Comics Through Time,* M. Keith Booker claims that the medium of webcomics is as reliant upon technological refinement as the digital platforms discussed in previous chapters:

> As of this writing, comics seem to have an exciting, if uncertain, future. This is especially the case of webcomics, whose full impact remains to be seen, especially as this general category includes not only comics that are produced specifically to be viewed online via the Internet, but also new forms of digital distribution of conventional comics for viewing on computer screens and on a variety of other digital devices [Booker, 4911].

Indeed, webcomics share attributes with both contemporary fan fiction and video games, such as their use of the Internet as a nonhierarchical space for publication and archiving, and their ability to construct fictional worlds that can be manipulated and expanded (in this case via hyperlinks, animations and other Web design tools). Moreover, just as fan fiction utilizes the same textual language as its print predecessors, webcomics follow mainstream graphic literature in their use of hybridized art and text, arranged into sequential patterns which form nominally linear narratives. Kukkonen points out that these panels serve the same literary function as the focalizing character or the cinematic eye of the camera: "What readers see in the panel images on the comics page are settings, characters and depictions of the events of the story as it unfolds. In other words, they show us the fictional world. However, comics panels do not show us the entire fictional world, but only a particular part of it. The image within the panel frame is a selection from the entire possible information which the fictional world holds" (Kukkonen, 215). Whether printed or digital, the content of these panels is decoded by the reader in accordance with parameters established in Barthes' *Image-Music-Text,* which notes that the simultaneous presence of textual and visual cues creates a three-tiered image containing "a linguistic message, a coded iconic message, and a non-coded iconic message" (Barthes, 36).

Much like Jakobson's communication model, Barthes' paradigm highlights the importance of the reader's interpretive process, attributing the parsing of different layers of the message (in this case, the sequential narrative) to the recipient. Jenkins further compounds these similarities by emphasizing the reciprocal nature of the relationship between digital works and their pre-digital antecedents:

> The Web represents a site of experimentation and innovation, where amateurs test the waters, developing new practices, themes, and generating materials that may well attract cult followings on their own terms. The most commercially viable of those practices are then absorbed into the mainstream media, either directly through the hiring of new talent or the development of television, video, or big-screen works based on those materials, or indirectly, through a second-order imitation of the same aesthetic and thematic qualities [Jenkins, 148].

This is not to suggest that webcomics operate in identical fashion to fan fiction; on the contrary, there are significant differences between the two. The proliferation of fan fiction follows a distinctly postmodern episteme, as the mode prioritizes multiplicities of texts and meanings splintering off from canonical originals which are subsequently rendered distant and irrelevant. Communal spaces permit and promote a near-infinite array of alternative interpretations, fueling further creation of fan works. By contrast, while some websites may host multiple webcomics, it is far more common for individual works to have their own distinct addresses online, serving as singular spotlights for specific creators rather than a broader array of thematically aligned works. That said, Robert S. Petersen points out that the very nature of these websites enables the same kind of instantaneous communication found in online fandoms: "Among the most common advantages that such Web comics offer is instant access to an archive of past material, making it possible to guide readers through more complicated plots. They also allow readers to interact, post comments about the strip, and recognize each other as belonging to the reading community of the strip" (Petersen, 234–235). Booker reinforces this claim by highlighting the continuing dissolution of the author/reader binary through sustained Internet use: "Webcomics also support a more direct and immediate relationship between creators and readers, embodying a communication style that is often welcomed and favored by users of other social media platforms" (Booker, 6507). In practical terms, this often manifests when creators place links on their own sites leading to other webcomics—an informal endorsement rather than the centralized categorization found in Archive of Our Own, yet still suiting Landow's definition of hypertextuality by directly linking readers from one webcomic text to the next: "The Internet works, however, appear in a very different context than do the print ones. Anyone who stumbles upon any of these writings is likely to find them linked to a personal or group site containing biographies of the site owner, explanations of the imaginative world, and lists of links to similar stories. The link, in other words, makes immediately visible the virtual community created by these active readers" (Landow, 8). Thus, while individual webcomics typically serve as singular showcases for their respective creators, they still invariably participate in a hyperlinked, hypertextual network to be navigated by the reader.

While webcomics do not directly present themselves as speculative derivations of existing works, prevalent tropes in the medium suggest a trend of reactivity and interactivity, aligning webcomics with fan fiction and video games as digital platforms informed by a desire for increased authorial agency. Specifically, many authors of long-running webcomics display an innate awareness of conventions and themes relating to the superhero genre in mainstream print comics—the most prevalent and ubiquitous form of graphic literature in the American market—regardless of whether the webcomics in question deal with those themes. Many such works explicitly subvert, satirize or comment upon the traditions of the genre, framing the act of creating and sharing webcomics as precisely the same anti-authorial rebellious impulse that motivates fan fiction. While Turk posits that "for fans who produce and consume fan works, the boundaries of the source text's fictional world are not fixed; rather, they are infinitely expandable" (Turk, 88), her attribution of this factor to the advent of television is problematic given that mainstream superhero comics were already displaying signs of advanced complexity and intertextuality in their own ongoing stories, long before television was popularly embraced as a viable narrative platform. Indeed, this chapter will put forth the claim that the overwhelming prevalence of superhero works is the primary catalyst for the creation of webcomics as an alternative space, one defined by resistance to oversaturation—at the time of writing, superheroes are featured in nearly 70 percent of all comics produced in America, with over 90 percent of major publishers DC and Marvel's output dedicated to the same. Consequently, where fan fiction relies upon a relatively simple process of cognitive extrapolation from source texts to achieve its aesthetic ends, the interdependent dynamics between superhero narratives and webcomics are more complex due to the unique nature of the medium. To understand how webcomics position themselves as a digital space of reaction and response to their print counterparts, a narratological dissection of the superhero genre is needed, as the direct antecedent to the style, techniques and content of many webcomics, as well as the technology that supports them:

...the Apple iPad ... upon its initial release in April 2010, was almost immediately hailed for its potential as a comics reader. That potential has only increased as the iPad itself has been improved. Major publishers such as Marvel, DC, and Dark Horse have dedicated apps for the iPad that allow the download and display of many of their comics, as the iPad and other tablet devices have increasingly come to be used for the reading not only of digital comics, but of digitized versions of conventional comics, including a growing archive of classic comics. This process has been furthered by the rise of websites such as Comixology.com, which caters to users of portable devices in providing a wide variety of digital comics. The digital comics phenomenon is only beginning, but it promises to have a major impact on the comics industry in years to come [Booker, 4911].

This chapter will begin with a breakdown of the superhero genre over its eighty years of history, focusing on elements Ryan defines as essential to all forms of narrative, regardless of medium: "Whether textual worlds function as imaginary counterparts or as models of the real world, they are mentally constructed by the reader as environments that stretch in space, exist in time, and serve as habitat for a population of animate agents. These three dimensions correspond to what have long been recognized as the three basic components of narrative grammar: setting, plot, and characters" (Ryan, 15). The enduring global popularity of figures such as Superman, Spider-Man and the like have produced unique variations on these basic concepts; this, in turn, has led readers of the ubiquitous genre to assume authorial powers in digital space, creating webcomics in direct response to those tropes.

In the interests of maintaining a focused throughline, discussion of the superhero genre will be limited to specific iconic characters produced by the two most prominent companies in the American comic book industry, DC and Marvel (to be detailed in the following chapter); the completed webcomics *Narbonic* (2000–2006), *Nimona* (2012), *Something Positive* (2001–present) and *SuperCakes* (2014) will then be presented as counterexamples. These works may seem unrelated to each other and their print counterparts, as only Kat Leyh's *SuperCakes* directly deals with superheroes while Shaenon Garrity's *Narbonic* is a science-fiction comedy, Noelle Stevenson's *Nimona* is situated in a fantasy setting, and R.K. Milholland's *Something Positive* is a slice-of-life dark comedy. But all four display their creators' awareness and invocation of superhero tropes, while at the same time exhibiting resistance to said tropes, consciously presenting themselves to the reader as viable alternatives to overly commercialized and overly familiar scenarios and icons. It is no coincidence that these alternatives are presented via the appropriation and repurposing of new technologies—rather, this further confirms that the pre-existing desire for authorial agency and reactivity is actively shaping not only the content being produced, but the methods through which they are distributed; and, furthermore, that webcomic creators are drawing on tropes and practices from other fields of digital creation to inform their own processes. As there has always been a trend of critique leading to new forms of creation—film fans becoming authors of the French Nouvelle Vague in the 1960s, the rise of New Hollywood and *der neue deutsche Film* in the 1970s and the contemporary trend of video game modders growing up to become developers—webcomics can be framed as a transmedia attempt to counter dominant trends in print by making inventive use of the same permissiveness inherent to the spaces and processes which enable fan fiction.

A History of Superhero Authorship and Reactivity

The presence of superheroes has endured in the face of changing social, political and cultural trends throughout the 20th century and into the 21st. Brian J. Robb notes that "from their secret origins in myth and legend, as well as in the adventurers of nineteenth-century pulp fiction heroes, the first comic book superheroes, Superman and Batman, gave rise to an all-conquering genre" (Robb, 15). The description is not hyperbolic—one of the genre's most distinguishing features is its longevity, which has generated singular cohesive storyworlds stretching over eight decades of continuous publication. This phenomenon has no parallel in other narrative media: even serialized works such as the James Bond films or American soap operas are subject to considerations of downtime, hiatus, and changing cast members (a process which effectively rewrites established physical characteristics as new actors replace the old). DC and Marvel publish dozens of issues on a monthly basis, all purporting to represent different points of view within the same fictional worlds, the "DC Universe" or the "Marvel Universe." These ontological megastructures will be examined in greater detail shortly, but it is critical to first explore the genesis of these constructs, and the long process that led to their formation.

Critics have assigned two distinct points of origin to the superhero genre. Richard Reynolds positions the initial presentation of these heroic characters in wartime America:

> The costumed superhero burst into seemingly fully-fledged existence in June 1938, with the appearance on American newsstands of *Action Comics 1*, featuring Superman's first ever appearance in print…. America's entry into World War Two gave the superheroes a whole new set of enemies, and supplied a complete working rationale and world view for a super-patriotic superhero such as Captain America [Reynolds, 8].

The 1930s and 1940s also saw the debut of iconic figures such as Batman, Wonder Woman and Captain America; at the time, though, the genre was a relatively minor presence in the American comics industry, overshadowed by pulp, crime fiction and romance titles. But Jeffrey K. Johnson argues that even in its earliest form, the genre was far more enmeshed in extradiegetic influences than its peers:

> Since Superman debuted in 1938 as a Great Depression hero, comic book superheroes have been linked to American hopes, desires, fears, needs, and social norms. Because superhero comic books have always been a form of popular literature, the narratives have closely mirrored and molded American social trends and changes. This means that superhero stories are excellent primary sources for studying changes in American society from 1938 until the present. They are an American mythology that is forever adjusting to meet society's needs. Superheroes are not merely comic book characters; rather they are social mirrors and molders that serve as barometers of the place and time in which they reside. Their stories help us to comprehend our world and allow us to better understand ourselves [Johnson, 2].

Indeed, the elevated perception of superheroes as a purely American mythological system may explain, in part, the "new wave" of the 1960s which saw the genre overtake any and all competitors in the market. Like Johnson, Mike Madrid frames this boost in popularity as an innate response to social and political upheavals occurring across the nation at the time:

> The self-proclaimed comic book revolution of the early 60's took place at a pivotal time in American culture. The 1962 death of Hollywood sex goddess Marilyn Monroe in many ways closed the books on the conservative 50's, as the world of petticoats, Elvis, and sock hops would give way to miniskirts, the Beatles, and discotheques. Marvel's flawed superheroes were plagued with real-life problems, and reflected the angst that Americans were feeling in an imperfect world fraught with intangible enemies, the world of the Cold War [Madrid, 107–108].

What these dual origin points demonstrate, first and foremost, is the high degree of reflexivity that lies at the heart of superhero publications. The narratives produced within the genre are viewed, at different historical points, as representations of whatever social norms and cultural trends were dominant at the time. This mirroring effect appears in other long-running serial narratives—television series *The Simpsons*, for example, has continuously run from 1989 and continues to reference contemporary events as they occur—but none cover such a broad swath of the 20th and 21st centuries. Moreover, *The Simpsons* is a single text representing one fictional world, whereas the ontological configuration of the Marvel and DC universes coalesced over time into broader cohesive megastructures.

In essence, what distinguishes superheroes from other pop culture phenomena which reflect extradiegetic trends is that any other text in any other medium corresponds to a set period of time, a specific place, or a particular event in history, whereas Superman and his successors exist in a state of "perpetual relevance," constantly updated to meet contemporary needs. With the resurgence of the genre in the mid- to late 1960s, a bilateral pattern of influence begins to emerge, similar in function (if not form) to the modes of direct interactivity seen in digital media. According to Johnson's historical survey, a marked increase in urban crime during the 1970s had a tangible impact on portrayals of superheroes—not only were new actants produced who embodied fictional responses to drug crimes and political corruption (Vietnam and Watergate having an obvious impact on American society as a whole), but existing characters were subtly modified and rewritten to serve the same purpose:

> As in most periods, superheroes epitomized the 1970s' social issues. Comic books entered a darker period in which creators presented more realistic stories as American society and popular culture was filled with many stark and unhappy images. Characters like the Punisher, Luke Cage, and even Batman began to address social issues and even openly disagree with those in authority. Comic books began to question the foundations of American culture and society and many superheroes were no longer simply champions of the "American way" [Johnson, 64].

Robb claims that this period in the genre's history is significant for another reason, one of great narratological value: "A new generation of storytellers was ready to take these now-venerable superheroes in new directions, or return them to their roots. This younger generation had grown up as comic book fans, so brought a return to the social awareness of the Thirties and Forties. This 'Bronze Age' stretches from 1970 to the mid–Eighties, when superheroes took a turn for the dark and serious. The origins of that revisionism sprang from the socially relevant Seventies" (Robb, 210). While this revisionism lacks the immediacy and efficacy of fan fiction simulacra and carries with it the official and explicit sanction of the texts' legal owners, the process Robb describes is nevertheless that of readers usurping original implied authors and imposing their own systems of values upon existing texts, worlds, and characters. The ubiquitous presence of superheroes as a constant emblem of the cultural zeitgeist ensured that, as new authors were hired to maintain ongoing publications, said authors inevitably approached the genre from within, as former readers. Danny Fingeroth substantiates this view of "Bronze Age" authors: "The fact that so many comics creators are from the ranks of fandom means that, while much of their work is filled with passion, it is passion that can generally only be appreciated by fellow fans, and so, despite lip service paid to the desire to expand markets, many comics produced at present serve that club—that family—of other aficionados, or fanatics, as the case may be" (Fingeroth, 112).

As a result of this gradual shift, new stories saw familiar characters repurposed to deliver commentary where, within the diegetic sphere, those concerns had not been previously expressed. Robb provides a specific example in the character of Green Lantern, a superhero whose prior focus had been light-hearted science fiction adventures; upon the arrival of writer Denny O'Neil and artist Neil Adams, the same Green Lantern suddenly found himself contending with issues more directly relevant to a new generation of readers:

> O'Neil and Adams explored social and political issues through the clash of ideas between these two, often depicting Queen advocating direct action while Jordan lectured about achieving change by working within the system. Travelling the country in an old pick-up, the pair witnessed the "real" America, and were involved in stories reflecting modern corruption, as well as stories based in racism, religious cults, the "generation gap," the plight of Native Americans, poverty, overpopulation, and environmentalism [Robb, 214–215].

This aptly demonstrates the significant power new authors wielded over pre-existing characters and fictional worlds; the unprecedented malleability evinced here would later play a pivotal role in the creation of webcomics as an act of response, subversion and reader empowerment.

The "promotion" of readers to writers was not the only factor that influenced the continuing evolution of the genre; technological innovation was also having direct and immediate effects. According to Laurence Maslon and Michael Kantor, this begins as far back as the 1940s, in which a major narrative platform—radio—would inform a recurrent element in the Superman mythos that continues to appear today:

> Forced by the conventions of radio to adapt Superman's adventures in an aural medium, the program introduced some innovations: Superman was given a teenaged comrade, a copy boy named Jimmy Olsen—because on radio he *really* needed someone to talk to, and to keep the suspense of the serials going; Clark Kent's paper was now the *Daily Planet*, run by a hard-boiled editor name Perry White; and a radioactive substance from his home planet, Kryptonite, pierced Superman's invulnerable carapace [Maslon/Kantor, 87].

Here, according to Maslon and Kantor, is a situation in which extradiegetic considerations demanded diegetic solutions, which in turn became inextricable components of the fictional world. The power of new media platforms over the source text would only be compounded further with the advent of television, and then with the 1978 cinematic adaptation *Superman*, a vehicle that reintroduced the character to yet another new generation of viewers (some of whom would themselves become authors of superhero fiction in subsequent decades). Technology was having an increasingly tangible influence on diegetic events: in the 1988–1989 *Batman* storyline "A Death in the Family," the fate of Jason Todd—an unpopular character who had assumed the mantle of Batman's sidekick Robin—was determined by a reader vote carried over telephone hotlines, with the final tally leading to Todd's death the following month. This would not be the last time a fictional character's circumstances were influenced by a trans-media network of competing, conflicting and collaborating narratives; Robb frames one of the most memorable story events of the early 1990s as a textual occurrence designed and executed entirely due to considerations relating to a forthcoming adaptation:

> The death of Superman—one of the biggest events in superhero history—only happened because the wedding of Clark Kent and Lois Lane was unexpectedly postponed. DC Comics' big plan for the early Nineties was to finally see the Man of Steel married off to his longtime admirer (they'd once been married in the newspaper strip, but that was later dismissed as "a dream"). However, as the television series *Lois and Clark: The New Adventures of Superman* was in development, the decision was taken to postpone the wedding in the comics to tie in with the new show. That left an empty slot in DC's planning for the year. In meetings to discuss alternatives, *Adventures of Superman* writer Jerry Orway jokingly said: "If we can't get Superman married, we ought to just kill him." Crazy as it seemed, the idea rapidly caught on among DC's editors [Robb, 261].

Of course, as will be discussed shortly, the ontological flux innate to the genre ensured the inevitable return of both Superman and Jason Todd; nevertheless, this event constitutes one of the many ways the malleable nature of superhero narratives could be construed as an early form of interactivity that preceded the technology to actualize more conventional expressions of that concept.

As Robb and Fingeroth state above, the entry of former readers into the industry as new writers had a profound transformative effect on narratives composed in the late 1970s and early 1980s. Robb, in particular, attributes the rise of the "deconstruction" movement within the genre to that same incoming wave of readers-turned-authors: "At the beginning of the Eighties a new generation of comic book writers and artists felt their work could aspire to more than mere entertainment, and that it might even verge on literary graphic art" (Robb, 237). Informed as they were by the implied authors of the source text—being the adventures of the same heroic figures circulating in the 1960s and earlier—these new writers approached their work with a greater level of insight and critique than their predecessors. Faced with the paradoxical task of updating these characters to match American's changing social and cultural landscape, while simultaneously preserving their pseudo-mythic iconic status, authors such as Alan Moore, Frank Miller and the aforementioned Denny O'Neil chose a deconstructive approach. Works such as *Watchmen*, *Batman: The Dark Knight Returns* and the aforementioned *Green Arrow/Green Lantern* disassembled the foundational concepts and underpinnings of the superhero genre via literary experimentation, designed to discern which aspects were no longer necessary and which could be reconfigured for a more contemporary readership. Terrence R. Wandtke links this trend to Landow's theories regarding hypertext:

> When discussing the type of readership created by the internet and digital culture…. Landow continues with examples that lead more directly into the art of the digital age such as fanfaction [sp], like that produced and distributed by *Star Trek* fans (before and after the advent of the internet). While Star Trek may be Landow's example, we can easily substitute superhero comic books as the basis for fanfaction [sp]. …fan writers of the early comic book convention scene regularly rose to be the new creators within the superhero industry. The influence of such fan writers has increased exponentially with ready access to computers and internet, as fans produce internet-based fiction, criticism, films, and of course, comic books. Whether it is direct by hiring the fans or indirect by incorporating fan ideas, the boundary between the reader and the writer is slim [Wandtke, 205–206].

Here we see again a porous delineation between reader, author and text, one which becomes even flimsier as the genre's popularity escalates and technology progresses further. Petersen indicates that, just as with fan fiction, the inherently postmodern fragmentation of the readership—and the ever-present possibility that individual readers of a text might someday become authors empowered to reshape the same fictional world of that text—has dramatically changed the way authorship itself is perceived and defined, in a genre simultaneously resistant to drastic change while being one of the most mutable forms of fiction available:

> The great proliferation of Web comics and DIY comics have vastly scattered readers who can communicate within their own specialized interests and using vocabulary, gestures, and images which they find appealing. Such diversity has fragmented the comics audience and made it difficult for critics to make meaningful assessments about comics as fewer and fewer artists find the kind of broad popular support Charles Schulz or Bill Watterson enjoyed. With the diffused and uncertain markets that comics now circulate in, it is also hard to imagine that any artist will ever be able to gain the same kind of reward and international fame as the leaders in the field a century ago were able to achieve [Petersen, 237].

This raises an interesting question regarding the nature of authorship as it applies to this type of narrative: what makes superhero stories so pervasive, and yet so easily subject to revision, deconstruction and postmodern reinterpretation? After all, reactivity in fan fiction and player participation in video games are still clearly restricted in that changes made to ontological simulacra, or "mods" of existing game code, cannot be back-ported and imposed upon the source material. The prevalent tendency in fan fiction to portray *Star Trek* protagonists Kirk and Spock as same-sex lovers (as detailed by Jenkins and Jamison) has had no effect on their appearance in subsequent core texts, firmly relegating fandom's views to the realm of the "alternative." By contrast, superheroes can be—and have been—drastically altered by the introduction of new implied authors, themselves the products of former readers; discussions of continuity, ret-roactive authorial fiat and conflicting diegetic representations are all com-monplace. How and why is such a state possible in this particular medium?

The answer lies in the mythical dimensions which the figure of the superhero has taken on in recent decades; indeed, a cursory examination of mythological systems produced by pre–American cultures easily invokes comparisons between characters such as Superman, Spider-Man, Wonder Woman and the X-Men, and the Olympians of ancient Greece or the Nor-dic Aesir. This is not to suggest a complete and direct correlation—as prod-ucts of popular culture, superheroes are commercial entities rather than sacred objects of worship, and they are not used as a lens through which we may understand natural or unexplained phenomena in consensus reality. Barthes' *Mythologies* uses the modern wrestler as an example of how iconic and symbolic performances may become a pantomime of mythical struc-tures without suggesting literal religious connotations:

> When the hero or the villain of the drama, the man who was seen a few min-utes earlier possessed by moral rage, magnified into a sort of metaphysical sign, leaves the wrestling hall, impassive, anonymous, carrying a small suitcase and arm-in-arm with his wife, no one can doubt that wrestling holds that power of transmutation which is common to the Spectacle and to Religious Worship. In the ring, and even in the depths of their voluntary ignominy, wrestlers remain gods because they are, for a few moments, the key which opens Nature, the pure gesture which separates Good from Evil, and unveils the form of a justice which is at last intelligible [Barthes, 35].

The application of human subjectivity to divine actants is, according to Edith Hamilton, one that largely originates in ancient Greece, as the Olym-pian Pantheon were viewed through an anthropomorphized perspective; rather than portray gods as beings beyond human comprehension, divine entities were frequently depicted as jealous, petty, spiteful and competitive, an echo of the people who worshipped them:

> The Greeks made their gods in their own image. That had not entered the mind of man before. Until then, gods had had no semblance of reality. They were unlike all living things. In Egypt, a towering colossus, immobile, beyond the power of the imagination to endow with movement, as fixed in the stone as the tremendous temple columns, a representation of the human shape deliberately

made unhuman. Or a rigid figure, a woman with a cat's head suggesting inflexible, inhuman cruelty. Or a monstrous mysterious sphinx, aloof from all that lives. In Mesopotamia, bas-reliefs of bestial shapes unlike any beast ever known, men with birds' heads and lions with bulls' heads and both with eagles' wings, creations of artists who were intent upon producing something never seen except in their own minds, the very consummation of unreality [Hamilton, 13].

This shift from abstraction and monstrosity towards humanized figures certainly appears to be upheld by conventional portrayals of superheroes. Fingeroth positions these beautiful men and women with innate (and, at times, distinctly elemental) abilities as successors to pre–American mythos: "Biblical and mythological heroes are clearly precursors of superheroes. Odysseus, Thor, Moses are individuals of courage, commitment and noble ideals, flawed though they may be as individuals. Somewhere in the evolution of the fictional hero, a subset of the heroic figure came to be possessed of *superhuman* qualities. It came to be understood that the hero was defined by *fearlessness*, as opposed to the ability to face and overcome fear" (Fingeroth, 16). The comparison is further strengthened by the static and enduring nature of the superhero and related generic conventions: "Like the gods of various pantheons, the superheroes do not change. Comics writers refer to their characters being allowed the 'illusion of change.' This is true of all serial characters, and may, strangely, be part of their appeal. We grow older, our friends and relatives grow older—even die, eventually— but the superheroes are always there. If they age at all, it's extraordinarily slowly" (Fingeroth, 34).

Of course, mythological narrative systems actively resist any possibility of an authoritative canon, a singular author, or a consistent chronotope. Classical icons such as Hercules, Achilles and Odysseus find themselves frequently reinterpreted and adjusted via eidetic variation to suit the purpose of whichever author has appropriated them—a process greatly aided by the lack of a definitive authorial presence (in contrast to literary characters such as Hester Prynn or Huckleberry Finn, who can be attributed to specific individuals). Superheroes are adaptively mutable in the same way: characters may die, return to life, or be de-aged; their abilities may change, then revert to the familiar; their origins may be revised to erase anachronisms. The pre-narrative history of Frank Castle, more commonly known as the Punisher, always includes a period of military service—however, over time the specific details of that service have shifted from Vietnam to Afghanistan, in order to maintain the character's perpetual age range. The ceaseless accumulation of narrative continuity and causality over decades of publication has, at times, required cosmological "maintenance" in the form of diegetic exercises designed to erase and doctor portions of that history:

Starting in April 1985, DC Comics published *Crisis on Infinite Earths*, a monthly 12 issue maxi-series that completely restructured the comic book publisher's fictional society. In the story, heroes from across multiple Earths and timelines band together to fight a villain, the Anti-Monitor, who threatens to destroy all of existence. The heroes eventually defeat the Anti-Monitor but not before an infinite number of living beings are not only destroyed, but many are erased from reality and deemed to have never existed. The end result is that history is altered and only one universe with one Earth survives. Heroes' backgrounds and origins are rewritten and DC's society is rebuilt completely anew [Johnson, 137].

By the genre's very nature, even such grand and sweeping gestures are themselves subject to the passing of time and the inevitable arrival of new readers and readers-turned-authors. The end result is a Textual Possible World (per Bell's terminology) that is in constant historical flux, exhibiting properties of postmodern fiction long before the term had even been codified.

The increase in superhero film adaptations since 2008 has also influenced the source texts and the current slate of implied authors. Marvel Studios' cinematic output over the past decade has focused on creating a series of interconnecting films all set in the same diegetic sphere; according to Liam Burke, the ontological structure of this Marvel Cinematic Universe is deliberately designed along genre lines: "compelled by the twin imperatives of fidelity and genre expectations, comic conventions have ridden the semiotic relay into cinema where they have gained wider use.... In his brief post-credit cameo in *Iron Man* (Favreau 2008), Samuel L. Jackson's Nick Fury heralded the arrival of the Marvel Cinematic Universe (MCU)— 'Mr. Stark, you've become part of a bigger universe. You just don't know it yet'" (Burke, 641). Burke attributes this innovative interlocking structure to the Internet permitting heightened communication between fans and creators, itself a factor in generating greater expectations of fidelity within the framework of adaptations. As of the time of writing, the MCU consists of over twenty films and a dozen television series, with more scheduled in the coming years; the conceit that all relevant works are set in the same shared ontological space, and that events in one may have direct consequences in another, is unprecedented in conventional media yet clearly derives from the existing template provided by the print precursor. That said, there is no question that the film series holds a place of primacy and priority within this transmedia array: "The two companies that drove the superhero revolution in pop culture are now huge commercial enterprises whose productions dominate summer movie screens. *The Avengers* (2012), based on a superhero team created in the Sixties for Marvel Comics, is the third-highest-grossing film of all time having taken $1.5 billion worldwide" (Robb, 15).

Consequently, it should come as no surprise that the comics have begun taking narrative cues (whether as "inspiration" or "instruction" is left for the reader to determine) from their adaptations. Characters who are well-received by film audiences are granted new titles, such as the popular monosyllabic Groot from 2014's *Guardians of the Galaxy*. In essence, the direction of influence has reversed itself—if at one time the source material served as the catalyst and blueprint for adaptation, highly-successful cinematic works now dictate new paradigms and conditions to which the original texts (under their current authors) must conform. Thus the nature of the superhero's fictional world has become even more permeable and subject to unpredictable shifts in content and context, aided in no small part by the appropriation of extant technology for the purpose of creating such shifts: "It took until the twenty-first century for digital effects to reach a stage where what had long played on the comic book page could truly be brought to the screen. Now, the biggest audiences for superheroes are in cinemas and on DVD, not reading the comics that first gave birth to them" (Robb, 15). Interactive bilateral processes are in full display: between author and fan, between fan and text, between source and adaptation. This is the baseline that webcomics will eventually be designed to comment upon, and in many cases, openly defy, bringing it into alignment with both the technologically dependent sphere of video games and the practice of counter-authorial reconfiguration extant in fan fiction.

Unstable Atopias and Chronologically Fluid Characters

Given that most superheroes have outlived their original milieu, their original readership, and in some cases even their original authors, it follows that the ontological structure depicted in these stories is highly atypical and almost impossible to replicate in other media. As previously discussed, initial publications by Marvel and DC in the 1940s and 1950s indicated that each title was set in a separate fictional world, with its own distinct chronotope and generic inclinations. Superman, for example, was more beholden to science-fictional adventures (as an alien visitor to Earth), whereas Batman's urban campaigns were more grounded and pseudo-realistic, and Wonder Woman's adventures connoted magic and fantasy. As the characters' popularity increased, both Marvel and DC began a protracted yet carefully calculated breakdown of these boundaries:

> Slowly, team-ups began: it was hard to resist uniting Superman and Batman. Similarly, a handful of stories in the past found it useful to feature alternative versions of Earth, but they were promptly forgotten once they'd served their

purpose. In the Sixties, as Marvel was successfully doing, DC attempted to unite not only its current roster of superhero comics and characters, but also all those of the past two decades into one coherent universe, even if the concept of a multiverse had to be invoked to shoehorn in Golden Age characters [Robb, 200–201].

By the late 1960s, any pretense of separation was set aside. Metropolis and Gotham, once thought to exist in entirely separate worlds, became sister-cities, their opposing architectural designs and embedded themes now serving as a source of explicit contrast for their heroic residents. William Uricchio claims that the various urban settings were themselves as subject to reinvention as their inhabitants:

> Like the character of the Batman himself, the representation of the city undulated throughout its long history, reflecting the concerns of the day: depression and urban decay; war and the need to look beyond urban conditions in the interests of fighting a larger enemy; the postwar era with its reorientation to civilian and above all family life; the uncertainties of the 1960s and 1970s manifest in the counterculture, the camp and beyond; the gritty 1980s marked by media representations of urban crime, governmental corruption; and the steady slide into darker, more obsessive concerns that have continued to the present [Uricchio, 122].

But the fluidity of the fictional landscape extends far beyond the reflexivity detailed previously. The merging of disparate settings into a theoretically cohesive whole also meant that any generic distinctions were subsumed into a larger universe: by the 1970s, Marvel's New York was populated by mutants (the X-Men), sorcerers (Doctor Strange), super-spies (Black Widow), urban vigilantes (Daredevil, Punisher), mythological figures (Thor, Hercules), science adventurers (the Fantastic Four), and cautionary tales drawn from the most foundational tropes of science fiction (the Hulk).

The resulting chronotope is a pan-generic nexus theoretically capable of sustaining any and all literary tropes simultaneously, with no innate contradiction in terminology or ontology. Heroes such as Iron Man, whose existence is predicated upon technology, may interact with entities mystical and divine, as friend or foe; the adventures of the X-Men have, at times, pitted them against demon sorceresses, time travelers, vampires, clones, aliens drawn from classic space operas, and so on. These generically intersectional spaces are then further informed by generations of readers-turned-authors updating embedded value systems to reflect contemporary concerns, per Arno Meteling's inspection of specifically coded cities depicted in comics:

> The superhero comic book shows two distinct strategies in dealing with political subjects and the strange confrontation between the archetypical and mythical character of the superhero and the modern urban setting. The first strategy

is the self-referential and esoteric worldbuilding of the DC Universe with its fictional cities, paradigmatically executed by *Starman* and thereby creating a mythologically coherent fantasy world. The second strategy is to implement extradiegetic political problems and to deal with them through the work of a superhero, as is done in *Ex Machina*. But these strategies are not mutually exclusive [Meteling, 145–146].

Over time, these ontological megastructures came to be referred to as fictional universes, an order of magnitude significantly larger than standard storyworlds: "Close links are established between characters and groups of characters. With enough team-ups (and there have been plenty) links are established between all the costumed characters published by a particular company. This intertextuality, forming in total the 'Marvel Universe' and 'DC Universe,' is the feature of superhero comics that most often surprises those who are not regular readers" (Reynolds, 38).

Taken in conjunction with the need for maintaining a nominal sense of continuity, causality and history, these overlapping factors may explain later contortions and convolutions of these diegetic spaces. DC and Marvel were not simply managing singular ontological systems; as Robb explains, stories that could not be encapsulated within the paradoxically permissive and constrained framework were relegated to alternate timelines and parallel dimensions (similar in narrative function and format to the AU genre of fan fiction). For Marvel, these were typically self-contained, self-nullifying storylines, as featured in their 1977–1998 title *What If?*, which took as its premise the conventional approach of glimpses into an infinite number of alternate universes, where familiar events took different turns, more often than not setting in motion destructive chains of events that could not be permitted to play out in the main setting. By contrast, DC attempted to contain the inevitable authorial clashes and contradictions by establishing the larger framework of the Multiverse, an array of co-existing parallel Earths which could hypothetically sustain any internal inconsistencies caused by the passing of time and creator turnover. Thus, where Marvel explicitly applied canonical authority on a selective basis, rendering AU divergences explicitly non-canonical and purely speculative/extrapolative, DC proposed that all stories that were or would be told could then be integrated into the megastructure of the Multiverse. Insofar as the reader was concerned, these events were all "real" and taking place "somewhere":

> By 1985, DC Comics had built up a fifty-year rich continuity that was complicated and convoluted. Across comics and characters continuity problems abounded, with many characters having multiple, often inconsistent, backstories or origins that had been retooled, embellished, re-imagined, and reconceptualized by a variety of creators, writers, editors, and artists. With a now well-established and vocal fandom collecting comics and offering feedback to

publishers, it became apparent there was an audience newly concerned about such things. Attempts to write around some of these problems resulted in the DC Multiverse, which allowed for variants of Earth within the DC Universe so conflicting versions of characters could exist independently of each other (and meet in crossover stories) [Robb, 253–254].

By the 1980s, the pressure of sustaining such a massive and complex constellation of fictional worlds became untenable for DC's writers and editors, prompting the aforementioned *Crisis on Infinite Earths*. As of the time of writing, both the Marvel and DC Universes have been "purged" of past continuity several times over, only to immediately begin accumulating history and multitudes of implied authors again. The end result of this cyclical process is a pair of settings which call for "ontological archaeology," in which the worlds themselves are built upon the remains of previous incarnations and inscribed with disparate fragments of long and storied pasts.

To fully grasp the significance of this configuration, both as an inherently postmodern construct and as the paradigm against which webcomics arose in response, the chronotope must be unpacked into its composite parts: time and space. According to Reynolds, situating individual story events in a causal or historical timeline is complicated by the amorphous nature of chronology in these story-universes: "New canonical texts are being added every month. Any definitive metatextual resolution is therefore definitely postponed. That is to say, the DC or Marvel universe is not finally defined until some future date when superhero texts cease to be published. In the meantime, new texts must be made sense of within continuity, or discarded as non-canonical" (Reynolds, 41). One consequence of continuous publication is an irreconcilable difference between diegetic and extradiegetic time: a single night in-story could span six months, and a year can be covered in a two-page montage. Revisions can selectively erase specific events or entire blocks of narrative history. This achronic, non-linear representation of temporality problematizes the concept of extrapolation—in effect, the superhero macro-narrative consists of beginnings followed by endless middle points. Endings are temporary, as a new adventure will invariably begin the following month and extend the timeline further; similarly, death is impermanent, subject to a given character's popularity and the fiat of successive authors.

Where other features of the genre align with mythological precedents, this use of repetitious cyclicality is a stark contrast to tales of the Trojan War or of Hercules, all of which derive meaning in part from their conclusions. Even those mythos which posit a scenario for the end of time—be it the Nordic Ragnarok, the Babylonian epic of Gilgamesh (in which the tale of Utnapishtim explicitly acknowledges the destruction of a previous world), or the New Testament's Book of Revelation—frame the apocalypse as a sequence of events triggered and sustained by causality. Any such sense of finality is completely absent from the superhero world, as "superheroes as metaphors and icons are here to stay. They are part of the DNA of our culture. The superhero will be around for as long as stories are told. Whether these stories will be told in comics, in films, on TV, on computer screens, or via some form of media that hasn't been invented, is the only uncertainty" (Fingeroth, 171). Individual plots and subplots may find resolution over months or years, but for all practical intents and purposes these constitute events in the endless "second act"; there is no final climax or denouement for these characters or the worlds they inhabit. And while the prominence and visibility of a particular character is dependent upon their popularity (itself determined by corresponding socio-cultural values at any given point in history), even obscure characters may return after decades-long absences: since the 1960s, Captain America's sidekick Bucky Barnes had been defined entirely by his death and absence from the protagonist's life, having been "killed off" at the end of World War II. The character returned in 2005 as the Winter Soldier and has been an active participant in ongoing stories and a deuteragonist in film adaptations since. This retroactively transforms the significant span of time in which the character was "dead" into a hiatus, rather than a permanent conclusion to his story arc.

Consequently, the actants of superhero narratives are situated in a paradoxical temporality, depicted by Meteling as a singularly unique cognitive challenge: "How do superhero comic books cope with the asymmetric clash of different historical epochs and what asynchronicities ensue when the anachronistic, mythical, and literally 'timeless' concept of a superhero confronts a recognizably modern and especially urban situation?" (Meteling, 135). On the one hand, superheroes are simultaneously present in all times—diegetically, the narrative of Superman constitutes one unbroken chain of events that spans the length of the character's existence, from 1938 to the present day, even as entire generations of creators and readers have come and gone in the interim. Superheroes have been present for every major event in American history after World War II: the Civil Rights movement, the Cuban Missile Crisis, the Vietnam War, Watergate, the Gulf War, the September 11 attacks, and so on. On the other hand, these characters can also be viewed as existing in "no-time," temporal stasis produced by the serial nature of the medium. For the most part, the lives of these fictional characters cannot be tied to any particular historical period, as the passing of extradiegetic time distances the diegetic world from integrated "present-day" events (barring specific examples such as Captain America and X-Men antagonist Magneto, both of whom have been given unique rationales for their innate ties to World War II as it fades further and further into our past). What emerges is a "drifting" timeline in which past, present and future are not fixed points in a stable chronology, but a fluid and porous system constantly adapting itself to its readers' contemporary reality. Increasingly distant historical correlations are excised from canon, either dismissed altogether or quietly revised. Reynolds indicates that these "updates" have become so utterly normalized as to produce a genre convention in itself: "The time that has passed since 1964 has been telescoped into continuity, which is openly non-historical and doesn't move forward at any set pace.... Clearly, intertextual and metatextual continuity create a subsidiary world in which the process of time can be kept under control. While this process does not exactly abolish history from superhero comics, it does divorce the superheroes' lives from their historical context" (Reynolds, 44).

As the chronotope is jointly informed by depictions of both time and space, the atemporality of superhero narratives directly correlates to its diegetic spatiality. As previously established, the fictional universes of Marvel and DC have become generic nexuses, junction points in which all categories and conventions of literature may manifest simultaneously, without producing internal logical inconsistencies. For example, the existence of both science and magic as parallel non-oppositional forces inform given characters' views of the universe, whether said universe is a simulacrum of our own (as Marvel's purports to be) or a fictionalized system of metaphorical constructs (Metropolis and Gotham as daytime/nighttime mirrors of New York, Star City replacing Boston and so on). That the city lies at the core of the genre is not coincidental: the pluralism and multiplicity inherent in modern urban space makes said space an ideal foundation for elastic storyworlds, as Elana Gomel details: "The microcosm of atopia is the global city, the postmodern metropolis where the extreme deformation of the social spacetime has gone so far as to generate the imaginary collapse of all distinctions into one impossible distorted continuum" (Gomel, 21). Thus the Marvel and DC universes, defined as they are in part by unstable chronology, are spatially deformed as well, both in the local sense of urban spaces layered with landmarks sourced in different (and at times diametrically opposing) genres, and in the macrocosm of multiple Earths and alternate timelines, all presented simultaneously to the reader, with ontological violations often occurring as narrative events. These spaces are an apt demonstration of what Gomel calls flickering topology: "In flickering, two or more epistemic frameworks are superimposed upon a single textual space, resulting in ontological indecipherability.... Flickering is about being lost in a world that seems willing to accommodate itself to any system of belief" (Gomel, 62).

Gotham City, the home of Batman, serves as an apt example of what effects a sustained flickering topology may have on narrative structures over an extended period of time. Uricchio's analysis of Gotham as a fictional urban space sheds significant light on the city's role as a spatial setting for superhero stories:

> And so to the question: What is Gotham City? Beyond trademarked property, narrative generator, and ideological conceit, it is an accumulation of narrative and graphic acts. We know Gotham through the actions of its inhabitants, and thus we know it not as an objective space, but as a highly selective and ever shifting accretion of parts, of encounters between characters, favorite episodes, rendering styles, even perspectives. Those few maps of Gotham that exist, attempting to define, fix, and represent a fictional entity from an objectivist perspective, are from this view absurd, unless positioned within the tight semiotic frame of a particular story [Uricchio, 130].

As with the "sliding" timeline defined largely by fluidity, the spatiality of the superhero chronotope is not (and cannot be) set in stone. Streets, blocks, alleys, skyscrapers—these shift and change with the same slow, understated frequency as the temporal position of the characters. The architecture of Gotham City, serving as both backdrop and foil for Batman himself, is subject to artistic reinterpretation, both in the source texts and in film adaptations: the 1989 and 1991 films *Batman* and *Batman Returns*, directed by Tim Burton, correspond to Burton's neo-Gothic sensibilities and contain a collection of darkly tinted, highly vertical and imposing shapes. By contrast, Joel Schumaker's *Batman Forever* (1995) and *Batman and Robin* (1997) replace this landscape with bright neon lights and bombastic statues, heralding the arrival of a new implied author for the cinematic approach. The ease with which Gotham changes to suit new extradiegetic developments demonstrates the inherent instability of the chronotope's spatial component: "Gotham City stands as an aggregation of the ever-changing events depicted on its rooftops, alleys and streets rather than as a stable and coherent street grid. It stands as an enacted space, a space whose identity and meanings are bound up in the dynamic logics of performance rather than the fixed terrain of material artifact" (Uricchio, 131).

Such spaces are impossible by definition, and unlikely in the context of other literary works—even imaginary urban hubs of paranormal activity such as Stephen King's Derry (*It*, *Insomnia*) or Joss Whedon's Sunnydale (*Buffy the Vampire Slayer*) are typically defined by fixed canonical landmarks which do not vary over time. By contrast, the continuing evolution of the Marvel and DC universes as organic, reactive constructs is perhaps most clearly evident in the textual response to the 2001 destruction of the World Trade Center. This extradiegetic event was depicted by both publishers, despite the diegetic presence of characters such as Superman or the Fantastic Four who could have—by the internal logic of the genre—prevented such an event. Both the attack and its impact on American society were translated intact; in some cases, the subsequent "War on

Terror" led to further revisions of existing characters, per David Roach's then-contemporary description of Captain America: "Cap's current incarnation, which again unerringly taps into the zeitgeist, sees the character reinvented as a four-color foot soldier in the fight against terrorism—albeit one facing serious moral quandaries—which only goes to show his longevity as a symbol of America itself" (Roach, 114). The Twin Towers were, and continue to be, absent from any subsequent artistic representation of New York.

Viewed in unison, the spatial and temporal configurations of the superhero narrative produce a chronotope that is not only impossible but atopian, per Gomel's description:

> The ultimate impossible space is the one which annihilates both temporality and spatiality. The physical incarnation of such a space is the black hole, or more precisely, the singularity at the heart of it. The human mind cannot actually imagine a black hole (though it is perfectly describable through the language of mathematics). But narrative can and does create fictional simulacra of the simultaneity that destroys linear time and homogenous space. The "death of history" is projected upon impossible spaces, in which distance and difference are abolished, and past and present coexist [Gomel, 37].

When applied to Bakhtin's arguments relating to the primacy of the chronotope, it is clear that the atopian atemporality of the superhero genre produces characters as unstable as the worlds they inhabit. E.M. Forster notes that one of the most basic traits of all literary actants is that "they are easily remembered by the reader afterwards. They remain in his mind as unalterable for the reason that they were not changed by circumstances; they moved through circumstances, which gives them in retrospect a comforting quality, and preserves them when the book that produced them might decay" (Forster, 36). In this, Foster is specifically referencing the notion that characters are "locked" in the mind of the reader as products of specific times and places: Ebenezer Scrooge, Anna Karenina, and even mythical figures lacking a central canon such as King Arthur are all powerfully associated with their respective chronotopes. As previously discussed, this is not possible with superheroes—as the storyworlds shift to accommodate historical, technological and social changes, their actants are similarly subject to whatever revision the current author (and the current culture) requires:

> So somehow, the superhero—more than even the ordinary fictional hero—has to represent the values of the society that produces him. That means that what, say, Superman symbolizes changes over time. In the 1950s, he may have been hunting commies. In the 1970s, he may have been clearing a framed peace activist against a corrupt judicial system. Either way—the hero does the right thing. Perhaps more importantly, *he knows what the right thing is* [Fingeroth, 17].

While Fingeroth focuses on Superman as an example of the superhero's transient nature, a more useful example of explicit, textual transformation motivated entirely by extradiegetic considerations would be the aforementioned Captain America—a character conceived, designed, and written from his earliest incarnation to represent what his creators deemed to be quintessential American values: "[Joe] Simon was clear that Captain America was a nakedly political creation: he wanted to reflect his own repulsion at the Nazi regime. He felt the anti-war movement was well organized, but those in favour of American involvement didn't have a platform. Captain America was his answer" (Robb, 112). While the character indeed served both textually and extradiegetically as a source of pro–American propaganda during World War II, David Walton's summary of the 1973 "Secret Empire" storyline reveals a drastically different use of a character who is nominally meant to be read as the same individual:

> Captain America's existential crisis came to a head when [Steve] Englehart transformed one of Marvel's clichéd, subversive organizations into a metaphor for government transparency, and recast its "Secret Empire" as the invisible merger of private, corporate and political interests.... Captain America discovered the Empire's reach extended as far as it had when he pursued their leader, Number One, from the White House lawn into the office of the President. There, an implied Richard Nixon unmasked off-panel, before committing suicide [Walton, 164].

In a clear example of authorial response to current events shaping a fictional narrative, Englehart's decision to incorporate the Watergate scandal into the Marvel Universe changed the most fundamental assumptions regarding Captain America's iconography: a character whose visual design, storyline and personality were tailored to physically embody American patriotism instead became a vehicle for criticism. Following the fictional Nixon's suicide, the subsequent issue of the *Captain America* comic explicitly depicts a rejection of patriotism due to disillusionment with the American government: "At last, he feels he's found his destiny! Captain America lies behind him, buried in the rubble that is politics, 1974 … but a life as a new breed of hero—a hero free to be his own man—ah, that lies ahead … and Steve Rogers quickens his pace to reach it!" (Englehart et al., 1). Adopting a new uniform and a new identity—"Nomad, the Man without a Country"—the character's adventures continued, albeit now distanced considerably from the values expressed by the original implied author. Status quo was reasserted soon enough, but Steve Rogers' transition from Captain America to Nomad and back again conclusively demonstrates that the ability of writers like Englehart, who had grown up in a culture saturated with this mythos, were granted the power to assimilate real-world events within mere months of their occurrence and extrapolate their effects upon a fictional world straddling the boundary between mimesis and fantasy. The concept (much less the practice) of literary interactivity was decades away, yet here we have a precursor to the notion that readers of a given text could exert some form of authorial fiat over said text.

Another example of this fluidity and its effect on presumptions of ontological cohesion may be seen in *Uncanny X-Men*. Originally produced by Stan Lee and Jack Kirby, the Marvel series launched in 1963 and featured a band of mutant superheroes with extraordinary abilities. The year of 1975 saw the arrival of new writer Chris Claremont, who reconceptualized Lee's depictions of human/mutant conflict as a metaphor for racism. In addition to battling supervillains and aliens (as the genre often requires), Claremont's stories featured the X-Men struggling against prejudice which would often turn violent, clearly paralleling the African American struggle for civil rights during the same period. X-Men founder Charles Xavier, with his dream of peaceful co-existence, was explicitly likened to Martin Luther King, Jr., while his aggressive and militant adversary Magneto drew inevitable comparisons to Malcolm X. One scene published in the 1982 graphic novel *God Loves, Man Kills* depicted Jewish X-Men member Kitty Pryde in an altercation with a bigoted classmate; when her African-American teacher instructs her to shrug off the racial slurs, Kitty responds: "Suppose he'd called me a nigger-lover, Stevie?! Would you be so damn tolerant then?!" (Claremont/Anderson, 9).

As with Englehart and Captain America, contemporary politics were also playing a part in Claremont's revisions: Stan Lee's Magneto, created in 1963, was a flat stereotype of motiveless malignancy, obsessed with world domination for no particular reason. Claremont rewrote the villain as a Holocaust survivor, instantly adding pathos to the character's struggle against the perceived threat of a second genocide, per Nicholas Pumphrey's description:

> In the *Uncanny X-Men* #150, the reader gets the first glimpse of Claremont's new Magneto, when he decides that the world would be at peace if ruled by a mutant. Instead of destroying the Homo sapiens, he has now moved to a modus of peace through absolute rule. When Cyclops tells him of Jean Grey's death and states that Magneto could not understand his grief, Magneto harshly replies, "I know something of grief. Search throughout my homeland you will find none who bear my name. Mine was a large family and it was slaughtered—without mercy, without remorse. So speak not to me of grief, boy. You know not the *meaning* of the word" [Pumphrey, 97].

The association becomes explicit in a later monologue: "I remember my own childhood—the gas chambers at Auschwitz, the guards joking as they herded my family to their death. As our lives were nothing to them, so human lives became nothing to me" (Claremont/Cockrum, 37). Lois Gresh and Robert Weinberg put forth the argument that this revision was necessary to maintain long-term interest and investment in characters who, after a decade of continuous appearances, required more depth and explanation for new readers: "Smug, arrogant villains lose their appeal after a time. Just as the heroes in comics need to change, evolve, and develop fuller personalities, so do the villains. In Magneto's case, his past is an empty book, and for years nothing of his previous life before he attacked Cape Citadel was known" (Gresh/Weinberg, 101). Claremont's depiction of Magneto as a victim of human atrocity shifted the character's primary motivation—conquest for its own sake—towards the desire to create "a society where the minority mutant population of Earth can live in peace and not worry about being persecuted by the majority of ordinary humans. In pursuit of this noble dream, he's fought many battles against human foes, following the old adage that the end justifies the means" (Gresh/Weinberg, 111).

Following Claremont's departure from the series in 1991, few of his successors substantially deviated from established definitions of the characters and the mutants' particular corner of the Marvel Universe. This would change in 2001, when writer Grant Morrison used his *New X-Men* series to methodically distance the franchise from Claremont's implied author. The premise of the series was slightly revised to allow the X-Men an additional function, serving dual roles of superheroes and teachers to an entire school of mutant children:

> A new generation of mutants is emerging, that much is certain. They will be called freaks. Genetic monstrosities. They will be mocked, feared, spat upon and accused ... of stealing human jobs, eating human food, taking human partners ... but they are emerging in the inner cities, in the suburbs, in the deserts and in the jungles. And when they emerge, they will need teachers, people who can help them overcome their anger and show them how to use their strange gifts responsibly. They will need us [Morrison et al., 14].

This coincided with a shift in the series' central metaphor: rather than be equated with ethnicity, as Claremont had done, mutants were now more closely linked to homosexuality and LGBT persecution. In one of Morrison's issues, long-standing team member Hank "Beast" McCoy deliberately creates a scandal by falsely "coming out" to the world's media: "I might as well be [gay]! I've been taunted all my life for my individualistic looks and style of dress.... I've been hounded and called names in the street and I've risen above it.... I'm as gay as the next mutant! I make a great role model for alienated young men and women! Why not?" (Morrison et al, 13). Here we see another example of a diegetic shift designed to negate potentially outdated forms of thinking in the readership, while accommodating matters more directly relevant to contemporary concerns.

As before, however, it is Magneto who best represents emergent inter-authorial conflict in this particular franchise: twenty years after Claremont redesigned the character as a sympathetic Holocaust survivor, Morrison's version plays the role of a monstrous genocidal villain actively seeking the complete destruction of humanity. When his plan to force the people of Manhattan into crematoria is explicitly linked to Nazism, Magneto replies: "Nazis? Do I look like a failed artist with a neurotic grudge against his father and the world? I am a force of nature, boy. I am Magneto" (Morrison et al., 4). We see here the exact paradox that played out with Captain America during the Watergate scandal, a conflict that has no direct parallel in other forms of literature: Claremont's Magneto of 1981 and Morrison's Magneto of 2004 are both diegetically and extradiegetically the same fictional character, with the same name, identity and iconographic design. The implicit textual assumption is that these vastly differing interpretations are situated along a timeline that is linear, causal and coherent, as would be the case for any other actant in any other fictional world. Yet the values these authors express in relation to Magneto are practically irreconcilable and reflect the genre's inherent use of what Filiciak defines as fundamentally postmodern paradigms: "The postmodern lifestyle is featured by lack of cohesion; it is fragmented. The postmodern man's personality is not quite definite, its final form is never reached, and it can be manipulated" (Filiciak, 127). However, this fragmentation is not an *ex nihilo* phenomenon, but rather originates with the superhero genre's amorphous chronotope—in an atopian, achronic ontology, instability and impossibility become common components of the narrative rather than anomalies, and inform not only temporality and spatiality but the intrinsic strategies of characterization as well: "When the even flow of time is churned and broken by the rapids of a revolution, space becomes rebellious, its uniformity challenged by strange and exotic topologies. Impossible narrative spaces are generated when a revolution is projected from the temporal axis onto the spatial axis of the narrative" (Gomel, 25).

Consequently, there is no way to view the heroes, villains and supporting cast members of superhero fiction as flat or round in the conventional sense; rather, the genre's serialized longevity has enabled a state of perpetual recontextualization (per Jenkins' terminology). This reaffirms the embedded desire for reactive and interactive fiction, and the authorial agency they provide, as seen with the other narrative platforms explored herein: here we have fictional worlds relegated to a relatively inflexible print medium, which nevertheless promoted ongoing mimesis by incorporating current events and adapting itself to contemporary readers. Ryan's assertion that the collapse and subsequent fragmentation of the storyworld exhibits precisely the flexibility and mutability which produced fan fiction and video games (to explore possibilities of authorial agency) bears true: "In the second half of the twentieth century, a process of shrinking, fissuring, split-ting, and multiplying worlds within a larger textual universe reduced big worlds to little worlds or dismantled them into heterogeneous fragments. Their scattered remnants could no longer build a coherent imaginary space and time, but they provided the perfect material for play" (Ryan, 176).

The superhero genre and the ontological systems it supports continue to grow and change, constantly incorporating extradiegetic events into their fictional landscape as they occur: the week preceding Barack Obama's inauguration as President of the United States (January 2009) saw the pub-lication of a backup story in *Amazing Spider-Man* #583 in which the titu-lar hero foils a supervillain's attempt to impersonate Obama and thus usurp the Presidency; New York State's 2011 legalization of same-sex marriage was followed by the wedding of gay superhero Northstar in 2012; in late 2016, British occultist John Constantine flees New York City "when a racist, short-fingered, failed meat salesman began circling the White House" (Oli-ver/Moritat, 3). Examples of diegetic reactivity are exceedingly common-place, as are instances in which fans of superheroes, starting out as readers of the genre (most commonly at a young age), become authors invested with the ability to rewrite the storyworld and its inhabitants to serve as expressions of their own systems of values.

Ultimately, the Marvel and DC Universes exist outside the boundar-ies of any specific social, historical or cultural framework, and defy conven-tional models of pre-digital narrative paradigms. In fact, while superhero comics are not hypertextual per the definitions of Landow and Bell, they nevertheless share many properties associated with that form: a network of linked texts (multiple ongoing series in concurrent publication, frequently intersecting and crossing over with each other); the absence of a singular centralized authorial presence; porous ontologies with multiple nonhier-archical points of entry; and finally, a growing dependency on technology for dissemination and access. Ironically, this would be the configuration against which webcomics would eventually come to define themselves.

Webcomics as a Digital Reaction to Superhero Fiction

By the early 1990s, the superhero was deeply embedded in Amer-ican popular culture. Their fictional worlds had become intricate, deeply intertextual universes spread across multiple monthly titles, and popu-lated by hundreds of iconic characters. Generations of creative turnover had produced dozens of competing implied authors, manifesting in ret-roactive continuity, alternate timelines, cosmological revision and other phenomena which shifted the narrative form from an assumed cohesive whole to a fragmented and modular network of texts (which were, at times, in direct competition with each other). Finally, an increasing number of film and television adaptations further cemented the paradoxical nature of these characters as both iconic and ephemeral:

> There's been a Superman for every decade since the character was created, as there has been a variety of Batmen, Wonder Women, and Spider-Men. And the medium you remember that character in could vary by the era, too. Is the Superman you remember from the comic book? The TV series? The films? The radio show? There is no "Moses for the 1940s," no "John Henry for the 1950s," no "swinging sixties Gilgamesh." Yet, superheroes keep being reinvented.... But whatever the version, the Flash is fast, Aquaman rules the undersea world, the Martian Manhunter is still a space-alien detective [Fingeroth, 20].

This was—and continues to be—the dominant paradigm against which modern webcomics would come to define themselves. The rationale is identical to that attributed to the production of fan fiction:

> Because popular narratives often fail to satisfy, fans must struggle with them, to try to articulate to themselves and others unrealized possibilities within the original works. Because the texts continue to fascinate, fans cannot dismiss them from their attention but rather must try to find ways to salvage them for their interests. Far from syncopathic, fans actively assert their mastery over the mass-produced texts which provide the raw materials for their own cultural productions and the basis for their social interactions. In the process, fans cease to be simply an audience for popular texts; instead, they become active participants in the construction and circulation of textual meanings [Jenkins, 24].

Once again, the unprecedented size of the potential corpus makes a complete survey of webcomics unwieldy at best, impenetrable at worst. Any analytical approach must be limited in scope to a set of particular texts; thus the four webcomics discussed in this section—*Nimona*, *Narbonic*, *Something Positive*, and *SuperCakes*—are to be viewed as representing broader trends in the field, even as each work distinguishes itself from its contemporaries.

Critics such as Petersen and Booker have established a general timeline that points to the medium's technological origins, with Petersen explicitly linking the rise of the underground comic (which preceded webcomics as platforms for "alternative" genres and narratives) to the same categories of fan-production Jenkins defines as the precursor to online fan fiction:

> An important part of the allure of the new underground comic art was the way it emerged from a handful of homespun projects that inspired many people to try their hand at comics for the first time. Much of this revolution in self-publishing was attributable to the first photocopy machines by Xerox that became widely available in the early 1960s, allowing for substantially better

quality and less expensive printing in small quantities.... Photocopy machines encouraged a number of small-format comics and fan magazines, or zines, to go into larger and broader production [Petersen, 210].

This again reinforces the notion that technology is at the forefront of a shift in methodology and motivation for the production of reactive fiction. Booker concurs with Petersen's analysis, pointing to the parallel pace at which developments in the art form coincided with refinement of the tools themselves: "The early webcomics evolved along with technology. Basic illustration and small image sizes were initially common, mostly due to the length of time it took to download or display large images. These restrictions improved alongside bandwidth capabilities, and webcomics became a medium where experimentation was welcome" (Booker, 6618). The distinction reveals both the similarities and significant differences between webcomics and other digital platforms: as with fan fiction, the absence of any authorized supervision pertaining to uploaded content permits a vast proliferation of new techniques and sub-genres, and ensures a nonhierarchical system of access that places no particular work above any other. Likewise, reliance on the Internet as a space of publication invests webcomics with a sense of impermanence, as they may be completely deleted for any reason (such as the sale or shutdown of the website hosting the comic), at any time, with no physical remnant left to reconstruct and analyze. Once removed, these works are effectively rendered non-existent, and may never resurface.

Of further interest is webcomics' use of experimentation as an indirect channel for critique and deconstruction of existing narrative paradigms. Where the central mechanism of fan fiction takes as given the desire to supplant and reconfigure a source text's implied author, very few webcomics attempt to produce visual simulacra of existing content (as these would, by definition, be considered explicitly derivative works of fan fiction themselves). And where any experimentation and provision of agency in video games are inevitably limited by the inescapable framework of programming code, webcomics require only basic combinations of linguistic and coded iconic messages to transmit their content. The four webcomics discussed herein make broad use of the same tools and techniques as their print precursors, and share the same goal of demonstrating ways in which the medium provides alternative and inherently critical spaces to work against the aforementioned dominance of the superhero genre—a motivation Petersen attributes to the nature of the digital medium itself:

The growth of personal computers linked together by means of the Internet has, over the past two decades, instigated a vast systemic change in the way information and entertainment are created and distributed. The full impact of the digital media revolution on publishing in general and comics in particular has yet to fully materialize, but its contours are becoming more evident as the means of digital creation, distribution, and sales have become standardized and accepted as a viable alternative to print media [Petersen, 227].

Of the four primary texts selected for this analysis, Kat Leyh's *Super-Cakes* is both the shortest and the most directly related to the classic narrative components of the superhero genre detailed earlier. Structured as a series of short stories, *SuperCakes* depicts the lives of heroines May Ai (also known as Tank) and Molly Lamarck (also known as Shift). From the very first page of the first story, "Pancakes," it is clear that Leyh is positioning her characters and the fictional world they inhabit as contrasts to the Marvel and DC Universes: "Pancakes" begins with a scene revealing that May and Molly are romantically involved, a scenario uncommon enough in the mainstream that its presence here lends credence to an interpretation of implicit critique. This becomes more overt as the focus of "Pancakes" is not on the conventional battle between good and evil, but rather the domestic lives of these women: the bulk of the dialogue is centered on Molly's suggestion that they move in together, and the story concludes with Tank and Shift, in their superhero costumes, flying off to face an unspecified—and utterly insignificant—threat. The story serves as an initial mission statement for Leyh's implied author: if the iconic, mythological dimension of mainstream superheroes was attained through (and remains dependent upon) spectacular displays of violence, *SuperCakes* distinguishes itself by shifting the emphasis of focalization and representation to the characters' interiority. Mundane concerns replace the high stakes and interpersonal conflicts that elevated Superman, the X-Men and their like to such prevalent positions in popular culture: the third story, "Manifest," details May's first use of her enhanced strength, and in stark contrast to the hyperkinetic show of force one might expect in conventional superhero narratives, the event occurs during a sparring match with May's father, during which she inadvertently injures him. However, Leyh further defies mainstream tropes when May's father uses his own ability to transfer physical injuries to inanimate objects and instantly recover. The protagonist is therefore prevented from developing the sort of guilt complex which serves as the primary psychological motivator for Batman, Spider-Man and other well-known heroic figures.

This deliberate aversion to established strategies of characterization continues in the fourth story, "Welcome to the Family," which eschews any notion of superheroic activity at all. Framed as a slice-of-life sequence, the story depicts Molly's first encounter with May's extended family at a Thanksgiving dinner. While Molly is warmly welcomed as May's girlfriend, she chooses not to reveal her own superhuman nature; this changes when she encounters Ames, a human-bat hybrid child adopted by May's uncle and his husband. Ames' sister Talula then presents a new interpretation of a commonplace childhood incident, as momentary excitement triggers an "accident"—in this case, Talula transmutes her entire body to water and splashes onto the carpet. It becomes clear both to Molly and to the reader that most (if not all) of May's family have superhuman abilities, though only May chooses to fight crime. The sense of normalcy Leyh imposes upon these revelatory scenes further distances SuperCakes from the iconography it borrows, and sets the text in direct opposition to the common values of the superhero genre: rather than find acceptance within a group of like-minded individuals (a scenario which typically produces "super-teams" such as the Justice League of America or the Avengers), it is the Ai family's diverse array of powers juxtaposed with the Rockwell-esque imagery of a holiday dinner that reaffirms Molly's status as part of a larger community.

The final story, "Bad Weather," takes this affirmation a step further by providing—for the first and thus far only time—a glimpse into the larger world of Tank and Shift. In the midst of struggling against a giant ice monster terrorizing the city, the protagonists question whether the creature is magical or technological in nature. Though this is treated as a casual inquiry, it reveals that the webcomic's ontological structure is meant to superficially echo the generic nexuses of Marvel and DC: as in those settings, Tank and Shift must contend with threats both mystical and scientific. The comparison is further compounded when the heroes team up with Grey Greave, another member of their community who serves as an analogue to Marvel hero Iron Man (this version being a baseline human woman empowered by a suit of machine armor). Both Grey Greave's presence and her ancillary role in the lives of Tank and Shift suggest that she is merely one of many heroes populating the cities and world of SuperCakes; but as seen in the previous stories, the community which has been so central to the elevation of superheroes as a pseudo-pantheon in Western imagination is only inferred here, and deliberately kept out of focus.

Practically every creative choice Leyh makes throughout the course of SuperCakes displays, on the one hand, a clear awareness of genre tropes that can only be attributed to familiarity with the source material, while on the other hand exhibiting a subversive system of values designed to undercut or criticize those same foundational, essential aspects of the genre. The webcomic features a lesbian couple as its protagonists, invoking Jenkins' previous arguments that representation of same-sex relationship paradigms within "marginal" narratives is frequently an act of resisting dominant trends of heteronormativity—in this case, the lacuna being exploited is one that can be statistically quantified, as "most superheroes who have declared themselves gay tend to be obscure or little known" (Robb, 287). Similarly, the implied author's prioritization of domesticity and the personal lives of May and Molly stand in direct opposition to the cataclysmic, ever-escalating events which typically accompany the everyday lives of superheroes. *SuperCakes* also exhibits none of the spatial or temporal anomalies that have come to define the ontological megastructures of Marvel and DC: the chronotope is stable; all aspects of plot and character are linear, consistent, and informed by the voice and values of a singular authorial presence; the macrocosm of the fictional world is limited, finite and clearly defined; and—most significantly—the narrative has set beginning, middle and end points. Though Leyh's exclusive control of the site hosting her work allows her to extend the series at a whim, the standing conclusion precludes any possibility of inter-authorial conflict. Any statement *Super-Cakes* purports to make in relation to the mainstream superhero genre is not subject to malleability or erosion for the sake of adapting to changing social and/or cultural concerns.

At first glance, Noelle Stevenson's *Nimona* seems a step removed from this comparison. Unlike *SuperCakes'* direct appropriation of terminology and iconography in order to subvert genre conventions, *Nimona* appears to opt for science-fantasy hybridity, most clearly seen in the subsumed contradictions present in visual representations of the diegetic space: an urban city ruled by a king, defended by a knight in golden armor who answers to an Institute more akin to a modern corporation. It is a storyworld in which magic and technology do not co-exist as distinct yet equal ontological forces (as is the case in the Marvel and DC Universes, where each is invested in specific characters who share the same diegetic space), but are instead merged together into a cohesive whole, producing another example of impossible spatiality per Gomel's definition: "In a fantastic text the structure of the fictional world vacillates between two mutually exclusive states depending on the perceptions of the reader.... The fantastic is created by the epistemological ambiguity, experienced by the reader and (often but not always) the narrator and/or protagonist as well" (Gomel, 61–62). Despite these differences, the plot, characterization and setting of *Nimona* all demonstrate Stevenson's acute awareness of, and innate response to, the superhero genre and its tropes.

The first chapter begins with the titular character applying for a henchman's position with Ballister Blackheart, a red-caped, black-bearded scientist with a robotic arm. Every element of Blackheart's coded iconic image casts him in the familiar role of the supervillain, explicitly confirmed by Nimona herself: "But I'm a huge fan of your work. You're Ballister Blackheart, the biggest name in supervillainy! You're an inspiration!" (Stevenson, 2). The enthusiastic teen is hired by Blackheart when she reveals her shapeshifting ability, but genre expectations are immediately confounded in the second chapter, when Nimona modifies Blackheart's proposal to kidnap and ransom the king in a theatrical display of supervillainy: "We could do with some more general chaos. I'm talking fire everywhere. We'll murder the King in front of everyone. Then you crown yourself the new King. And since Sir Goldenloin is sure to try and stop us, I'll disguise myself to get close to him and take him out before he even knows what's happening" (Stevenson, 4). Blackheart rejects Nimona's plan, establishing the atypical contrast between them wherein the supposed "sidekick" is more bloodthirsty and violent than her employer. Indeed, Stevenson's implied author rejects conventional paradigms at every opportunity, while also indicating the characters themselves have at least a partial meta-awareness of the rules that govern the fictional world:

> NIMONA: And now they've got you locked into a system where you can't win! Doesn't that make you mad?
> BLACKHEART: It's not about winning. It's about proving a point.
> NIMONA: You don't need to prove a point. You need to destroy them.
> BLACKHEART: As I said, Nimona, I go by the rules. Not their rules. Mine [Stevenson, 6].

Blackheart's references to the systems and rules which determined the role he currently plays in the kingdom is, according to Wandtke, a product of postmodern sensibilities: "As the inseparable cultures of digital and postmodern theories have changed the way we think about the creator, text, and audience, the self-conscious aesthetics of superhero comic books have assumed a comfortable place in culture. With major architects of superhero comic book universes invested in the practices of new traditionality, the psychology of new traditional culture is even more fully presented and represented" (Wandtke, 219). This awareness affects both the reader's perception of Blackheart as the supposedly stereotypical master villain and the character's own internal struggle with an identity he does not fully embrace, a clear divergence from the traditional image of the cackling, overconfident mad scientist.

The plot continues with the introduction of the aforementioned Sir Goldenloin—again, as with Blackheart, the character's appearance is tailored after iconic representations of heroic individuals: long blonde hair, golden armor, square jaw, and so on. Goldenloin's repeated clashes with Blackheart and Nimona in the first half of the narrative seem to follow Fingeroth's assertion concerning the symbiotic nature of the relationship between hero and nemesis, and the reason these conflicts are so essential to the genre: "In confronting supervillains, therefore, superheroes enact our own inner and societal dialectics about issues of life and death. Again, the superheroes both reflect and are reflected by the world that produces them. They are very much the dream life—including the nightmares—of our society" (Fingeroth, 166). However, as the story continues to unfold, it becomes apparent that the stalemated status quo between "good" and "evil"—produced, in superhero fiction, by enforced temporal stasis—is here the indirect product of a past romantic relationship between Blackheart and Goldenloin, as revealed to the reader by Goldenloin's supervisor: "Really, Goldenloin, do you fancy yourself sly? Your motivations are quite transparent. I know what the nature of your relationship was. I made it clear at the time that I disapproved" (Stevenson, 124). As with Tank and Shift in *Super-Cakes*, the use of a same-sex relationship achieves the same subversive effect by providing an alternate cause for the genre-required artificially-induced détente: where Batman and the Joker remain in eternal conflict because their stories continue to be published (a clear example of extradiegetic considerations dictating basic diegetic causality), the status quo Nimona seeks to disrupt is one sustained by the characters' shared pre-narrative history, a purely diegetic factor. Just as Leyh focuses on domesticity in place of violence, Stevenson's rooting of the conflict in a schism between former lovers deflates the mythical dimension of the superhero formula that otherwise informs much of the textual and visual elements of *Nimona*.

This also distorts said formula's traditional moral binary, as the titular protagonist and her employer are visually and textually coded as "evil" while the story's antagonist is coded as "good." Per Jenkins' established categories of fan fiction, Stevenson's depiction of these characters falls under the heading of moral realignment:

Perhaps the most extreme form of refocalization, some fan stories invert or question the moral universe of the primary text, taking the villains and transforming them into the protagonists of their own narratives. Characters like Servalan, Paracelsus, the Master, Darth Vader, and the Sheriff of Nottingham are such compelling figures that fans want to explore what the fictional world might look like from their vantage point; such tales blur the original narrative's more rigid boundaries between good and evil [Jenkins, 171].

While the deliberate inversion seems embedded in the very premise of the narrative—focalizing as it does through a nominal supervillain and his henchwoman—the implied author invests the work with an intentional sense of ambiguity, as seen in chapter 9 when Blackheart addresses the people of the kingdom and reveals what he claims are his true motivations:

My name is Ballister Blackheart, but I'm sure you know that already. You may think of me as your enemy, but I have only ever fought against the Institution, not against you. Your true enemies are the ones who have beaten you down and kept you in compliance through fear. They took your children and raised them as soldiers. They mongered war at the expense of their people. They've locked us into a system where they hold all the power. In return, they promised you safety, but they've broken that promise. In their quest for war, they've endangered the very people they swore to protect. They took away your power. It's time to take it back [Stevenson, 135].

In addition to its postmodern subversion of conventional moral binaries, *Nimona* also takes steps to complicate the standardized formula of "the origin story," another longtime staple of both the superhero genre and its mythological precursors. Like Hercules, Achilles and their classical peers, the modern superhero's pre-history is typically presented to the reader as the initial step of the Hero's Journey, detailing their personal motivations and the various sources of their superhuman abilities. In chapter 4 of *Nimona*, Blackheart asks his assistant how she acquired her talent for changing shape, to which she replies: "Aw man, do I HAVE to do the backstory thing? It's kind of a downer. 'Course, I bet you love downer stories, don't you?" (Stevenson, 24). Nimona then proceeds to tell her employer that, as a child, she encountered a witch trapped in a deep hole; to facilitate her rescue, the old woman transformed Nimona into a dragon, but neglected to reveal how to return to her original form. Forced to retreat to the woods, Nimona eventually mastered her gift and wandered the forest in a multitude of animal guises. Though initially skeptical, Blackheart is satisfied with this account until a later discussion reveals Nimona's deception: "You made it up.... You forgot your own backstory, Nimona. It wasn't TRUE. I took it for granted that this was your natural form. But it's not, is it?" (Stevenson, 169–170). In the course of the narrative, Stevenson presents not one but four possible backstories for the character, each more outlandish than the last, none of which are ever verified. The deliberate ambiguity serves to defamiliarize both Nimona herself (by retroactively revealing her to be an unreliable narrator of her own history) and the function she is meant to perform, that of the loyal sidekick. By the end of the story, Stevenson's implied author has forced an inversion of the characters' prescribed roles: Blackheart is hailed as a hero, Nimona is revealed to be a terrifying beast, and Goldenloin is rendered a powerless victim of the world that attempted to enforce genre-defined identities on all three lead actants.

Stevenson's work defines itself in stark opposition to the long-running tropes of superhero fiction, and in doing so provides response and commentary to said tropes within the diegetic space itself. At the time of writing, *Nimona* has also been distributed in print form by established publisher HarperCollins—however, this transmedia shift does not undermine the narrative's oppositional nature, as its resistance to the established norms of mainstream comics remains deeply embedded in its plot structures, themes, and values expressed by the implied author. This proves Ciccoricco's claim that cybertexts (such as webcomics) do not necessarily forfeit their innovative or subversive qualities when translated into non-digital media: "Cybertext creates a template based on textual function that takes precedence over how these functions manifest in particular media. The medium, in this sense, is 'immaterial,' and the way to read a hypertext document may in theory be identical to the way one reads a text in print if their typological functions are the same" (Ciccoricco, 24).

Shaenon Garrity's *Narbonic* evinces a similar dynamic to *Nimona*, as another webcomic which distances itself from the superhero genre even as it enacts a dialogue with those same generic tropes. Broadly categorized as science-fiction comedy, *Narbonic* begins with the introduction of Dave Prescott, a computer science major hired as a lab assistant by mad (if genial) scientist Dr. Helen Narbon. As the main focalizer, Dave is positioned as an outsider to the genre he has stumbled into and is frequently the target of Dr. Narbon's experiments—over the course of the series he is transformed into a zombie, a woman, a digitized intelligence; he becomes unstuck in time, cloned, sent to Hell, and physically altered into a doppelganger of Helen's rival Professor Lupin Madblood. However, just as the status quo of the quasi-mythical superhero always reasserts itself over time, Dave inevitably appears to return to his original state in time for the next misadventure. Despite initial appearances, it becomes apparent as the series progresses that Garrity has eschewed the cyclical, achronic narrative structure in favor of a linear and stable time/space configuration: each subplot affects the next, culminating in a sequence which reveals Dave's own latent supervillainy—a development which recasts Helen's previous manipulations as one ongoing experiment in the creation (and potential prevention) of another "mad genius." This is only possible due to the narrative's finite nature, which allows for the creation and maintenance of a causal chain that builds towards a set conclusion. The sequential nature of Narbon's experiment also ensures that each storyline in *Narbonic* features tropes common to superhero adventures—raiding a moonbase, infiltrating a secret facility, rescuing abducted Nobel Prize laureates from a floating island, and many more. At the same time, the repetition of familiar premises and sequences is complicated by the same moral realignment used in *Nimona*: characters coded as traditional villains (in this case, the mad scientist and her minions) are resituated in the roles of protagonist and deuteragonists, creating a powerful sense of cognitive estrangement by reversing the meaning of recognizable iconography.

Where Stevenson's experimentation and commentary in *Nimona* exists wholly on the diegetic level, Garrity's use of the Internet as her medium of publication permits a level of experimentation beyond the strict confines of the storyworld. At its original site (the webcomic has changed locations at least once, again proving the ephemeral and transitory nature of the digital text), the name of the file containing the comic strip for November 12, 2002, had a word appended to it. From that point through to the conclusion of the comic in December 2006, Garrity layered an entire self-contained narrative in the filenames of the strips, one to three words at a time. This text represents a diegetic event not depicted in the core series, in which Helen is informed of her mother's violent demise and suffers a psychotic break which sets her on the path to becoming a mad scientist. For all practical intents and purposes, the sequence constitutes Helen's origin story, a crucial piece of pre-narrative history that is only revealed to users savvy enough to inspect not the panels themselves, or the text and art contained within, but the names of the JPEG and GIF files (which are not normally visible when browsing websites). This further substantiates Gomel's position that "as the chronotope of embedding develops through the twentieth century, writers begin to join it to other narrative techniques. As its narrative sophistication increases, embedding becomes increasingly used for metafictional purposes: figuring the process of constructing the storyworld" (Gomel, 102). For Kukkonen, the additional layer of storytelling constitutes a metaleptic effect intrinsically tied to pre-digital practices and conventions in mainstream comics:

> Metalepsis draws readers' attention to the representation conventions of comics and thereby foregrounds the traces of the real world in a work of fiction. As characters cross the panel frames, they leave the fictional world. As characters interact with drawing styles, paratextual elements and the physical nature of the comics pages, they perform a writerly or a readerly function. Such metaleptic foregrounding has been current in English language comics since the beginning of the twentieth century. It is not necessarily at odds with the popular culture status of comics. In fact, it ties in well with genres like the superhero comics with their fantastic fictional worlds and outlandish battles [Kukkonen, 229].

Helen's origin story is not the only experimental feature in *Narbonic* which is unique to the medium: at the conclusion of every calendar year during the webcomic's publication (from 2000 to 2006), a "Dave in Slumberland" sequence would be published in a notably different art style, based on Winsor McCay's *Little Nemo in Slumberland*. Though framed as glimpses into Dave's nonsensical dreams, each of these annual strips would contain subtle hints and foreshadowing for the following year's storylines. Most significantly, these would frequently break the established four-panel horizontal format of the ongoing series, making use of what Scott McCloud termed the "infinite canvas," which "advocated for an eventual shift away from the basic orientation of a comic on a page and offered innovative possibilities new comics could explore" (Petersen, 234). In *Narbonic*, this is represented by extremely long or asymmetrical vertical narratives, requiring the reader to scroll down through the page in order to continue reading. This feature, used to dramatic effect in the final "Dave in Slumberland" episode to simulate a character falling from a great height, can only be experienced online, as digital space is devoid of the strict requirements and limitations of the print medium:

> It is traveled by jumps and seemingly instantaneous transportation (known as teleporting) rather than being traversed point by point like Cartesian space. It is not finite, but infinitely expandable: claiming a territory as one's own (for instance, by creating a home page on the Net) does not diminish the amount of cyberspace available to others. Being non-physical, it is equidistant from all points in the physical world.... Since it expands and changes continually, it cannot be mapped [Ryan, 86].

The development and deployment of such innovative storytelling techniques further demonstrates the permissiveness of online space vis-à-vis narrative experimentation. Unburdened by clear editorial mandates or supervision, the Internet allows individual authors to push back against any boundary, real or perceived, and produce literary phenomena unique to digital space. Additionally, the deliberate deployment of counter-tropes, underrepresented perspectives and meta-generic awareness can be read as a shared commonality with *SuperCakes* and *Nimona*—as with those texts, the narrative structure of *Narbonic* displays an explicit awareness of dominant paradigms in mainstream print comics (specifically, the ubiquitous superhero genre) while taking full advantage of every possible opportunity to resist those paradigms. As the tools continue to advance, and "many of the former criticisms of the medium (bandwidth issues and technology gaps) have been overcome" (Booker, 6630), even Garrity's metaleptic techniques may become outdated, with new permutations soon to take their place.

While the three aforementioned texts are disparate in both their narrative configuration and the specific criticisms they levy against the superhero genre, all three are nevertheless situated within the mode of writing frequently referred to as "the fantastic," and may therefore share some formulaic commonalities with the subject of their subversive approach. By contrast, R.K. Milholland's *Something Positive* distances itself almost entirely from science-fictional or supernatural elements within its diegesis. A slice-of-life comedy series, *Something Positive* consists of episodes from the lives of Davan MacIntire and his close circle of friends as they navigate domestic issues, financial concerns, local scandals and ennui. Of the four webcomics examined herein, Milholland's text would seem to be furthest from any possibility of dialogue with the iconography and traditions of the superhero; but Davan and many of the supporting cast members define themselves as fans of the genre, frequently commenting on current pop culture events in general and mainstream comics in particular.

While critique of superhero fiction initially remained in the form of idle conversation between characters, the May 2011 storyline "Heroic"

and its subsequent repercussions implement a far more direct incorporation—and subversion—of coded iconic and linguistic features taken from
mainstream comics. "Heroic" features Mike, a character introduced in the
series' formative years as an antagonistic embodiment of the worst stereo-
types associated with pop culture fandom: abrasive, misogynistic, pedan-
tic and deeply anti-social. Initially serving as comic relief, the later years of
Something Positive saw Milholland craft a moderately successful redemp-
tion storyline for the character, as he matured, reunited with his estranged
girlfriend and raised a child with her. Though not completely free of his
existing personality flaws, by 2011 Mike had reached a relatively stable point
in his life. A complication arises when, in a casual meeting with Davan's
friend Aubrey, Mike witnesses a costumed individual escorting an elderly
woman across the street. Aubrey explains: "That's Captain Feelsafe. He
dresses like a superhero and goes around making sure the elderly are okay. I
guess there's this movement now of people who wanna be real superheroes.
They have websites and clubs and all that crap. Guys like him aren't so bad.
He's helpin' out and calling attention to a need" (Milholland, May 24, 2011).
In this, Milholland is "re-fictionalizing" a phenomenon that exists in reality today: since the mid–2000s, individuals across the globe have adopted
costumed identities for the purposes of community service and activ-
ism—documented examples include the United Kingdom's Shadow, Italy's
Entomo the Insect-Man, Australia's duo The Fauna Fighters and more (naturally, there is a significantly higher number of such individuals active in
the United States). Milholland's note at the end of this introductory comic
strip is "These people … they are real" (Milholland, May 24, 2011).

Mike, having idolized superheroes his entire life, wastes no time in
constructing his own heroic alter ego, creating (and immediately subverting) a scenario in which fictional characters such as Batman have inspired
"real-life superheroes" such as Mr. Xtreme and Geist, who are in turn
retranslated back into the fictional world of *Something Positive* as templates
to inspire Mike's transformation. As with any superhero story, the first step
establishes the character's primary motivation: "I want to be a superhero. A
real one. I think I could do a lotta good" (Milholland, May 31, 2011). At the
same time, the implied author maintains the strict separation of diegetic
and hypodiegetic spheres: "If I may have a moment of self awareness, I am
the last person to tell people to keep their tempers in check. How do I jus-
tify that with my past actions? … I'm a real person, not an imaginary alien.
I want to do good and not end up in an asylum" (Milholland, June 6, 2011).

The story of Mike and his alter ego, the Pythagorean, serves a dual
purpose for the text's implied author: as a realistic storyworld, there are no
fantastic elements playing into this narrative, thus placing hard limits on
what Mike can actually achieve. There can be no expectation of spectacular

violence or mythical adventures, reducing the iconic superhero to a (fictional) flesh-and-blood individual. At the same time, Mike is deeply aware of the reality in which he is situated—as befits a character in a postmodern comic, per Wandtke—and explains his goals in such a way that his depiction remains essentially heroic nonetheless:

> A lot of people are just angry or depressed or just really unhappy. Maybe they need someone to vent to. Maybe they need someone to yell at. I can help with that. 'Cuz I understand it. I... I tend to take my anger out on people who don't deserve it. I dunno why, but I get the need. And if I can give someone an outlet that isn't someone else who doesn't deserve it, great. Or maybe I can help 'em in ways that don't involve being a rodeo clown. Maybe I can help with a few errands, make 'em laugh, or just listen. Thing is, I've caused a lot of problems. It would be nice to help people deal with 'em for once [Milholland, August 30, 2011].

Indeed, while Mike's new identity is initially played to humorous effect, as the character repeatedly fails at his chosen tasks, his growing aptitude and experience begin to reshape his storyline into a structure strongly resembling the basic patterns of the superhero narrative: his determination inspires two of his friends, Nancy and Jhim, to join him as masked crusaders; he stumbles into an underground community of fellow heroes who support each other's efforts; and he is taught a valuable lesson by older hero Factoid: "No one's perfect. We all fail, sometimes no matter how hard we try. You're human. The best heroes tend to be" (Milholland, December 16, 2011).

Given the overwhelming prevalence of mutants, cyborgs and other posthuman subjects in the superhero genre, and the dominant tendency among artists to give these larger-than-life characters bodies that are hypersexualized and idealized, Milholland's implied author here suggests a preference for quintessentially normative depictions of heroism: it is the frail, physically unimposing Mike who comes to represent the traits most frequently associated with the superhero. As the webcomic continued, this point would be further emphasized whenever the focus returned to Mike: in 2012, a local politician attempts to use the Pythagorean's popularity to boost his own by hiring an actor to take Mike's place at a rally, only for the audience to revolt when they realize the impostor is not the man who has helped them on so many occasions: "I met that Pythagorean gentleman when the senior center forgot to send my ride for my eye doctor appointment. He hailed a taxi, rode with me to the doctor's office, waited with me, and then took me to lunch on the way home. You are not the nice young man who did all of that" (Milholland, April 30, 2012). Only the arrival of the true Pythagorean prevents a violent riot, as Mike appeals to his supporters in an attempt to diffuse the situation: "It has been my honor to help this community out. I was born here and I expect to live my whole life in Charlestown. But it breaks my heart to see the people I love—good people—turn so fast. We're better than that. There's no need for violence. Especially not over me" (Milholland, April 30, 2012). The story concludes with Mike being ambushed by Captain Feelsafe, the same figure who inspired Mike's transformation (and not coincidentally a character who uses Superman's color scheme), and who stands revealed as a jealous hypocrite: "You and your lot make me sick. Here I am, bustin' my ass for six years, trying to get noticed ... get appreciated. And then some ugly, gangly screw-up shows up and he's the one everyone loves?! I'm the one who read to all those awful li'l sick kids! I'm the one who helped hundreds of old geezers with their groceries! I've tolerated every asshole in this town" (Milholland, May 10, 2012). And so, as every superhero must, the Pythagorean gains a nemesis.

Unlike *SuperCakes*, *Nimona* and *Narbonic*, *Something Positive* remains in active publication as of the time of writing; thus, the Pythagorean's story is still ongoing, and constitutes only one small portion of Milholland's storyworld. But the dynamic of resistance and subversion continues to evolve, providing an ongoing commentary that can only be defined in opposition to the subject of critique, as readers unfamiliar with superhero fiction will be at a loss to decode the meaning of Mike's trials and tribulations, and the values that inform them. These are clearly the product of an author who was (and may still be) a reader of superhero comics, and who uses the same techniques Jenkins attributes to all modes of fan-production.

Embracing Subversion and Normalcy in the Infinite Canvas

Two facts are apparent when viewing the current state of webcomics in tandem with the current state of the superhero genre: first, as mainstream heroic figures become more deeply embedded in popular culture via an exponentially increasing transmedia presence, equal and opposite reactions are being produced by webcomics, which continue to proliferate and carry with them a multitude of new voices and new implied authors. Second, and more significantly, experimentation with narrative form and function in webcomics is still evolving parallel to new technological developments; as improved devices become available for public use, they are almost immediately assimilated and adapted to produce new forms of story, which in turn warrant additional critical scrutiny. The full ramifications of digital narratology are only beginning to become apparent, and existing theoretical systems are not quite capable of encompassing these new permutations:

While these experiments with web-based technology and new media have reached a wide audience and have records of success, critics continue to question their value. Scott McCloud rejected the "gimmick" response in his 2009 revision of the infinite canvas theory, noting that; he continues to see technology-enhanced comics as the future of the medium. In 2009, the blog Comics Worth Reading raised questions about the value of motion comics; one such question has been applied to transmedia comics as a whole: "When you add camera tricks and a soundtrack to a comic, is it still a comic?" (Carlson par. 4). This question taps into long-standing debates about what makes a comic, and will likely continue to be a topic of debate as technology advances. Still, despite the criticism, mixed-media comics continue to have an impact on the industry. The Comixology platform, for example, has become a top distributor of digital comics. Sites like Top Web Comics and The Webcomics List catalog thousands of webcomics by genre. Further, the use of mobile device technology has spawned a new genre of mobile comics, viewable only through downloaded apps and designed to utilize the navigation patterns of a given device [Booker, 6630].

While webcomics can (and should) be incorporated into analytical paradigms shared by other digital platforms, any such attempt is somewhat complicated by the medium's ongoing reactive relationship to its textual precursor. The desire for agency and interactivity is self-evident: just as fan fiction can only exist by virtue of readers generating simulacra of source texts and usurping implied authors, and games make active player participation a necessity by default, so too do webcomics express the assertion put forth by Hellekson and Busse that "it may not be coincidental that the specter of authorial intention, cast out with the rise of poststructuralism and postmodernism, coincides with fan fiction's beginnings. The interpretive power shifted away from the author and even the text. Instead, it resides in the process of reading and interpretation" (Hellekson & Busse 2014, 19). Jenkins, Jamison and King all concur that these forms are determined in part by pre-digital models—fanzines, tabletop role-playing games and print comics, respectively—to which new technologies were applied in order to enhance those same provisions of authorial power. The key difference is that the lineages of the former two can ultimately be traced back to singular, linear textuality, as fan fiction directly draws from source works while tabletop gaming derives its conventions from Tolkienist fantasy literature.

But if webcomics are to be framed as a digital response to superhero fiction, what then do we make of the latter's inherently postmodern configuration? As detailed earlier, the foundational narrative components of the DC and Marvel Universes exhibit clear markings of postmodern fragmentation and multiplicity in their chronotopes and tropes, with a corresponding shifting and malleable ontology. The multitudes of authors, implied authors and temporal/spatial distortions position the genre beyond any fixed socio-historical context, yet all are assumed to be part of theoretically coherent storyworlds despite these worlds being achronic, atopian and perpetually self-adapting to contemporary cultural concerns. The paradox continues to hold true as of this writing, over eight decades into the genre's continued domination of its medium. Superman is always the last survivor of an alien race; Spider-Man is always empowered by an irradiated spider bite; Batman is always a vigilante traumatized by the murder of his parents. Yet even as these characters persist in their state of temporal stasis, the world around them changes with each incoming generation of readers-turned-authors. Originally a disparate cluster of fictional worlds segregated by genre, the DC and Marvel Universes of today are sprawling transmedia megastructures, exhibiting what can only be described as generic schizophrenia, populated as they are by vampires, aliens, time travelers, demons, mutants, sorcerers, zombies, cyborgs and more. Gomel's model of the "simultaneous city" is here writ large, the basis for entire fictional cosmologies: "A *simultaneous city* is one in which two or more spaces are superimposed upon each other as in Freud's Rome. Since the human mind cannot cope with simultaneity, narrative has to manipulate the narrator's/characters' perceptions so as to enable a more or less coherent narrative sequence" (Gomel, 181). At the same time, critics such as Reynolds reject the notion of sequential continuity, arguing instead that these supposedly causal narratives have been—and continue to be—written as a chain of modular narratives closer in form to classic mythology, just as the tale of the Trojan War may be told independently of the heroic exploits of Orpheus or Perseus:

> The comings and goings of major artists and writers on key titles are events in their own right, existing parallel to the progress of continuity, and yet able to affect the seamless intertextual fiction in a premeditated way. Thus John Byrne's arrival at *Superman* or Moore's scripting of *Swamp Thing* are decisive events in the evolution of those particular characters. We can legitimately speak of Byrne's Superman or Messner-Loebs' Flash as being different from other writer's conceptions of these characters, without negating the assumption of continuity on which the prosecution of the continuing saga rests [Reynolds, 47].

And so, where other forms of digital fiction embrace postmodern narrative techniques and strategies to differentiate themselves from their textual and cinematic precursors, webcomics—having evolved from a form of literature already heavily influenced by authorial pluralism, multiplicities of meaning, decentralized access and fragmented ontologies—instead adopt a stance more aligned with traditional literature: a single authorial presence and consistent implied author, a thematically-cohesive storyworld with a fixed and stable chronotope, and a finite plot. The very possibility of conventional narrative becomes, in itself, subversive when positioned as a response to the practices which dominate the mainstream. Most significantly, the lack of editorial or corporate oversight (which so frequently dictates the creative direction of established franchises) allows individual authors such as Leyh, Milholland, Stevenson and Garrity the agency needed to produce texts which exist in a marginal space relative to the print market, enabling a direct dialogue with (and appropriation of) pseudo-mythical iconography. This agency is inherently reactive and interactive, as it takes its cues from diegetic and extradiegetic changes in near-real-time, as seen with the Pythagorean's storyline in *Something Positive*. While these four webcomics constitute a mere fraction of a fraction of significant works in the medium, they share key features both between them—all free, all accessible to readers using any device capable of browsing the Web, all organized within their respective archival spaces—and with other online and/or virtual products. Any attempt to discern the common elements attributed to new forms of digital fiction must therefore take the medium of webcomics into consideration as another actualization of pre-existing desires for authorial agency and interactivity, expressed via extant technology.

Moreover, this trend towards a "return to normalcy" in webcomics, expressed as a movement away from postmodern complexity towards simplified chronotopes and fundamentally singular storyworlds, demonstrates a broader principle in contrast to the development of fan fiction and video games: reactivity is not teleological by default. The latter forms of digital narrative push towards fragmentation and dissolution of perceived narrative boundaries, because advancing technology permits such a response to existing conventions of narrative. As the Marvel and DC ontological configurations had evolved past that point long before digital technology was widely available, the inevitable response is oriented away from those attributes, while nevertheless expressing the same desires and achieving the same goals as other forms of technologically produced narrative.

4

A New Way of Framing
the Pursuit of Interactivity
and Agency

Herman characterizes narratological theory as a series of critical attempts to explore the ways in which stories are understood, and their potential effects on their audiences: "Narratology's grounding assumption is that a common, more or less implicit, model of narrative explains people's ability to recognize and interpret many diverse productions and types of artifacts as stories. In turn, the *raison d'etre* of narratological analysis is to develop an explicit characterization of the model underlying people's intuitive knowledge about stories, in effect providing an account of what constitutes humans' narrative competence" (Herman, 29). Like Fludernik, he also puts forth the argument that innovations and developments in the field are not the result of clean, organized and linear processes, but rather an organic array of factors simultaneously contributing to new understandings over an extended period of time: "the history of early developments in narrative theory should be viewed, not as a series of events linked by a single causal chain and lending themselves to neat periodizations (Russian Formalism, New Criticism, narratology, etc.), but rather as fields of forces sometimes unfolding in parallel, sometimes temporally staggered, but emerging at different rates of progression and impinging on one another through more or less diffuse causal networks" (Herman, 31).

It follows, then, that the advent of digital technologies, particularly as platforms for authoring and distributing works of fiction, should lead to a new set of variables for narratological analysis; indeed, each of the three forms of digital fiction explored in this book has been the subject of independent critical scrutiny, from the transition of fan fiction from print to online space to the mechanics of hypertext; from the centrality of simulacra to the multitextual narrative structures of games; from modern mythological ontology to a "new ordinary" produced in response; these examinations have provided vital insight into the disparate processes of producing and consuming digital fiction. However, the singular focus of existing scholarship portrays such phenomena as isolated, self-contained modes of production, suggesting little or no common ground between them. As this book demonstrates, the new narrative platforms of the digital age are undeniably interrelated, sharing practices and technologies and motivations, sustained by a consistently expressed desire for authority agency and greater diegetic interactivity. Thus it is possible—and even necessary—to view fan fiction, video games and webcomics as parts of a greater whole, sharing attributes, narrative throughlines, experimentation and even specific creators who easily shift from one mode to the next. These are communal experiences made available and accessible through decentralized channels; they are largely reactive in nature, frequently producing new generic rules and forms in response to extradiegetic events; and they are deeply intertextual and hyperlinked, necessitating a closer relationship between author, text and reader—a connection which blurs the boundaries between the three. Gomel aptly points out that these new functions are a manifestation of our current reality, and are further bolstered by the constant introduction and refinement of new technologies:

> Increasingly, we live in sorts of space that may not be grasped in Bachelard's sense—or rather, may not be grasped by the narrative paradigms inherited from the nineteenth-century realistic novel. Video games, movies, the Internet, and global transportation constantly reconfigure our spatial perception.... With the shift from realism to modernism and eventually postmodernism, impossible spaces have become central to spatial representation. It is only the "naturalistic" bias of narratology that enforces their marginalization [Gomel, 5–6].

As such, the question remains: how can narratology best accommodate these new developments? Works of fan fiction may be revised and erased with no trace of a previous incarnation, and may themselves become substitute source texts for further extrapolations; webcomics are similarly transient, and can be encoded with additional layers that defy textual representation (animation, sound and music, file name manipulation); video games may be experienced differently with each engagement, whether these be ludic variations such as passing a difficult challenge after multiple failures, or expressions of pseudo-authorial agency along branching plot structures, modular choice/consequence systems and determinant characters. In each instance, multiplicities of meaning are rooted not only in the act of interpretation but in the variable nature of the text itself. Future attempts to track new digital phenomena within the framework of narratological analysis must therefore take these factors into account and consider access to digital platforms as a practical guarantee of textual response, and of a broader network of intra- and inter-fandom communication informing circumstances of both production and reception. Virtual ontologies must be regarded not as singular, self-contained entities but objects which exist in dynamic states of active response, greatly influenced by (and, in some cases, explicitly designed to) the pseudo-authorial designs of the player in much the same way fan fiction imposes new meanings and values upon a text. And the artistic merits and technological manipulations of webcomics must be considered in light of the cultural dominants against which they define themselves. When these commonalities are centered in the critical eye, comprehensive analysis becomes not only possible but viable.

Ciccoricco speaks of the almost-symbiotic relationship between the dissemination of new devices and their implementation in the process of creating narrative: "Emerging media technologies are continually informing fiction and poetry, both in the sense of 'influencing' (not *determining*) and 'giving form or structure to.' The process reciprocates, evident in the modes of fiction and poetry that were both shaped by and gave shape to the medium of film over the course of the twentieth century. Thus there is little doubt that writers will continue to write fiction and poetry that are informed by the computer medium" (Ciccoricco, 3). But this does not take into account evidence provided by other critics that emerging technologies *do* in fact determine not only the manner in which digital narratives are delivered, but the potential content of said narratives as well. The appropriation of Web-based technologies for the establishment of fan fiction archival spaces has led to the formation of codified categories, a clearer sense of genre rules and regulations (self-policed by the fan communities themselves), and dynamic hyperlinked and hypertextual systems of exchanges, countertexts, and second-order derivations, all of which impact methods and content of fan-production according to Bell: "online fan fictions also exist within an intertextual network within which the relationship between works of art is essential. Websites such as fanfiction.net host thousands of stories written as parodies, prequels, sequels or alternatives to the original canonical print works. Fan fiction works thus very much rely on their epistemological connection to their sources and influences" (Bell, 191). This is particularly evident in the aforementioned discussion of fan fiction challenges such as Yuletide and The One Ring: it is the existence of the archive itself (and the community that sustains it) which precedes the production of narrative. Absent a digital platform characterized by absolute freedom of content, it is unlikely these texts would enjoy equal circulation and consumption, taking into account the existing discussion on the hard limitations of pre-digital fan fiction creation and consumption.

By the same token, increased sophistication of graphical engines, computer memory and data containment media (from floppy disks to CD-ROMs to DVDs to purely digital streaming) have been driven, at least in part, by game developers striving to boost the immersive multitextual potential of their products:

> video games do not just exist on consoles. They appear on mobile phones, in arcades, within web browsers and, of course, on computers—formats that lack the distinct generational divides of consoles. Hardware is merely the vehicle for the creativity and vision of the video game developers who have spent the last 50 or so years moulding a new entertainment medium where, unlike almost all other rival media, the user is an active participant rather than a passive observer [Donovan, 4].

Here, teleological progression is in full evidence: motion capture technology has been appropriated to create more lifelike avatars and actants, in turn increasing the options of identity and sexual role play per Consalvo and Filiciak; faster Internet bandwidth and persistent connectivity allow for quick and easy access to large libraries of games; and greater storage capacity leads to more complex worlds, potential branching paths, and transmission of narrative data across games (as seen in *The Banner Saga* and *The Walking Dead*), built on gigabytes of data that could never have been stored on floppy discs or CD-ROMs. Whatever purpose these tools may have been designed for, whatever the original intent of these advances, there can be no question that the end result of their appropriation by video game developers is a net increase in interactivity, player agency and narrative sophistication.

Several conclusions may be drawn from this examination of the deep reciprocal link between narrative and technology. The first is that the author, already pronounced dead by Barthes, has been fully disintegrated in the digital age, an entity whose component atoms have been absorbed and assimilated by the multitude of readers. Empowered by extant media, these readers are able to assume—to varying extents—the temporary role of a pseudo-author, generating works that do not exist in a context-less vacuum, but rather derive meaning from intertextuality and connectivity to other narratives, whether these be products of the same fan community or the simulacra's template itself. Even in webcomics, where the pretense of a singular author may have nominally been reconstituted, it is clear that these creators still participate in the particular dynamics of the pseudo-author, as their works are primarily defined as reaction and resistance to a greater cultural dominant; to them, the use of the Internet as a "free space" follows the same principles and connotations of those fan fiction writers who, according to Hellekson and Busse, take advantage of nonhierarchical space to produce slash narratives as protests of enforced heteronormativity.

The second conclusion is that perceived limitations on the scope of fictional worlds have, until recently, been based on the hard constraints of non-digital media such as the novel's page length or the film's runtime.

According to Ryan, this is no longer the case, as the theoretically infinite depths of cyberspace can now produce ontological structures with no fixed boundaries: "From a cognitive point of view, the answer to the fullness of fictional worlds depends on the texts' power of immersion. If a text manages to make a world present to the mind, inviting the user to imagine much more than its signs can describe or imply, then it projects a full world" (Ryan, 17).

Finally, one of the most essential features common to all narratives—the chrono-spatial configuration, or chronotope—has been molded into new experimental forms due to the permissive nature of the Internet as a postmodern narrative laboratory, in which no legitimizing body can impose hierarchical values: "The formulation and playing with alternative complex projections or future scenarios in all fields is the resultant pervasive contemporary preoccupation, supported by computer technology, where many options can be considered side by side simultaneously and where everything is quite literally virtual" (Margolin, 163). What once was only possible over decades of continuous serialized publication—and which, as evidenced, came about largely by accident—can now be produced deliberately and practically instantaneously.

At the time of writing, the emerging theoretical field of unnatural narratology has only just begun to investigate the full implications of these phenomena, how they affect our reception and perception of narrative, and what new permutations may arise in the near future. In a joint paper by Jan Alber, Stefan Iversen, Henrik Skov Nielsen and Brian Richardson, unnatural narratology is defined as "directed against what one might call 'mimetic reductionism,' that is, the argument that each and every aspect of narrative can be explained on the basis of our real-world knowledge and resulting cognitive parameters" (Alber et al., 115). Thus far, proponents of unnatural narratology have focused on deconstructive representations of impossibility within conventional media—Edgar Allan Poe's "The Tell-Tale Heart" as an example of unnatural narration, Virginia Woolf's *Orlando* as a deconstruction of mimetic time, and so on. In digital and virtual textuality, unnatural narratology may find its richest, fullest expression. The underlying impetus that continues to drive both technological developments and subsequent evolutions of form and function is key to deciphering what the future holds for contemporary narrative in general and digital fiction in particular.

Bibliography

Aarseth, Espen. *Cybertext: Perspectives on Ergodic Literature.* Baltimore: Johns Hopkins University Press, 1997.

Abbott, H. Porter. "The Future of All Narrative Futures." *A Companion to Narrative Theory.* Eds. James Phelan and Peter Rabinowitz. Malden: Blackwell, 2005.

Alber, Jan, Stefan Iversen, Henrik Skov Nielsen, and Brian Richardson. "Unnatural Narratives, Unnatural Narratology: Beyond Mimetic Models." *Narrative* 18, no. 2 (May 2010).

Allen, Graham. *Intertextuality.* New York: Routledge, 2000.

Anthony, Brad, Bryan Stratton, and Stephen Stratton. *Mass Effect Official Game Guide.* Roseville: Prima Games, 2008.

Bakhtin, M.M. "Forms of Time and of the Chronotope in the Novel: Notes Toward a Historical Poetics." *The Narrative Reader.* Ed. Martin McQuillan. London: Routledge, 2000.

The Banner Saga. Stoic Studio, 2014. Video game.

Barthes, Roland. *Image, Music, Text.* Trans. Stephen Heath. New York: Hill and Wang, 1978.

_____. *Mythologies.* Trans. Annette Lavers. New York: Hill and Wang, 1974.

_____. *S/Z.* Trans. Richard Miller. New York: Hill and Wang, 1974.

Bartle, Richard A. "Alice and Dorothy Play Together." *Third Person: Authoring and Exploring Vast Narratives.* Eds. Pat Harrigan and Noah Waldrip-Fruin. Cambridge: MIT Press, 2009.

Barton, Matt. *Dungeons and Desktops: The History of Computer Role-Playing Games.* Natick: A.K. Peters, 2008.

Batman: Dead End. Directed by Sandy Collora. Collora Studios/theforce.net, 2003.

Baudrillard, Jean. *The Perfect Crime.* London: Verso Books, 1996.

Bell, Alice. *The Possible Worlds of Hypertext Fiction.* London: Palgrave Macmillan, 2010.

Berens, Kate, and Geoff Howard. *The Rough Guide to Videogames.* London: Rough Guides, 2008.

Blade Runner. Directed by Ridley Scott. Warner Bros., 1982.

Blood Omen: Legacy of Kain. Crystal Dynamics, 1996. Video game.

Bolin, Kate. "Beauty." http://dymphna.net/fanfic/beauty.html. Accessed 4 Sept. 2016.

Booker, M. Keith. *Comics Through Time: A History of Icons, Idols, and Ideas.* Santa Barbara: ABC-CLIO, 2014.

Booth, Wayne. *The Rhetoric of Fiction.* Chicago: University of Chicago Press, 1961.

Burke, Liam. *The Comic Book Film Adaptation.* Jackson: University Press of Mississippi, 2015.

Campillo Arnaiz, Laura. "When the Omega Empath Met the Alpha Doctor: An Analysis of the Alpha/Beta/Omega Dynamics in the *Hannibal* Fandom." *The Darker Side of Slash Fan Fiction: Essays on Power, Consent and the Body.* Ed. Ashton Spacey. Jefferson: McFarland, 2018.

Cavelos, Jeanne. "How The Rebel Princess and the Virgin Queen Became Marginalized and Powerless in George Lucas's Fairy Tale." *Star Wars on Trial.* Eds. David Brin and Matthew Woodring Stover. Dallas: BenBella, 2006.

Ciccoricco, David. *Reading Network Fiction.* Tuscaloosa: University of Alabama Press, 2007.

Claremont, Chris (w), and Brett Anderson (p/i). "God Loves, Man Kills." *Marvel Graphic Novel* 1, no. 5 (January 1983).

Claremont, Chris (w), Dave Cockrum (p), Josef Rubenstein (i), and Bob Wiacek (i). "I, Magneto..." *Uncanny X-Men* 1, no. 150 (October 1981). Marvel Comics.

Close, Samantha, and Cynthia Wang. "Erotic Imaginaries of Power in Fan Fiction Tropes." *The Darker Side of Slash Fan Fiction: Essays on Power, Consent and the Body.* Ed. Ashton Spacey. Jefferson: McFarland, 2018.

Consalvo, Mia. "Hot Dates and Fairy-Tale Romances: Studying Sexuality in Video Games." *The Video Game Theory Reader.* Eds. Mark J.P. Wolf and Bernard Perron. London: Routledge, 2003.

Costikyan, Greg. *Uncertainty in Games.* Cambridge: MIT Press, 2013.

Crawford, Chris. "Interactive Storytelling." *The Video Game Theory Reader.* Eds. Mark J.P. Wolf and Bernard Perron. London: Routledge, 2003.

Deltarune. Toby Fox, 2018. Video game.

Doki Doki Literature Club. Team Salvato, 2017. Video game.

Dolezel, Lubomir. "Fictional and Historical Narrative: Meeting the Postmodernist Challenge." *Narratologies: New Perspectives on Narrative Analysis.* Ed. David Herman. Columbus: Ohio State University Press, 1999.

_____. *Heterocosmica: Fiction and Possible Worlds.* Baltimore: Johns Hopkins University Press, 2000.

Donovan, Tristan. *Replay: The History of Video Games.* Lewes: Yellow Ant, 2010.

Dragon Age. BioWare, 2009–2014. Video game.

Dragon Warrior. Enix, 1989. Video game.

eleveninches, Febricant, hellotailor, M_Leigh, neenya, and tigrrmilk. "Steve Rogers at 100: Celebrating Captain America on Film." http://archiveofourown.org/works/1599293. Accessed 4 Sept. 2019.

Engleheart, Steve (w), Sal Buscema (p), and Vince Coletta (i). "The Coming of the Nomad." *Captain America* 1, no. 180 (December 1974). Marvel Comics.

Fallout 2. Interplay, 1998. Video game.

Fencott, Clive. *Game Invaders: The Theory and Understanding of Computer Games.* Hoboken: John Wiley & Sons, 2012.

Feyersinger, Erwin. "Metaleptic TV Crossovers." *Metalepsis in Popular Culture.* Eds. Karin Kukkonen and Sonja Klimek. Berlin: De Gruyter, 2011.

Filiciak, Miroslaw. "Hyperidentities: Postmodern Identity Patterns in Massively Multiplayer Online Role-Playing Games." *The Video Game Theory Reader.* Eds. Mark J.P. Wolf and Bernard Perron. London: Routledge, 2003.

Fingeroth, Danny. *Superman on the Couch: What Superheroes Really Tell Us about Ourselves and Our Society.* New York: Continuum International Publishing Group, 2004.

Fludernik, Monica. "Histories of Narrative Theory (II): From Structuralism to the Present." *A Companion to Narrative Theory.* Eds. James Phelan and Peter Rabinowitz. Malden: Blackwell, 2005.

Forster, E.M. "Flat and Round Characters." *Aspects of the Novel.* New York: Harcourt, Brace & Company, 1927.

_____. "'The Story' and 'The Plot.'" *The Narrative Reader.* Ed. Martin McQuillan. London: Routledge, 2000.

Fowler, Charity A. "A Bad Bromance: Betrayal, Violence and Dark Delight in Subverting the Romance Narrative." *The Darker Side of Slash Fan Fiction: Essays on Power, Consent and the Body.* Ed. Ashton Spacey. Jefferson: McFarland, 2018.

Friedman, Susan Stanford. "Spatial Poetics and Arundhati Roy's *The God of Small Things.*" *A Companion to Narrative Theory.* Eds. James Phelan and Peter Rabinowitz. Malden: Blackwell, 2005.

Gaider, David. "Ascension README." *Baldur's Gate II: Throne of Bhaal.* Black Isle Studios, 2001. Video game.

Garrity, Shaenon. *Narbonic.* http://narbonic.com/. Accessed 4 Sept. 2019.

Gomel, Elana. *Narrative Space and Time: Representing Impossible Topologies in Literature.* New York: Routledge, 2014.

Gorman, David. "Character and Characterization." *Teaching Narrative Theory.* Eds. David Herman, Brian McHale and James Phelan. New York: Modern Language Association of America, 2010.

Gresh, Lois H., and Robert Weinberg. *The Science of Supervillains.* Hoboken: John Wiley & Sons, 2005.

Hamilton, Edith. *Mythology.* New York: Little, Brown, 1942.

harmonyangel. "I Never." http://harmonyangel.livejournal.com/263355.html. Accessed 4 Sept. 2016.

Hellekson, Karen, and Kristina Busse. *The Fan Fiction Studies Reader.* Eds. Karen Hellekson and Kristina Busse. Iowa City: University of Iowa Press, 2014.

Herman, David. "Introduction: Narratologies." *Narratologies.* Ed. David Herman. Columbus: Ohio State University Press, 1999.

Hodgson, David S.J. *Mass Effect 2 Official Game Guide.* Roseville: Prima Games, 2010.

ICEY. FantaBlade Network, 2016. Video game.

Jakobson, Roman. "Closing Statement: Linguistics and Poetics." *Style in Language.* Ed. Thomas A. Sebeok. Cambridge: MIT Press, 1960.

Jamison, Anne. *Fic: Why Fanfiction Is Taking Over the World.* Dallas: Smart Pop, 2013.

Jenkins, Henry. *Convergence Culture.* New York: New York University Press, 2006.

_____. *Textual Poachers.* London: Routledge, 1992.

Johnson, Jeffrey K. *Super-History: Comic Book Superheroes and American Society.* Jefferson: McFarland, 2012.

Keogh, Brendan. *A Play of Bodies: How We Perceive Videogames.* Cambridge: MIT Press, 2018.

King, Brad. *Dungeons and Dreamers: The Rise of Computer Game Culture from Geek to Chic.* Emeryville: McGraw-Hill/Osborne, 2003.

Knight, David, and Alexander Musa. *Dragon Age: Inquisition Official Game Guide.* Roseville: Prima Games, 2014.

Kodat, Catherine Gunther. "I'm Spartacus!" *A Companion to Narrative Theory.* Eds. James Phelan and Peter Rabinowitz. Malden: Blackwell, 2005.

kormantic. "That Night She Dreamt of Stars." http://archiveofourown.org/works/754918. Accessed 4 Sept. 2016.

Kukkonen, Karin. "Metalepsis in Comics and Graphic Novels." *Metalepsis in Popular Culture.* Eds. Karin Kukkonen and Sonja Klimek. Berlin: De Gruyter, 2011.

_____. "Metalepsis in Popular Culture: An Introduction." *Metalepsis in Popular Culture.* Eds. Karin Kukkonen and Sonja Klimek. Berlin: De Gruyter, 2011.

Lahti, Martti. "As We Become Machines: Corporealized Pleasures in Video Games." *The Video Game Theory Reader.* Eds. Mark J.P. Wolf and Bernard Perron. London: Routledge, 2003.

Landow, George. *Hypertext 3.0: Critical Theory and New Media in an Era of Globalization.* Baltimore: Johns Hopkins University Press, 2006.

Lanser, Susan S. "The 'I' of the Beholder: Equivocal Attachments and the Limits of Structuralist Narratology." *A Companion to Narrative Theory.* Eds. James Phelan and Peter Rabinowitz. Malden: Blackwell, 2005.

Leyh, Kat. *SuperCakes.* http://katleyh.com/comics/. Accessed 4 Sept. 2016.

Lummis, Michael, Rick Barba, Chris Burton, and Thom Denick. *Dishonored: Signature Series Guide.* Indianapolis: BradyGAMES, 2012.

Lutas, Liviu. "Narrative Metalepsis in Detective Fiction." *Metalepsis in Popular Culture.* Eds. Karin Kukkonen and Sonja Klimek. Berlin: De Gruyter, 2011.

Madrid, Mike. *Supergirls: Fashion, Feminism and the History of Comic Book Heroines.* Ashland: Exterminating Angel Press, 2009.

Margolin, Uri. "Of What Is Past, Is Passing, or to Come: Temporality, Aspectuality, Modality, and the Nature of Literary Narrative." *Narratologies.* Ed. David Herman. Columbus: Ohio State University Press, 1999.

Maslon, Laurence, and Michael Kantor. *Superheroes! Capes, Cowls, and the Creation of Comic Book Culture.* New York: Crown, 2013.

Mass Effect. BioWare, 2007–2012. Video game.

Meteling, Arno. "A Tale of Two Cities: Politics and Superheroics in *Starman* and *Ex Machina.*" *Comics and the City: Urban Space in Print, Picture and Sequence.* Eds. Jörn Ahrens and Arno Meteling. New York: Continuum International Publishing Group, 2010.

Milholland, R.K. *Something Positive.* http://somethingpositive.net/. Accessed 4 Sept. 2016.

Morrison, Grant (w), Frank Quitely (p), and Tim Townsend (i). "E Is for Extinction (Part 1)." *New X-Men* 1, no. 114 (July 2001). Marvel Comics.

Morrison, Grant (w), Keron Grant (p), and Norm Rapmund (i). "Kid Ω." *New X-Men* 1, no. 134 (January 2003) Marvel Comics.

Morrison, Grant (w), Phil Jiminez (p), and Andy Lanning (i). "Planet X (Part 4): Phoenix in Darkness." *New X-Men* 1, no. 149 (January 2004). Marvel Comics.

Murray, Janet H. *Hamlet on the Holodeck: The Future of Narrative in Cyberspace.* Cambridge: The M.I.T. Press, 1998.

Oliver, Simon (w), and Moritat (p/i). *The Hellblazer: Rebirth #1* (September 2016). DC Comics.

Pavel, Thomas. *Fictional Worlds.* Cambridge: Harvard University Press, 1986.

Perron, Bernard, and Mark J.P. Wolf. "Introduction." *The Video Game Theory Reader 2.* Eds. Bernard Perron and Mark J.P. Wolf. New York: Routledge, 2009.

Petersen, Robert S. *Comics, Manga, and Graphic Novels: A History of Graphic Narratives.* Santa Barbara: ABC-CLIO, 2011.

Phelan, James and Peter Rabinowitz. "Introduction: Tradition and Innovation in Contemporary Narrative Theory." *A Companion to Narrative Theory.* Eds. James Phelan and Peter Rabinowitz. Malden: Blackwell, 2005.

Pumphrey, Nicholas. "From Terrorist to Tzadik: Reading Comic Books as Post-Shoah Literature in Light of Magneto's Jewish Backstory." *The Ages of the X-Men.* Ed. Joseph J. Darowski. Jefferson: McFarland, 2014.

Quest for Glory. Sierra Entertainment, 1989–1998. Video game.

Rehak, Bob. "Playing at Being: Psychoanalysis and the Avatar." *The Video Game Theory Reader.* Eds. Mark J.P. Wolf and Bernard Perron. London: Routledge, 2003.

Rettberg, Scott. "Corporate Ideology in *World of Warcraft.*" *Digital Culture, Play and Identity: A World of Warcraft Reader.* Eds. Hilde G. Corneliuss and Jill Walker Rettberg. Cambridge: MIT Press, 2008.

Reynolds, Ren. "Competing Narratives in Virtual Worlds." *Third Person: Authoring and Exploring Vast Narratives.* Eds. Pat Harrigan and Noah Waldrip-Fruin. Cambridge: MIT Press, 2009.

Reynolds, Richard. *Superheroes: A Modern Mythology.* London: B.T. Batsford, 1992.

Richardson, Brian. "Beyond the Poetics of Plot: Alternative Forms of Narrative Progression and the Multiple Trajectories of *Ulysses.*" *A Companion to Narrative Theory.* Eds. James Phelan and Peter Rabinowitz. Malden: Blackwell, 2005.

Roach, David A. "Captain America." *The Superhero Book: The Ultimate Encyclopedia of Comic-Book Icons and Hollywood Heroes.* Ed. Gina Misiroglu. Detroit: Visible Ink Press, 2004.

Robb, Brian J. *A Brief History of Superheroes: From Superman to the Avengers, the Evolution of Comic Book Legends.* London: Constable & Robinson, 2014.

Roga. "Whole New World." http://archiveofourown.org/works/142845. Accessed 4 Sept. 2016.

Roine, Hanna-Riika. "How You Emerge from This Game Is Up to You: Agency, Positioning, and Narrativity in *The Mass Effect Trilogy.*" *Narrative Theory, Literature, and New Media: Narrative Minds and Virtual Worlds.* Eds. Mari Hatavara, Matti Hyvärinen, Maria Mäkelä and Frans Mäyrä. New: Routledge, 2016.

Rosen, Philip. "*From* Change Mummified." *Film Theory & Criticism, Seventh Edition.* Eds. Leo Braudy and Marshall Cohen. New York: Oxford University Press, 2009.

Ryan, Marie-Laure. "Cyberage Narratology: Computers, Metaphor, and Narrative." *Narratologies.* Ed. David Herman. Columbus: Ohio State University Press, 1999.

_____. "Introduction." *Cyberspace Textuality: Computer Technology and Literary Theory.* ed. Marie-Laure Ryan. Bloomington: Indiana University Press, 1999.

_____. "Narrative and Digitality: Learning to Think with the Medium." *A Companion to Narrative Theory.* Eds. James Phelan and Peter Rabinowitz. Malden: Blackwell, 2005.

_____. *Narrative as Virtual Reality: Immersion and Interactivity in Literature and Electronic Media*. Baltimore: Johns Hopkins University Press, 2001.

_____. "Texts, Worlds, Stories: Narrative Worlds as Cognitive and Ontological Concept." *Narrative Theory, Literature, and New Media: Narrative Minds and Virtual Worlds*. Eds. Mari Hatavara, Matti Hyvärinen, Maria Mäkelä and Frans Mäyrä. New York: Routledge, 2016.

Sarkhosh, Keyvan. "Metalepsis in Popular Comedy Film." *Metalepsis in Popular Culture*. Eds. Karin Kukkonen and Sonja Klimek. Berlin: De Gruyter, 2011.

Searle, Mike. *Dragon Age: Origins Official Game Guide*. Roseville: Prima Games, 2009.

Shaw, Harry E. "Why Won't Our Terms Stay Put? The Narrative Communication Diagram Scrutinized and Historicized." *A Companion to Narrative Theory*. Eds. James Phelan and Peter Rabinowitz. Malden: Blackwell, 2005.

Skolnick, Evan. *Video Game Storytelling: What Every Developer Needs to Know About Narrative Techniques*. Berkeley: Watson-Guptill Publications, 2014.

smercy. "For Our Own Benefit." http://multiverse5000.livejournal.com/12158.html. Accessed 4 Sept. 2016.

Spacey, Ashton. "Introduction." *The Darker Side of Slash Fan Fiction: Essays on Power, Consent and the Body*. Ed. Ashton Spacey. Jefferson: McFarland, 2018.

Spengler, Birgit. *Literary Spinoffs: Rewriting the Classics—Re-Imagining the Community*. Frankfurt: Campus Verlag, 2015.

spock. "don't even recognize the stranger." http://archiveofourown.org/works/2784878. Accessed 4 Sept. 2016.

Star Trek: New Voyages. Developed by James Cawley and Jack Marshall. https://www.youtube.com/user/startrekphase2DE. Accessed 4 Sept. 2016.

Star Wars: Revelations. Directed by Shane Felux. Panic Struck Productions, 2005.

StarTrek.com. Interview with David Gerrold. "Trek Writer David Gerrold Looks Back—Part 2." http://www.startrek.com/article/trek-writer-david-gerrold-looks-back-part-2. Accessed 4 Sept. 2016.

Stevenson, Noelle. *Nimona*. http://gingerhaze.com/NIMONA. Accessed 12 Dec. 2012.

Tavinor, Grant. *The Art of Videogames*. Chichester: Wiley-Blackwell, 2009.

thedeadparrot. "Dreams of Electric Sheep." https://archiveofourown.org/works/1196. Accessed 4 Sept. 2016.

TheSecondBatgirl. "I Never (The But Just This Once Remix)." https://archiveofourown.org/works/31131. Accessed 4 Sept. 2016.

Tolkien, J.R.R. *The Lord of the Rings*. London: HarperCollins, 2009.

Turk, Tisha. "Metalepsis in Fan Vids and Fan Fiction." *Metalepsis in Popular Culture*. Eds. Karin Kukkonen and Sonja Klimek. Berlin: De Gruyter, 2011.

twentysomething. "DILF." http://archiveofourown.org/works/487739. Accessed 4 Sept. 2016.

Uricchio, William. "'The Batman's Gotham City™': Story, Ideology, Performance." *Comics and the City: Urban Space in Print, Picture and Sequence*. Eds. Jörn Ahrens and Arno Meteling. New York: Continuum International Publishing Group, 2010.

The Video Game Theory Reader. Eds. Mark J.P. Wolf & Bernard Perron. London: Routledge, 2003.

The Walking Dead. Telltale Games, 2012. Video game.

Walton, David. "'Captain America Must Die': The Many Afterlives of Steve Rogers." *Captain America and the Struggle of the Superhero: Critical Essays*. Ed. Robert G. Weiner. Jefferson: McFarland, 2009.

Wandtke, Terrence R. *The Meaning of Superhero Comic Books*. Jefferson: McFarland, 2012.

Warhol, Robyn R. "Neonarrative; or, How to Render the Unnarratable in Realist Fiction and Contemporary Film." *A Companion to Narrative Theory*. Eds. James Phelan and Peter Rabinowitz. Malden: Blackwell, 2005.

Warr, Philippa. "The Banner Saga 2: On Combat and Continuity." https://www.rockpapershotgun.com/2015/07/09/the-banner-saga-2-interview/. Accessed 4 Sept. 2016

What Remains of Edith Finch. Annapurna Interactive, 2017. Video game.

Wolf, Mark J.P. "Abstraction in the Video Game." *The Video Game Theory Reader*. Eds. Mark J.P. Wolf and Bernard Perron. London: Routledge, 2003.

Wolf, Mark J.P., and Bernard Perron. "Introduction." *World of Warcraft*. Blizzard Entertainment, 2004–present. Video game.

Yuletide FAQ. http://archiveofourown.org/collections/yuletide2015/profile. Accessed 4 Sept. 2016.

Zelda Starring Zelda. Kenna W, 2013. Video game. http://kennastuff.blogspot.co.il/2013/03/zelda-starring-zelda-story.html. Accessed 4 Sept. 2016.

Zimmerman, Eric. "Gaming Literacy: Game Design as a Model for Literacy in the Twenty-First Century." *The Video Game Theory Reader 2*. Eds. Bernard Perron and Mark J.P. Wolf. New York: Routledge, 2009.

Index